A
RHONDDA
ANTHOLOGY

A RHONDDA ANTHOLOGY

Edited by
Meic Stephens

Introduced by
Dai Smith

SEREN BOOKS

SEREN BOOKS is the book imprint of
Poetry Wales Press Ltd
Andmar House, Tondu Road, Bridgend, Mid Glamorgan

Selection and editorial material © Meic Stephens, 1993
All other material © the authors or their Estates, as specified

A CIP record for this book is available
at the British Library CIP Office

ISBN 1-85411-089-6

Printed in Palatino by The Cromwell Press, Melksham

Contents

Editor's Preface

'Revolutionary and riotous; religious and musical; sporting and artistic, coal-bearing Rhondda. The starting-point of hunger marches, religious revivals, and Communist miners' delegations to Russia. Place of origin of champion boxers, talented musicians and composers, famous choir conductors, operatic stars and novelists...'. That's how Jack Jones begins his novel *Rhondda Roundabout*, and — as near as dammit, as Jack himself might have said — I think he got it just about right, for 1934.

Here in Wales the Rhondda Valleys, Fawr and Fach, are perhaps the most famous valleys of all, and in the view of many elsewhere, in England and beyond, they have sometimes seemed to be the very epitome of industrial south Wales. Certainly for me, as a boy growing up a mere sheep-walk or engine-shunt away in Pontypridd during the 1950s, the Rhondda (singular in more than one sense) was a magnet every bit as powerful as Cardiff, and whenever I took the red bus up through Trehafod of a Saturday afternoon it was always in a spirit of patriotic adventure. The townships, the streets, the pits, the chapels, the rivers, the hills and the panoramic vistas were, in my eyes, the landscape of an authentic Wales: a very special place.

My connection with the Rhondda over the subsequent forty years may have been intermittent, but I have never ceased to feel involved in its affairs, even while living at Merthyr Tydfil in the valley of the Taff. I have read as much about its history, politics, and culture, as I have been able to lay my eyes on. More recently, in the autumn of 1990, I was teaching at Tonypandy Comprehensive School. From there, on the last day of term, the 21st of December, during an extended dinner-hour, I drove over Penrhys into the Rhondda Fach with my colleague and friend Jeff Powell to take part in the ceremony which marked the closure of the Mardy, the last pit in the Rhondda.

It was during that extraordinarily moving experience I had the idea for making this anthology, as a token of my admiration for the people of the Valleys, past and present. Long may the Rhondda continue, not only as one of the great literary landscapes of Wales but also as a proud administrative entity where the old sense of community, rising to the challenge of changing times, remains as strong as ever.

Meic Stephens

DAI SMITH
Introduction

The literary value of a place that is turned into literature owes most to those who imagine it afresh in their writing. Invariably, though, it is the literal worth of the life of the place which has forced the writer's hand. No one could read this anthology without recognising both traits. And what a range of material the Rhondda has elicited — novels, lyrics, epic poems, verse-drama, essays, autobiography, travel-writing, memoirs, short stories, and plays. It is a literature of criticism and comment as much as one of praise and stirring narrative. It comes from the native-born, the incomer and the visitor; it is in Welsh and English and, in a sense, in the language Rhondda fashioned as its own. It speaks to and about its own but it travels widely and well for it is a product of a history whose intense localism never disguised its universal implications. When we read Malkin we can dream, as generations of Rhondda schoolchildren did, of the mythical squirrel who could leap from tree to tree without ever touching the ground between Porth and Blaenrhondda; yet that is to conjure up a Rhondda which never existed as a fully peopled settlement. The Rhondda of the imagination is one which feeds on the later reality of the world's most significant coal-mining patch. This is the Rhondda Meic Stephens gives us in these skilfully culled pages.

They begin and they end with Rhondda's supreme literary figure, Gwyn Thomas, who had in common with most of the inhabitants of his world the sheer accident of birth in that particular place. His father had actually been born in America. The family returned to coal-booming South Wales. This was a fact that once caused Gwyn to speculate, almost longingly, on his missed fate as a writer on the great urban experience of America — of the East Side of New York, say, or, as he mused of Algren and Bellow, of Chicago. He was almost wistful before, decisive as a tack, he added that he could have wished for no better stuff to work into words than that provided for him by the Rhondda. It was, he said, reaching out to convince and impress, 'a more significant Chicago'.

For him it certainly was. We can detect, too, in this selection how the Rhondda's concentrated human existence gave a density to its life. Writers could tap into this just as colliers mined the wealth-yielding seams squeezed close, but haphazardly, across geological fault-lines in the pits which gave the settlements their primary purpose. The more important, secondary purpose, was to be discovered in what was packed tight into such a short span of time — an exuberant if bewildering mix of religion and politics, of domestic respectability and desperate sexual repression, of release and yearning, of boom and slump and hard-won, unsustainable recovery. As early as the 1950s we can read laments for the loss of that vitality, even implicit reprimands of a more secure, less millenarian present. The cacophony of voices is, in some measure, a reflection of the varied life of these two valleys. We reduce it to a single tone at the risk of losing its babylonian melody.

The revealed history of the Rhondda is presented in both its public and its private guise. Alexander Cordell drops his characters into Edwardian upheavals of riot and rebellion that put Tonypandy into the card-index of every modern British historian. That strand, leading out from the Rhondda to inform and influence three generations of Socialist politics and union militancy, is present in the biographies of A.J. Cook, of Arthur Horner and Bill Paynter. In turn, their lives reverberate in the fiction of contemporaries like Lewis Jones and Jack Jones. The former now has European recognition as a writer of innovative 'proletarian fiction' which Jack Jones, a much clumsier chronicler, seemed to a metropolitan audience to have been in the 1930s. Either way, both provide us with the ways back into a world whose shape was always more protean than passing journalists thought. Poets, like Idris Davies and J. Kitchener Davies, often despaired of a Rhondda, vulgar and secular, that others celebrated; younger men, like Duncan Bush, indict a contemporary world over-eager to put it all to rest.

The knowable scope of Rhondda lives, perhaps in most accessible form, seeps through the synaesthetic memories of those like Brinley Jones, Gareth Alban Davies and Mary Davies Parnell, who recall a Rhondda whose upbringing — in school, on the street, in shops, at worship, at play — moulded them. Their adult lives, they tell us, owed an enormous amount to observation and imitation of the adult lives which framed their childhood and adolescent years. My own Rhondda dovetails into their sense of the two valleys. After 1945 both the uncontrolled growth and the devastating decline had levelled off. We were left in a post-war world of relative security. Our Rhondda was not a dull world for all that. Into our lives came the cultural explosion of film and television. Those who were and are nostalgic for earlier, communal cultural endeavours can attract sympathetic understanding but should not be allowed to obscure the excitement of the novel, still common culture we now shared. If your feet are on the ground there is nothing wrong in wanting to look at the stars. We were aware, in the eyes and in the words and in the family histories all around us, of where we had come from but, in our connection to a future, we also knew where we were going.

So, whatever diminution of social energy is subsequently visible, even palpable, in the decades that followed, it should be comprehended not as some kind of sullen retreat, a betrayal of golden aspirations in return for the tawdry gilt of popular culture, but as a phenomenon linked to the economic nemesis which Ron Berry nominates for faceless guilt in *Flame and Slag*. His novels are about as wistful for Rhondda 'glory days' as a gob in the face; they explore, with cold contempt, what happens to praised 'community spirit' and 'culture' when others chip away at the foundation of jobs. We go underground, in more ways than one, in his fiction in order to hold the surface reality in check. This Rhondda Anthology is particularly valuable for all the hidden history it brings to light. Paramount amongst the writers who do this are Alun Richards, brilliant dissector of the social mores of Pontypridd, Rhondda's reluctant capital, and Rhys Davies whose short-stories are acid-etched into the plain glass of Rhondda's self-promotion. Both novelists, confronted by the muffled silence of those whose small witness greater rhetoric has stifled, turn to women as truth-tellers. Posture is savagley pricked; what Raymond Williams memorably called 'a structure of feeling' is exposed and indicted. The result, paradoxically enough, is the restoration of a fuller humanity through the fiction than was often, and for too many, available in past lives. The achievement, by empathetic insight and then imaginative reconstruction of reality, is so stunning that we can hail it as the retrospective literary vindication of what Rhondda struggled to mean against all the odds.

More straightforwardly we can feel the tensile pull, this way and that, in Rhydwen Williams' mock-heroic poem and in Gwyn Thomas' boastful lament that he had 'never had any truly passionate wish to be elsewhere'. Reading this volume we can begin to see why. I can think of no more vital task for those of us who believe that Rhondda's tributary of experience should continue to merge with and invigorate the whole life of Wales, than to place a copy of this book in the hands of the jaded, the elected, the cynical and those young and hopeful enough to be no such thing.

BENJAMIN HEATH MALKIN
The Parish of Ystradyfodwg

In my first excursion, the direction I took from New Bridge [Ponty-pridd] to Brecknock [Brecon] was through the parish of Ystrady-fodwg to Pontnedd Fechan; and I question whether any part of my tour is better furnished with its apology, if an untrodden track may excuse an author for supposing that his observations are of sufficient value to come before the public. I have already mentioned the bridge that crosses the Rhondda Fawr at its confluence with the Taff, close by New Bridge. The scenery from this bridge to the first and only known and frequented water-fall on this river, which is a salmon-leap, and frequently mistaken by strangers for the cascade before described on the Taff, is highly interesting, singular and impressive. The progress of this river, narrow and rapid, is still more turbulent, and more impeded by rocky fragments, than that of the Taff.

The vale is very much confined, admitting only a road and a few fields on one side, and on the other, the cliffs rise perpendicularly from the water in all their naked grandeur, but are clothed on the top with some of the choicest and most majestic timber that Glamorgan-shire produces. The union of wildness with luxuriance, and of sub-limity with contracted size and space, is here most curiously exemplified. The distance to the water-fall is about two miles. About a quarter of a mile before you arrive at it, there is a very long and tremendously lofty Alpine bridge, constructed with trunks of trees laid together, and supported in a sort of reeling equilibrium by a prop of timber in the middle of the river, without which the ricketty con-trivance could not abide. It is picturesque in proportion to its rude-ness. The fall disappoints those visitors whose admiration is adjusted by measurement, and whose accuracy of computation teaches them that there must in all cases be one third more of the sublime in thirty feet than twenty. But the scene addresses itself with peculiar charms to those who have other inducements than to tell their friends in London, with travelled self-complacency, that they have seen a cas-cade or a mountain. I have had the pleasure of visiting this spot at three different times; and once when the river was very full of water. The composure and solitude of the place, undisturbed by any thing but the roar of the projected stream and the dashing of the spray; the rocks intruding on the precincts of the flood in massy portions, smoothened by attrition and worn into fantastic shapes; the river placid and shady for a lengthened reach above the fall, but thrown as it were unexpectedly down the steep, collecting itself in dark and profound pools among the fragments, and then driving its impetuous course from the scene of its disturbance; — all these are circumstances and features which aim at our sensibility, more than they command our wonder. When the season suits, the fish-basket, flung across the fall from a pole supported by the rocks, affords a specimen of rustic ingenuity that adds to the pleasures and speculations of the moment.

The character of the scenery remains the same when you pursue the road beyond the salmon-leap; but the river, instead of rippling over rocks, becomes deep and darkly placid, but transparent. Indeed, a principal beauty of the rivers in this rocky country arises from their perfect clearness, uncontaminated, unless in very heavy floods, by the least tinge of muddy soil or any other fortuitous discolouring. It may be necessary to observe that travellers in any sort of carriage are precluded from adopting this interesting route: for about a mile and a half above the first water-fall, the Rhondda Fawr for a space becomes broad and shallow, over a bed of large, loose stones, and the road on the right bank only leading to some coal-pits close by, the traveller, who wishes to pursue this way towards Ystradyfodwg, is obliged to ford at this place. The almost impassable road then continues on the left side of the river, overhanging it at a considerable height, with opposite scenery precisely of the same description, as what engages the attention in the way to the ford. Yet it is curious to observe that the mere circumstance of changing sides, without any heightened features, gives it all the effect of novelty, and creates for it an increasing interest....

The traveller has scarcely turned his back on this, before his ears are saluted with the sound of a third fall, at the distance of not more than a quarter of a mile. It altogether differs in character from the other two. It is less beautiful, but larger and more grand. Immediately below it, massy rocks thrust themselves almost across the river, leaving it a very narrow, but deep and clear passage; and the depth of course gives a darkness to the hue of the water that communicates a degree of sublimity to the general tone.

The ascent from this fall is steep and lofty, and after a short space presents a new scene, at the junction of the two rivers, Rhondda Fawr and Rhondda Fach, which by their confluence form a more important stream, whose banks we have hitherto skirted. There is a bridge of a single arch over the Rhondda Fawr, highly ornamental to the distant prospect, which is here of considerable extent. The Rhondda Fawr lies

in the parish of Ystradyfodwg, and we shall, with occasional devia-
tions, trace it to its source, through country of uncommon wildness.
The Rhondda Fach takes its source in Aberdare, and flows through a
district of less romantic character, but very considerable beauty. I
have no doubt but that an excursion to Aberdare would be equally
interesting in this direction, as in that which it suited my arrange-
ments to adopt: but I had no opportunity of trying the experiment,
and here took my leave of the Rhondda Fach. There is here a grove
of oaks, remarkable for their height, occupying the side of a declivity,
from the road to the river. It may be observed generally that among
these mountains, the oak, if it grows at all luxuriantly, is drawn up to
an uncommon tallness.

From the spot just described, the road turns to the left, up a steep
and barren hill, without any thing to interest, till you meet the direct
road from Llantrisant through these wilds; on which you turn due
north, when the mountain scenery of Ystradyfodwg breaks upon the
view. There is here a gate, which marks the entrance of the parish;
and the way lies at the foot of a rocky ridge, grand in its elevation,
and most whimsical in the eccentricity of its shapes. The almost perpendicular side is clothed nearly to the top, with dwarfish, stunted
oaks, scarcely exceeding the size of garden shrubs. The foliage re-
lieves the eye, but the impoverished vegetation of the place detracts
little from the repulsive grandeur of the landscape. Towers of limestone occasionally start up, which overhang the road, and seem to
endanger the traveller; while a pleasing, though not rich valley on the
left, softens the general dreariness, and reminds us that there are
men, with the habitations and the works of men. The descent down a
long hill brings the traveller to a little brook, abounding with fish,
which joins the Rhondda Fawr a little way to the eastward; and at a
very short distance from the brook, after descending another hill, you
cross a bridge over that river, which has disappeared since its junction with the Rhondda Fach; but from this place the sound of it is
never lost, though frequently the sight, till you arrive close by its
source at the top of the parish, distant about ten miles. Here, however, it ceases to be the leading feature of the prospect. It fertilizes the
valley with its pure, transparent stream, rolling over loose stones, but
is no longer encumbered, yet ennobled, by massy projections, or
stately and aspiring cliffs. Hereabouts, and for some miles to come,
there is a degree of luxuriance in the valley, infinitely beyond what
my entrance on this district led me to expect. The contrast of the
meadows, rich and verdant, with mountains the most wild and ro-

mantic, surrounding them on every side, is in the highest degree picturesque.

The next object of interest, for such it is in a proportion equal to that of a palace in a better inhabited country, is a substantial farm-house, placed in a most pleasing solitude, as beautifully situated as any thing in the parish. Its name, for it is dignified with a name, is Llwyn y Pia, signifying the magpie's bush. It is occupied by Jane Davies, a widow, but its situation seems little calculated for the feebler exertions of female industry. Though, in truth, the delicacy and supposed corporeal imbecility of the fair sex are little respected in these mountains. The women at least divide the severest labour, and seem, by their hardy, robust constitutions, to triumph over the bleakness of their winters, and the ruggedness of their toils. On the farm of Llwyn y Pia, standing alone by the road side, there is the tallest and largest oak that ever I have happened to meet with. There is also on the same estate, if you pass through a gate on the left, a little beyond the house, a very beautiful field, with a magnificent grove at the upper end of it, under the shelter of a towering rock. A second bridge over the Rhondda, on the other side of which the road winds to the left, furnishes a most interesting point of view, embracing the country just traversed on the one part, and on the other the wilder grandeur of what remains to be explored.

I had met with but one person of whom I could ask a question since my entrance into the parish; and then only through the medium of my attendant, whose services as an interpreter were not to be disregarded. My ears, therefore, were not unpleasingly assailed with a shout, which I found to have proceeded from a few people, with most powerful lungs, who were exulting over the lifeless remains of three or four snakes they had just killed. Soon afterwards I heard another clamour, seeming to resent the imputation of solitude, from some labourers at work in the woods. Such sudden salutations almost startle the wanderer, who can scarcely suppose that so much voice could be collected in the district, deserted as it appears to be by human habitations. The people are, indeed, thinly scattered, as well as miserably poor: but one would think they were determined to shake the throne of silence, and atone for the rare occurrence of social intercourse, by giving a loose to loud and boisterous loquacity. I have mentioned the miserable accommodations of the peasants in the parish of Aberdare; in Ystradyfodwg, wilder, less inhabited, without manufactures, and altogether cut off from the commerce of the world, they are in all these respects still worse, though better than in some parts of Cardiganshire and Carmarthenshire; and it is a striking instance how little the state of the animal spirits depends on the possession of external comforts, where the influences of fashion and competition are excluded, that none of the languor, indifference, and stupidity, so generally expected among the inhabitants of such regions, is to be found here. Though ignorant and unpolished, they are far from dull; they have enough of boisterous pleasantry, though it is a pleasantry exclusively their own; and however the fastidious stranger may lament what seems to him their misery, I question whether his pity would be justified by their complaints, or rewarded by their gratitude.

About a mile from the bridge just described, is the church, near the centre of a parish more than ten miles in length. I had inquired with some anxiety for the church, taking it for granted that there I should find a village, as at Aberdare; but I only got laughed at by my rustic informant, who seemed to wonder I should know so little of Ystradyfodwg, as to expect to find a village: and, indeed, how can a man be said to know the world, without knowing Ystradyfodwg? My error was, however, soon rectified, and every house in the parish, with its situation, was enumerated to me in a detail, the length of which was in no danger of burdening my memory. There is only one house within sight of the church, which was formerly a sort of inn; but now there is neither resting-place nor refreshment for man or horse in a fatiguing, though in general far from dreary space of about thirty miles, from New Bridge to Pontnedd Fechan. The church is one of the most miserable in its structure, and most neglected in its preservation, of all that have come within my knowledge in travelling through the mountainous parts of South Wales. The churchyard, unlike the gay absurdity of Aberdare, is wild and overgrown, little occupied by the dead, and little tended by the living. Nettles and thistles supply the place of those flowers with which the more refined inhabitants of the cultivated vales adorn the last dwellings of their departed friends. Yet even here, all was not silent or solitary: the drowsy hum of mountain scholars, twanging their guttural accents to their Cambrian pedagogue in the church porch, informs us that ignorance does not reign supreme and unrivalled, where knowledge would appear to be least producible, and most difficult of attainment. These children, numerous as they were, must many of them have come from great distances for their instruction; and the attendance on divine service, if indeed it is much attended, must be highly inconvenient; for the church, though centrically situated with respect to the local extent of the parish, is nearly at the extremity of the inhabited part.

After you pass the church, the fields and meadows of the vale are found to be narrower and less fertile: the rocks and hills gradually close in, becoming bolder and more fantastical in their appearances, while the sides of many are clothed with an apparently inexhaustible opulence of wood. The continual water-courses, down those that are naked, break the uniformity of the perspective with their undulating lines, and assist in communicating a characteristic interest, to what may not improperly be termed the Alps of Glamorganshire. The bottom is much encumbered with brushwood, through which the Rhondda Fawr takes its course, sometimes visible, and sometimes concealed; the sides are formed of a rocky chain, as has been described, alternately bare and woody; and the front of this narrowing dell is filled up by a single cliff, high, broad to the top, and as it were regularly and architecturally placed, appearing as much the result of design, as those on the sides seem to indicate the fortuitous vagaries of sportive nature. The height of this mountain seems much greater than it is, from its rising abruptly from the level ground, unencumbered by hillocks at its foot, the perpendicular nearly unbroken from the summit to the river that passes at its base. The mountain cattle, which find their way from the other side, grazing on its brow, add greatly to the general effect. By one of those mistakes, which may be deemed fortunate by the traveller who wishes to see as much as possible of a country, I took the road which seemed the best, and forded the river in front of this mountain, crossing to the left side. At the distance of more than a mile, among the most romantic scenery, a narrow brook precipitates itself from one of the highest mountains, and finds its way to the Rhondda Fawr below. My visit to Ystradyfodwg was in the early part of the summer, when the rains had not long ceased; but this and similar beauties must be nearly lost in a dry season.

It was long since I had met with any trace of habitation, not since I quitted the church, but there was a solitary cottage at the foot of this cascade, and the master was at home. He informed my servant in Welsh, that instead of passing in front of the before-mentioned cliff, and crossing the river, we should have pursued a scarcely perceptible track up another mountain on the right; and that the path we were now upon would only carry us a few hundred yards further, and then desert us. We therefore traced back our steps, and before we began our ascent, fortunately met with some cottagers milking, from whom we derived a very seasonable refreshment, after travelling all day without any opportunity of procuring more substantial sustenance. I should not have introduced our taking a draught of milk by way of an anecdote, had it not been for the purpose of illustrating the disinterested character and simple manner of these mountaineers, who could not help testifying their surprise at my offering a reward for what they so willingly spared; and it was only by transferring it to the children that its acceptance could be reconciled with their hospitable feelings.

The path up the mountain, which is the highest in Glamorganshire, is winding and difficult; it crosses two torrents near the top, which demand considerable care from the inexperienced traveller; and from the mountain opposite the Rhondda Fawr tumbles, though not in an uninterrupted fall; distinguished from the other cascades of the district by glittering through the woods that overhang its course, the only ensign of vegetation within ken; — this view alone well repays the labour of the journey to those who affect the grander scenes of nature. On gaining the summit, the freshness of the breeze, the extensive view of the mountain valley, the reach of the Rhondda Fawr on the opposite height, seen to its very source, with its projection down the crag, all bring to the mind the best descriptions of Alpine scenery, though on an inferior scale.

from *The Scenery, Antiquities, and Biography of South Wales* (1804)

GWYN THOMAS
This is my Rhondda

Come up towards the Rhondda from Llantrisant. The hills grow less gentle. The fields lose grace and lushness. The first coal tips sit fatly on torn slopes. Black pyramids set up by nimble-witted Pharaohs who had the theatrical guile not to get themselves enclosed within. The housing takes on a sombre, barrack-like monotony that even has the mice complaining and keeps the average modern architect in a deep faint and glad to be there. Pass Tonyrefail. You'll pass it if you survive that astonishing slope on the edge of the town. So many cars have stalled on this place that many people of the district still think that Ford backed a loser, and even the goats have been known to knock on the vet's door with a burned gear-box after tackling it.

Then you reach the broad, reedy moorland, the Waun. It is a gaunt place, this, a lonely place where even ravens and gulls have a way of trading crumbs for nerve tonic. And beyond the Waun, the great barrier ridge that marks the southern limit of the Rhondda. There is a deep hostile stare about that wall of grey and green. These mountains do not like what has been done to them. Too much has been taken from them. They proclaim it in sight and sound. Their rims are shot through with outbreaks of defensive rock and most of the winds that blow off them are husky with recollections of storm, outrage and ancient battles that nobody could possibly have won.

We come to the crown of the ridge. Here on one side is the road to Tonypandy, sharply, abidingly to the left. Straight ahead, across the deep bowl in which Porth stands, is Penrhiwgwynt mountain. It is curiously pastoral with its lay-out of many coloured fields. From our kitchen window we could see the fringe of trees on its top. They were small trees, tilted back by the winds from the sea. They suggested gasps of astonishment, as if they had taken one look at Porth when they got tall enough and had been trying to get away ever since. From Porth the spokes of terraces and work-places shoot up to Treorchy and Maerdy, and down south to Pontypridd. Society and nature have come together here to achieve some amazing patterns and they should be told not to do it again.

And between Porth and Trebanog lies my village, Cymmer. My life between two and ten years of age wore itself wild and bandy-legged on that fierce and fascinating slope. You'll pardon my harping on this question of gradients, but the lack of flatness between Porth and Trebanog was a thematic thing in our lives. Before the buses came there were elderly people by the score rusted down by habit or rheumatism who stuck to their kitchens and never ventured from Trebanog or Upper Cymmer down into Porth. The walk down was one thing but it was not always easy to recruit somebody to push you back up a gradient of two in three, and the rickshaw service, with so much time given over to digging and singing, was patchy.

The day the bus service started up through Cymmer and Trebanog and Tonyrefail was an occasion of excitement and meaning. We children had turned out as if for some climactic summer treat, dressed in our best and in a vocal trim to blow the bus up that mortal phase of the slope if the wheels, for some reason or another, vanished in Lower Trebanog. They had mobilised some of the saddest and least active of the elderly population, and they were installed in the bus for the pioneer trip. The first journeyers to the moon will look no tenser than that little phalanx of adventurers. The bus roared into action. We ran as a body just behind it, singing for joy, touching the glossy red paint and getting drunk in the petrol fumes.

A fussy councillor, regretting the calm of the horse age, kept shouting 'Back, children, back. It may slip. This is a juggernaut.' As we chugged through mid-Cymmer, and we had now switched from singing to mimicking perfectly the bus's every noise, a woman whose voice had once been a golden legend in the lower Rhondda, leaned out of the bus to a point where she could have kissed the pavement and had two panicky passengers hanging on to each leg. She bawled to some relations and friends, "Wave to me. I'm in a bus." And no one had ever stood a better chance of suddenly not being so.

But gaiety turned to something like terror when the machine approached the foot of Farmer's Hill. The engine coughed and snorted as if it were trying to get out and walk. A local sage, Waldo Aberystwyth, gave the driver a most distracting tap and asked him if Rolls and Ford had been told of this particular gradient up to Trebanog before exposing humanity to this nonsense of internal combustion.

To the left of the hill's peak is the field where the rugby team recruited from Cymmer and Trebanog used to play. It was the least level pitch in Christendom. Those who survived it got a diploma from Darwin. It was the only rugby field where the players were allowed to dip their bits of lemon in adrenalin while sitting in an oxygen tent at half-time, and the referee was allowed to call in a relative or use a motor horn if he lacked the breath to make the pea move inside the metal. The Trebanog and Cymmer boys mastered the slope. They were badly defeated but once and then the victors were found to have two Sherpas on the wing on loan from Tibet.

Most of the houses in Cymmer are of the traditional cottage type endemic in our mining villages. They were built in blocks of forty to fifty, each block large enough to evolve a personality, a culture, a pattern of stars and scars, all its own. In many of them the structure was flimsy to the point of being flippant. Start hammering in the top house and someone was hanging on to the looser fittings in the bottom one.

How tiny and inadequate most of the houses look now. Like units in a game of blocks in a House of Correction. Take our kitchen. To the eye of childhood it had the size of the Albert Hall and the converging tumults of Crewe. We were not content to be a large number of brothers. We had a phalanx of friends who loved my sister's cooking. On a good day it was like an overflow meeting from Doctor Barnardo's. Today its walls are about an inch away from my shoulders and the loud bustling cormorants have fled.

But the eye returning to this place sees most acutely the things, the great meaningful things that the years have led into silence. The rubbery, flaming-eyed band of tireless young yahoos with whom I romped through High Street, Graigwen, Lincoln and Argyll Streets, have gone and their games have been replaced by antics which I do not at once recognise as play. The huge colliery in the middle of the village, its rich, sinister heart, finished work in the late thirties. Just behind our house was the vast tip built up from the endless honey-combing of pitwork beneath us. The rattle of trams up and down the tip, through the day and notably through the night, clad each of our dreams in a cloak of sharp and cruel omens.

When we played on the tip it was jet-black, proud and growing. The engine-house at its top, which played out the hauling cable, was full of wheels that sang wonderful velvet, greasy songs. In those days we did not notice the tip's colour, its blasphemous lack of green. The young are great acceptors and the tip, like the pit, was the centre of our world. But grass of a sort grows over it now, a dim, grudging grass over the dramatic undulations, like a landscape of the moon. The old tracks of the tramlines down its flank are a contracting, sardonic furrow. The engine-house is now an empty shell upon its eminence. The winds blow through it and the ferns creep back into their old kingdom.

We had no cinema in Cymmer itself. Our place of pilgrimage on a Saturday afternoon was The Grand or The Dog as we knew it. It was not difficult, with some hastily done chore on a Saturday morning, in my case the cleaning of cutlery for a family of twelve, to get the penny admission to The Grand. But there was another method that had a yard more panache to it. It was to take a couple of jars to the jam factory next door and get a penny on each. We followed the example of the hard boys of the upper age group whose fad was to buy with the second penny a fresh batch of bread and a swede. And we, with limping baby jaws, did likewise. The racket of that swede-chewing was immense. When the talkies came the clients had to agree to synchronise their dental swing to let an odd line of the dialogue through to the critics in the back.

Not long ago I looked at the dun, padlocked doors of that palace of delight. I think I could have stood before the Parthenon and felt relatively blithe, for the gods of the Greeks did not cry through my childhood. But in The Dog, locked up there, huge and articulate phantoms, were a countless parade of evenings that had shaped the eventual pattern of my mind, whatever it is. I was taken there for the first time by the daughter of a neighbour, a lovable but remiss maiden and daft on the pictures. I was about eighteen months old at the time. The temporary nurse had wrapped a shawl around me and I, as a male, had escorted her into the cinema. She stood in one of the side aisles, gawking at the epic being currently unrolled. It was a naval film. Some of it I saw over the shawl. Some of it I saw through the shawl. Good sight or poor shawl. The memory of that evening has stood so vividly by me through the years that I cannot even think of the navy or see the sea without having a strong taste of wool on my lips.

And in the middle of Cymmer is the chapel. A large chapel. Off-hand I would say one of the largest in the Rhondda, a place where piety has begotten more shapes in wood and stone than anywhere else in Britain. Of that chapel I was a member. Theologically, as a child, I had a tangled time of it. I was one of the Rhondda generation whose language, with an almost malignant ease, had changed from Welsh to English. But the chapel's teaching had remained in Welsh. I and my mentors blinked at each other across a wider gulf of heretical overtones than anything since Luther. But I cannot look at that building with anything but a deep, good love. For music does not concern itself with the base Machiavellianism of doctrine and vocabulary. Nations are torn apart, languages fall silent but the young will always sing. We could all learn enough Welsh to give a unique passion to the hymns we sang at the festivals of Easter and Whitsun.

And if Cymmer produced nothing else it was an abundance beyond praise of beautiful sunlit voices, soprano and especially alto. I say 'especially' because it was in that brazen section of the juvenile gallery that I and my brothers found ourselves. The chapel is now abandoned. Mice and the odd mutter of subsidence pronounce their own coda on the packed festivals of yesteryear. But in those days when it knew our triumphs of innocence and immaculate harmony, our Easter mornings of voices arising and hearts fulfilled, it and the men and women who made it raised a banner of loveliness and joy.

Now let's go back up the hill again. Down that side street to the left is the Library and Institute. There I had my first taste of what have been the great merits of life. Masses of books, good talk, concerts. There of a Sunday evening the Cymmer Military Band would play under their impressive bearded bandmaster, Mr Martin. He was a grave, Moses-like figure and it would never have surprised me to see his sheet music turn into tablets of stone. And there, too, in the draughts- and chess-room I sat in the company of sage and outrageous wags who seemed to see themselves merely as part of a vast cosmic jest. Those lads who set my thoughts swinging to a satirical chime that will never be amended,

Just over to the left is St John's Hall which for years shuttled between being a centre for grand opera and the headquarters of the Ministry of Labour, both in those days demanding large casts and sombre synopses. And slightly higher up is the old graveyard. The earth of this musty and haunting patch was torn out of plumb by subsidence years before my time. The memorial tablets are painfully aslant and stare at each other in the most overt confusion. After a fairly jumpy life we thought the least a citizen can expect is a stable headstone.

Further along the road is the chip shop that was the hub of the late winter evenings. It was a place bulging with light, warmth and turbulent gossip. Often, in the intervals of waiting, clutches of junior artists fresh from the Band of Hope and vestry rehearsals and hot with a sense of worldly carousal, were recruited and hoisted on to the lemonade boxes and asked to sing. My own strong suit was songs of tender yearning and such sweetness I was accused more than once of taking the tang off the vinegar. I also had a batch of ballads from Sankey and Moody that would have moved a mule to remorse. With 'Have Courage My Boy To Say No' I was always sure of a bag of hot scrumps. With 'Where Is My Wandering Boy Tonight?' I got a cutlet to go with them.

A few weeks ago I walked around the green patch by the old steam fan where we played and talked and ate the lotus through the fat, delicious summers of childhood. I stopped to watch some boys playing. I pondered the violent tumble of events that had shattered the face of reality between my birth and theirs. One of them said, 'I wonder what he wants.'

So do I...

And now, in the closed mind what are the voices, the visions that continue to hang about?

Most of them are bound to relate to the period when the whole region seemed to be teetering on the edge of violence. The swift decline of economic power after the First World War had given a spearhead of fanatical decision to the vague, evangelical socialism and syndicalism that had formed the South Welsh political idiom since the beginning of the century.

Even around my cradle I seemed to detect angry fists and raised voices. The miners and their masters had elected to tear the entrails out of each other. About this there was nothing new. For a hundred years the valleys had been given over to industries that were brutally dangerous and dirty, with repression and revolt glaring at each other like imbecile twins. My gripe-water was flavoured with chopped pamphlets. As a pre-sleep tactic, my father would let me stroke a slight lump on the back of his head. This, he claimed, had been caused by some ruffianly cossack of a constable who had broken his truncheon on my father's pate during the Tonypandy Riots.

My elder brothers, bitter myth-deflaters to a man, swore that the contusion had been caused by a thrown coconut during a drunken revel at Barry Island. But I accepted my father's story and gave him my full sympathy when he rattled off the names of at least six men who had got on to the Council merely for having been within earshot of the riot.

The great strikes of 1921 and 1926 still operate as massive traumas in the less public parts of my psyche. In 1921 some Whitehall Napoleon despatched a force of infantry, the Yorks and Lancs, to nip insurrection in the bud and protect the rentiers and virgins of the land from spoliation. The soldiers were small, unsoldierly and amorous fellows. Copulation throve and in our boyish games among the ferns, tripping over lovers and the attendant troupe of telescope-toting *voyeurs* became a fixed hazard. Often one would see a passionate Lancastrian being harangued by one of the miners appealing to him not to exhaust utterly the local supplies of warmth and to revert, for pity's sake, to the role of running dog of imperialism.

Through that summer we were fed in soup-kitchens, housed for the most part, and for the extra laugh, in vestries. The diet differed from that of a gaol only in being served by smiling and splendid women. Never was the sweet tooth of youth so thwarted. Soup bombarded with monstrous doughboys was the dish of the day. And this was usually followed by a type of tough, unsugared rice pudding which was later taken over by Japan as the Mark One of their buna product, synthetic rubber.

Off and on some jesting sadist would run around the village shouting, 'Fruit salad down the vestry.' We would swoop like gulls around the gates of the little kitchens and watch the conventional two acres of rice being lifted out of the ovens. This may earn me a frown from the American Senate but there was Russian money behind this flow of dainties. The miners of the Don basin had a whip-round and sent the valleys a cheque to the tune of 'Solidarity for Ever.'...

When the 1926 battle came around I was in the County School and outside the orbit of public charity. In most kitchens miracles of division and sharing swarmed like flies. The more astute got the middle cut of the sardine. Our earliest sexual stirrings were shadowed by so consistent a hunger that for years to come the zone's libido had a stammering tongue. The strike, begun in late spring, did not end until the autumn. The weather was flawless. Every day opened and closed like a great flower. The valley slipped back to its primal calm. The hillsides were murmurous with groups talking, singing, gambling with buttons or pins.

At school every class witnessed a bijou but solemnly bitter civil war. The miners' sons were for conflict unto death. The sons of tradesmen and other people not affected by the fight were malignantly opposed to the whole business, especially during the General Strike part of the affray, when they had to go without buses and trains. They did the long walk down the valley, working up a fine, reactionary head of steam. I recall, one day, trying to explain to the son of a draper, a torpid, powerful boy, the content of a speech I had heard the night before in the concert room of the Library and Institute. The speaker had given us the exact shade and time of arrival of the Red Dawn. The draper's son listened patiently. He brooded over it for about a week. Then he asked me to repeat what I had said. I gave him the message once more, festooned with a few fresh Trotskyist axioms dredged up from the Institute. He hit me flat. Over the years the wound between us has healed somewhat. But even now I cannot be in his presence without feeling that the world is a little more fissile than it has the right to be.

The thirties gave South Wales their political peak. Coal, already a ruptured industry, had stepped down from first place as a battle cry. The world's brow was hot and we were out to fan it with banners. We suggested a possible definition of Wales as a non-stop protest with mutating consonants. Navels distended by resting banner-poles became one of the region's major stigmata. During the demonstrations against the Means Test and other bits of crass social legislation that put Britain in deep-freeze during the Baldwin period, we marched almost as a way of life. We were trying to shout a little wisdom and compassion into the world's ear and the world was as deaf as a post.

Our slogans covered every contingency. Many banners would show a pair of staring eyes, indicating man's need of greater insight, and a pair of clasped hands, to symbolise unity. We must have been the first spot outside Asia to send warm greetings to Mao Tse-tung. Smaller causes would always find spokesmen. 'Keep Chepstow Welsh!' 'Remember Builth Wells!' 'Free Beer!' 'Hands off Cwmparc!' 'Keep Wales vocal!' 'Revive Tonic Sol Fa!' 'What about Colenso Jones?' This Colenso Jones was a paranoid bookmaker from Ferndale, who had accused the police of hounding him and his runners with undue zeal. He had been put away in an asylum and his case had overtones of the Dreyfus Affair.

For the police were not loved in those days. They had a way of flipping you with their white gloves if groups of three or four stood on a pavement putting the comb through the world's tangled plight. And at all the major meetings, where you would nearly always get a fast gale of republican rage, anyone with a strong voice and a way of banging it like a torpedo against the back of the hall was nourished by the thinkers at the Institute with nuggets of information about every lapse in royal conduct all the way back to Ethelred and even further. And whenever they started beating out their Robespierre routine the constabulary, in their quaint, Prussian-seeming helmets, could be seen making heavy weather of the shorthand notes that would help, later, to send one or more of the lads to stiffish terms in gaol. It is a cooling experience to see neighbours vanish into prison for the simple offence of frankness. The totally new relationship between people and police is as pleasant a sight as the factories that have sprouted on the disused tips of yesteryear. I never thought that they or I would make it.

The political marches were great musical occasions. The period that saw the incredible eruption of chapels witnessed also a vast spawning of bands. It was as if the darkening industrial context inspired a wish to react loudly. If life looks to insolently at you, blow right back in its face. If you have a euphonium to do it with, all the better. Whenever the multitudes thronged the valleys to suggest a sweeter ethic to the Herods of Whitehall, bands, their rehabilitated instruments reeking with metal polish, would come pouring from every street. It was the highest ratio of musician to marcher ever seen. And no two bands ever played in any related way. The band ahead of you might be splitting the sky with 'Colonel Bogey'. The one behind would be tenderly suggesting 'Hits from the Lilac Domino'.

In 1935 some climax of disgust brought the entire valley population onto the streets. As one watched the huge streams of protesters pouring up and down the two gulches on their way to Tonypandy, one could have sworn that the very blood of the place was on the boil. One of the visiting contingents was of members of the October Club, a very militant outfit at the University of Oxford. I had been a student there, on some of the most tenuous State-aid ever devised, until the previous year. The October boys called on me and requested that for Oxford's sweet sake, I should march behind their banner. I had to decline for I had already arranged to take my place with my large and entire family in the front ranks of the Porth phalanx. The Oxford boys were just behind. They had one band in front of them and one immediately behind. The conflicting tunes played hell with the rhythm of the afternoon. They were the only persons I have ever seen marching towards the New Jerusalem in strict waltz tempo.

Now the volcano lies still. The valleys now give out as little political clamour as those ghostly little villages of North Wales where slate was quarried and lead mined. The banners have been furled and put away. A quiter, healing hedonism has set off a proliferation of bingo and drinking clubs as impressive in its way as the almost solid wall of conventicles and trade union lodges brought into being by the psychoses of poverty and dread. And just as well.

from *A Welsh Eye* (1964)

RHYS DAVIES
I was Born in Clydach

Half-way up the main Rhondda Valley one of the tributary vales swerved away steeply from Tonypandy, rising for a couple of miles between reasonably attractive mountains. Clydach Vale was too steep for negotiation by the tramcars running through all the ten rude miles of the main valley, which finished beyond Treherbert, where beetling mountains closed round, and which opened at Pontypridd, a bustling town with a market day, busy police court and proper hotel where, as in England, bedrooms could be rented. Each of the other tributary vales running out of the Rhondda had its own colliery. Clydach was the one which had, at its high top reach, one of the big collieries of the Cambrian Combine, its fighting boss D.A. Thomas, the man who was to become Viscount Rhondda.

Cardiff, well-stocked with pale English people, lay a score of miles distant. The mining valleys streaking Glamorganshire behind the great port were not of good social and civic repute down there. In addition to the annoying strikes and constant industrial strife, rough men swept down from the mountains on Saturdays, especially on rugby-match occasions, and roaringly made their presence known. Without those coal-rich valleys, however, Cardiff would have lain moping in an unimportant past and modern Wales have scarcely existed. Myopic journalists, especially in England, usually referred to these packed valleys as 'villages' and reached for such random words as 'grim'. The villagers of the Rhondda, and of its companion valley of Merthyr, in addition to breast-feeding the puling Socialist babe, enjoyed bi-annual visits by the Carl Rosa Opera long before the Kaiser's war, filling the plush seats of the Tonypandy Empire Theatre — a substantial edifice which stood next to a pioneering shop of Marks & Spencer and, past clanking tramcars, not far from Mr Ladd's photograph studio, with its camera on stilts, a black cloth over Ladd's head, and handsome scenery palms and mansion chairs for displaying the sitter to elegant advantage. Indictable murders were almost unknown in these seething 'villages'. Only wages and God were grim.

The Rhondda, because of its long size, fidgety population and battles for economic reform, was the best-known of all the wealth-producing districts lying among the hurl of mountains crowding the county's middle. Clydach Vale, like the other culs-de-sac running off the valley, was rough and well- behaved, religious and drunken, but never earned a nickname such as the vale that in due course was to be called Little Moscow. Lined with terraces and streets of standard dwellings all the way to the two-shafted Cambrian colliery, Clydach had a turbulent stream of mountain water changing at regular intervals from Cambrian black murk to a glassy purity of blue. The place gave birth to a champion boxer, preached magnificent sermons and, inescapably, it sang. I knew only one of its three hard-worked midwives — well-informed Mrs Bowen Small Bag, rightly a great gossip, who brought me expertly into the world while the new century was still taking stock of its advantages, and to whom I never thought of sending a bunch of flowers until too late. Like all the Rhondda, Clyd-ach trumpeted an affirmation of the constructive urge in man.

In the last decade of Victoria's reign my optimistic father had opened a grocery shop in the centre of the vale's long main road and called it, for some far-fetched reason, Royal Stores. With several other shops, it stood opposite the Central, a massive pub of angry-red brick and dour stone which ran around its corner position to where a secret back door opened into an additional bar, an ill-lit cave exclusive to courageous women. A two-horse brake, its floor covered with straw in winter, stopped outside the Central at fixed times, plying from and to Tonypandy railway station with as many as eight passengers, its horses remaining alive until after the Kaiser's war, when a strong, single-deck bus appeared. A hansom cab could also be hired.

Within sight of my father's shop were two Welsh Nonconformist chapels, Noddfa and Libanus (there were five others up and down the vale), also St Thomas's church (English), a police station with cells for violent Saturday night men and rioters in strike time, and the Marxian Club (not called 'Marxist'). A doctor's surgery sent a warning smell out to the pavement night and day. There was a shop for locally slaughtered meat and one for ironmongery, flower-seed packets and punishment willow canes; also Ada Lloyd's shop for fruit and vegetables and, in her parlour behind hanging bunches of bananas, spiritualist seances; also a shop for sweets and ice-cream, kept by an Italian couple to whose daughter I suffered a token marriage; also Evans the Boot, selling what his nick-name implied; and Eynon's for moleskin pit trousers, singlets, buttons, American oilcloth, and 1s. 11d. per yard Welsh flannel out of which shirts and other distressing garments were made.

My favourite was the shop in which *The Magnet* and *The Gem* arrived efficiently on their proper day. I read everything coming my way, including my mother's *Home Companion* and *Weldon's*, finding cookery receipts and fashion notes almost as rewarding as Billy Bunter in *The Magnet* and — my father's slip of judgement — Horatio Bottomley's humbugs in *John Bull*. Fish and Penclawdd cockles arrived twice a week in a seaside-smelling donkey cart; and the Crier with his handbell stopped almost as regularly outside the Central to bawl announcement of some coming event. Of all the shops in the centre of Clydach Vale only the corner butcher's suffered wreckage in the riots and lootings that were to come; down in Tonypandy it was a different tale.

We lived for years behind and above our busy shop; a living-room, pantry and scullery behind, three bedrooms above. It was a 'credit' shop and a history of family fortunes. On a lectern desk panelled with a frosted glass screen lay an enormous black ledger, six inches thick, a double page for each customer. Its chronicle of strike-time debts was my mother's bible and bane, and in my mind it remained the Ledger of Old Accounts, durable as a lichened tombstone. My easy-going and popular father fed the multitudes in bad times; he also made some current money in good times. We could afford a domestic servant; Esther, the one I knew best and who stayed the longest, came from 'the country' like so many hopeful invaders of the Rhondda. We also kept a horse and cart, with a part-time man to drive them. A succession of schoolboys, together with my unpaid self, helped with menial jobs natural to our low status.

The shop smelled of wholesome things. Golden sawdust, thrown fresh every morning on the swept floor between the two long parallel counters, retained its breath of sawn trees. There was one chair, for stout old women panting on arrival from up or down hilly Clydach in our wonderful bad weather. There were lettered canisters of black and gold, an odorous coffee-grinding machine, mounds of yellow Canadian and pallid Caerphilly cheeses, rosy cuts of ham and bacon, wide slabs of butter cut by wire for the scales, and bladders of lard. Behind the counter over which my mother presided stretched wall-fixtures stacked with crimson packets of tea, blue satchels of sugar, vari-coloured bags of rice, dried fruits and peas, weighed and packaged by hand out of chests and canvas sacks on quiet Monday. Soaps gave their own clean smell, especially the favoured kind which arrived in long bars and, cut into segments, was used both for scrubbing houses and washing pit-dirt from colliers' backs and fronts. Slabs of rich cake lay in a glass case on an intersecting counter stacked with biscuit tins. Packets of Ringer's tobacco, black chewing shag, spices, almonds and dried herbs occupied a row of drawers under a counter, though not in the one always chosen by our cat for her frequent *accouchements*, filling me with wonder that she could force her heavy body through the narrow aperture at the back; an intelligent puss, she accepted the quick drowning of her load with experienced resignation and plodded on to the next adventure....

Our glossy trap made us seem stylishly well-off in comparison with nearly all the shop's customers. But my mother, who had been a trainee schoolteacher before marrying, kept an increasingly despairing eye on the Ledger of Old Accounts. Sometimes she warningly curtailed the extravagant orders of families known to be feckless and drinkers. 'They've no shape in their ways,' she would discover, always unerringly, a woman with an instinctive sense of symmetry. Untainted by the romantic gullibility of my father, she swooped drastically now and again. Some particularly dodging family would find itself 'put into court'. This suit for recovery of debt usually followed news, gained invariably from her knowledgeable midwife friend, that the family had inherited a sum of money from an expired relative in the country. Such a family seldom paid up its old strike-time debt unless sued; and sometimes not even then. Hailing from a less raw and dangerous place than the Rhondda, it took my mother some time to subdue her puritanic irritation with the turbulent valley. But I was born into it.

from *Print of a Hare's Foot* (1969)

LEWIS JONES
First Day in the Pit

Six months had passed since the air of the valley had been shattered by the explosion. All the bodies that could be brought up the pit had been taken by the people to the distant cemetery. The remaining hundred or so were left as cindered dust in various parts of the colliery. Imperceptibly the explosion had sunk from the surface of men's minds and become a memory, though in many homes it was a black one. The explosion distress fund that had been organised throughout the country immediately following upon the catastrophe was now declared to be running low, and the widows and orphans were informed that their relief scales would have to be reduced as a consequence.

One day Big Jim came home from his repairing work at the colliery, and after dinner casually told Shane: 'Well, gel bach, we will be starting to fill coal in the old pit next week once again.'

Shane turned to him. 'That be good news,' she said.

'Ay, but I have got even better than that. I have arranged with Williams, the under-manager, for our Len to start work with me next week.'

Len sat up in his chair with a start and looked at his father with wide-opened eyes that sparkled with interest.

'Aye, aye. It be quite true. You be starting to work with me next week. Your mam wanted you to keep in school, but since you be not willing for that there be nothing left but for you to work.'

The week following this brief announcement Len was so excited he hardly knew what he was doing. He told his mother one day: 'I'm glad, mam, that I'm starting to work. School's no good to me, I can't learn enough there. I want to be with dad in the pit. I'm not afraid. The other boys have told me it's not so bad when you get used to it.' And, looking slyly at his mother, he added: 'They get pocket-money from their mothers on top of trumps from their butties.'

Shane pretended not to notice, but a tiny smile flickered for a moment on the corners of her mouth.

Len became a hero in the eyes of his schoolmates. He made them envious with tales of what he intended to do, the things he would buy, the places he would visit when he started work. He conjured up for them a romantic vista of what work meant, and the days went by so slowly he thought the week would never end. But at last the final night arrived.

His mother had bought him the usual white-duck trousers that marked the end of his boyish breeches. The large tin box and jack, to carry his food and water, were given to him by his father, who had already used them for years. Shane sent him to bed early, intending him to get plenty of sleep. Excitement and anticipation, however, prevented this and he was still awake when the first morning hooter blew at five o'clock. About ten minutes later his mother called him. She had already lit the fire and had breakfast waiting. Jim was half dressed in his pit clothes when Len entered the kitchen. The lad soon clothed himself in his strange rig-out, and sat down to drink a cup of tea, for food was out of the question in the state to which he had worked himself. When the half-past five hooter gave the signal that it was time they were off, Shane passionately pressed her son to her body. She kissed him tenderly and whispered in his ear, 'Do everything your dad do tell you, my boy. Don't move from his side. You be starting to-day what only the grave can steal you from.' She said this more to herself than anyone else and put the canvas apron to her eyes. Then shaking her head sharply, she turned to Jim.

'I know you will take care of him, James. 'Member he be only a baby after all, the only one us have got left.' With another hungry kiss she sent them into the dark, wet street with a 'Good morning' that stuck in her throat and was never uttered.

The rain poured down as Len and his father, like a giant and a pigmy, trudged up the hill towards the pits. Jim made his son walk as closely behind him as possible. It was some time before Len realised this was done to shield him from the main force of the rain driving down the valley. His head bent to the drops that evaded his father's body, Len vaguely noticed the long string of silent men, like shadows, making their way in the same direction as himself. Each of them, dragging his feet, used the man immediately in front to shelter him from the rain.

Len followed his father across the bridge into the cabin where authoritative-looking men scanned him over curiously as if he were a calf.

'So this be the boy, James?' asked the most officious.

'Ay, this be him,' responded Jim, whereupon Len had to write his name and age in a big book.

He took a round piece of metal handed him by one of the men, who told him, 'Take care of that, my lad; it is your lamp check with your number on it.'

A few further words passed between the group before Jim led the way to the lamp room, a long corrugated-iron structure containing hundreds of lighted lamps arranged on a series of trestles. Len followed his father to one of the pigeon-holes, where Jim handed in the check and received a lamp in exchange. Len did the same and at once felt himself a man, although the lamp dangling from his hand nearly touched the floor. They left the lamp room and walked to a cabin, where another man with an air of authority examined the lamps. Having unscrewed the top and blown all round the pots, he handed them back with a final twist of the bottom, to ensure that the lamps were stuck fast.

Big Jim and his son left the cabin and went straight to the pit-head. The shaft in which Len was to work was called the 'upcast', because all the air from the pit was sucked up through it by a fan of huge dimensions. To prevent the air being drawn up before it had time to circulate all round the workings, the shaft was closed in with heavy wooden 'droppers', only leaving a space for the rope to wind its way through, so that when the two cages were in the pit the air howled and screamed through this tiny outlet.

Len was rather frightened by the terrible tumult on the pit-head, and he had to shout to make himself heard above the din. While they were standing in the queue waiting to go down, he felt for his father's hand and pressed it to his side in a gesture of love and confidence, but Big Jim, sensing the boy's mood, said nothing, thinking to himself that the lad had to 'find his own feet'.

When the ascending cage lifted the wooden barriers from the pit-top the released gusts of heated air rushed through with a roar. Jim cautiously led his son over the little gap between the cage and the pit edge. Eighteen other men and boys followed before the man in charge declared that the box was full and placed a thin iron bar across the entrance. This was a measure of precaution supposed to prevent the men falling out.

Once inside the cage, Len held his breath and waited. He heard the knocker clang three times, and the tinkling of a bell far away in the engine-house. Then suddenly he felt the floor of the cage press against his feet as it lifted off the stanchions that held it to the pit-head, and in another second the breath was torn from his lungs by the sudden drop as the cage plunged its way into the depths of the pit.

Even in his panic Len heard the clatter of the droppers falling into place above him, and he felt that a door had been bolted between himself and the world. Regaining his wind after the initial shock he put his arms round his father's leg, finding courage in the human contact it provided in the black, falling void. Warm air rushed past the cage with wicked squeals, and just as Len was beginning to get accustomed to the sensation of dropping, the bottom of the cage again pressed against his feet. This was due to the brakes in the engine-room being applied to the great winding drums and marked the half-way line between the pit bottom and the surface. The lad felt the cage rising under him and wondered why they were returning to the pit-head, but before he had time to think it out the cage, with a few preliminary jerks, jarred on the planks that covered the water sump at the bottom of the pit.

The men slowly got out, Len behind his father. His curious eyes noticed at once that the little lamps appeared to give out a greater light here than they did on the surface, due to the more limited space they had to illuminate. He was also surprised that he could see underground as well as he could above, for he forgot there was no daylight when he left the pit-head and that his eyes were already inured to the darkness before he descended. He stumbled against a rail and glanced around the semi-elliptical passage-way that led from the pit bottom. Looking behind, he saw a similar passage going in the opposite direction, the other side of the pit, then, threading his way carefully between the long line of coal-laden trams on the one side and an equally long line of empty ones on the other, he eventually came to the end of this double roadway.

'Look where you be going to now, Len bach,' advised Big Jim, as they turned off into a narrow and gloomier passage.

'There's different this place do look, dad, without no whitewash on the sides.'

'Never you mind about the sides. You watch these ropes in the roadway.'

Len took his father's advice and kept his eyes glued upon the ropes. Not another word was said until they came to a large cabin dug into the side of the roadway, where their lamps were again taken from them and tested.

Big Jim received certain instructions from the man in the cabin, and Len listened to their talk of 'shots' and 'rippings'. After receiving instructions and having their lamps returned to them, Big Jim remarked to Len: 'Come on. We have got a hell of a plateful for to-day, so you'll have to look sharp.' Without a word Len followed his father. The roadway was becoming narrower and lower with every stride, and steel girders gave way to timber as supports for the roof.

In his anxiety to keep pace with Big Jim Len had no time for talking;

it was his father who broke the silence.

'Are you all right, Len?'

Len started at the sound of Jim's voice. 'Ay. I'm all right, dad. How much further have we got to go?' he asked tremulously.

'We got a good bit to go yet.'

'Have we come two miles so far?'

'Thereabouts, boy bach,' replied Jim, turning to Len. 'You don't feel tired, do you?'

'Of course not,' bragged the lad, forgetting the tired ache in his legs and pulling himself to his full height.

Jim walked on again. 'Many is the time I have travelled this old roadway,' he mused. 'Duw, duw, I be sure to have done hundreds of miles along it.'

They proceeded in silence for a while, Big Jim thinking of the good old days that had gone, while Len thought of the days that were to come. Suddenly the former warned: 'Look out by here, Len bach. This be a nasty old trip.'

Len continued down the steep road that reminded him of the path leading from the mountain top.

'I 'member coming over this trip once with old Dai Cannon,' said Jim, 'when all of a sudden we did hear a rush behind us. Dai and me stopped like statues for a minute. But not for long. The rush come louder and louder and, muniferni, you did ought to see us jump for the side. Ha-ha! Dai gived one howl, mun, and before I did know what was happening he fell back on 'is arse in the middle of the road. Ha-ha-ha! Arglwydd mawr, boy, I was bound to laugh, mun, if Dai did kill me for it. Arglwydd, you should have seed the look he did give me! "That's right," he did say, "laugh you silly beggar. Go on. Enjoy yourself although I have broked my bloody neck".'

Jim burst out into another uproarious guffaw at the memory. When this had subsided Len asked: 'But what was the matter, dad?'

'Why, some of the horses, coming down from the top of the trip, got a little bit restless and was stamping their feet like hell. 'Oops a daisy, we did think, the devils be running wild. Dai jumped for the side and bumped right into a low piece of timber, and that was why he did land flat on his arse. Ha-ha!'

The descent now became even steeper. Len compared it to the sheer mountain drop near the quarry, and the thought made him long for the first time that morning to be back again in the sun. He had never dreamed of this interminable tramp in the darkness of the pit. Thinking of the world above prompted him to ask: 'How far be we down, dad?'

'They do say 'bout two thousand feet. But never mind 'bout that, now. You look after yourself; the roof be getting pretty low by here.'

Jim was walking with his body bent nearly double and Len, taking the tip, dug his chin deep into his chest and bent his head low. After a while they came to a part of the road where the roof was higher. Jim, knowing the spot, straightened his body and walked erect, but Len, fearing to raise his head, was not aware of this and walked on in solemn silence with his head bowed like a man in a funeral. The ropes beneath the lad's feet were moving when Jim called out, 'Come into this manhole, boy bach.'

Len hurried into the tiny hole in the side of the roadway and squeezed himself alongside his father in the limited space. 'What's the matter, dad?' he asked, thinking that something serious was about to happen.

'It's only the journey,' Jim assured him. 'You see those ropes by there,' pointing into the roadway, where the ropes were slithering along like snakes, one sizzling along the ground while the other ripped through the air nearly to the height of the roof, 'Well, those do belong to the journey'.

Len hesitated a moment, then asked, as a low rumbling sound came to his ears from the distance, 'What's that noise, then, dad?'

Jim started to explain when thirty empty trams rushed past the manhole with a deafening clatter. The terrific din sent Len cowering against his father's legs. Without further explanation Jim caught the lad by the arm and drew him out of the hole. 'Come quick,' he shouted above the rattle of the receding trams, 'let us get to the parting before the full journey come out.'

Len did not understand the meaning of these instructions, but he obediently ran headlong after his father. Gasping and perspiring, they stopped after they had run about a quarter of a mile. Still panting from his exertions, Len noticed that the roadway had widened and was blocked by two strings of trams, one of which was empty, the other full of coal.

Safe in another manhole, the lad watched with interest two men change the rope from the string of empty trams and place it on the full ones. When the change was completed he heard a whistle blow further on, and one of the men near him responded to the signal by rasping the two thin wires above his head with the blade of a knife. The wires connected with the engine-house at the bottom of the pit. The ropes began to move and slowly tightened on the first tram of the string, then the others, attached to it with steel shackles, were drawn forward with increasing speed and clamour until the last was lost to sight in the darkness of the roadway.

Len and Jim emerged from the manhole and again continued their walk, the former beginning to think that it was to be endless. He noticed places where huge holes gaped in the roof. At other places he saw large masses of stone overhanging into the roadway without any visible support.

He turned to his father and asked in a quavering voice, 'Be that safe, dad ?'

'Safe? Ay, boy, safe as houses. It will take more than Gabriel's trumpet to blow that down."

Len was too fatigued to ask any further questions. He was glad when Jim stopped and said, 'Here we be. Strip off and get yourself ready. A little whiff will dry up all that sweat on you.'

Len's exhaustion vanished with the knowledge that the interminable trudge was over and that he was now in his father's working place. He started to pull off his coat, when Jim interrupted him testily. 'Not by there, boy bach. Shift under those timbers, where you will be safe.'

Len did as he was told, and putting his box and jack carefully at the foot of a strong-looking prop, he pulled off his coat and shirt. He paused at this until he saw Jim pull off the singlet next his skin; then he did the same, and immediately felt the air beat more cool and pleasantly upon his naked chest.

'Duw, that be nice, dad,' he said, revived by the contact.

'Huh,' grunted Jim. 'Take the tools off the bar. Here be the key.'

Len did so, then, with a shovel in his hands, he followed his father on hands and knees through the coal-face. The glistening coal, reflecting the gleam from the two lamps, fascinated Len. He watched Jim crawl, practically on his stomach, up the long stretch of the coal face until only the dim light of his lamp was visible. Scared to be left alone, the lad followed, only to be gruffly ordered back.

'You keep by that empty tram and don't move till I tell you.'

Len turned back and for the first time gave conscious thought to the tram. It stood end on to the clear-cut roof, or 'rippings', which had to be blown down as the coal-face advanced, so that the tram could follow the coal.

A deep feeling of loneliness enveloped Len as he wondered what would happen if his father were not near and he were left entirely on his own. All round him he could hear little movements, as if the place were alive. He had an uncanny feeling that the roof was moving, and each creak of the timbers, as they unwillingly took the weight of the settling strata, sent a quiver through his body. He had yet to learn that the pit had a life of its own, that it was never still or silent, but was always moving and floating in response to the atmosphere and pressure.

Suddenly he felt a burning sensation on his stomach. His hand flashed to the spot automatically, his fingers clutched some object and tore it away, and opening his hand he saw a huge red insect with innumerable hairy legs and hard, shiny wings. Although crushed in his convulsive grip, the ghastly legs still beat the air, and looking down at his belly, he saw a thin stream of blood running down it where the cockroach had gripped the flesh and torn it away. A sick giddiness swept over the lad for a moment, while the perspiration burst from every pore in his body, lathering it in a mixture of coal-dust and moisture, but before he could recover from the shock he heard his father crawling back. This proof that he was not alone encouraged the lad and he was smiling when Big Jim emerged on the roadway.

'We will work in the right hand cut today, Len bach,' he said, 'so that we can free the whole face for to-morrow.'

Len did not understand the technique underlying the remark, but he asked with assumed indifference, 'What be I to do, dad?'

Jim replied: 'You will come up the cut with me and throw the coal back towards the tram.'

The lad obeyed, and followed his father, and for hours he worked on his knees with the back of his head rubbing against the roof. He began mentally counting each shovelful of coal his father cut and which he had to throw back to the tram. His arms grew heavy as lead, cramp caught him in his bent legs, and his back felt as though it were broken. The coal-dust that filled the air got into his nose and eyes. It made him sneeze and blink and, working into the sweat-opened pores of his body, set up an intolerable irritation. He felt it impossible to lift another shovelful of the coal he now detested, but somehow he kept on, until at last his father said: 'That will do for now. Let's go back and get a bit of tommy.'

The lad dragged his weary, painful limbs back into the roadway, where he stretched himself full length in the dust. He saw his heart pumping against the bones of his naked chest, and felt pins and needles run through his flesh in spasms of excruciating agony.

Big Jim, sensing what was happening, urged him to his feet. 'Come on. Get up before you go stiff.'

With infinite care Len dragged his limbs together and slowly rose to his feet. He opened his food box and sat down. The bread-and-butter looked dirty and unappetising, but the water in his jack was like nectar. Jim stopped him before he had emptied the tin of its contents. 'Don't do that again or you will get cramp in your belly. Get on with your food.'

The lad tried to obey, but the hundreds of savage-looking cock-roaches that buzzed and fussed around turned his stomach, while the dust he had already swallowed curdled in his inside.

After a while Big Jim rose and made his way back up the face, telling Len: 'You stop there till I shout for you. A bit of a whiff 'on't do you any harm now.'

During the rest the lad slowly recovered from his exhaustion. The black dust under his body seemed softer and more sweet to him then than even the green grass on his beloved mountain, and his mind wandered to the end of the shift. Before his eyes floated a picture of the envious glances of his schoolmates when they saw him striding, black-faced, down the hill in his working clothes. He saw the glad look in his mother's eyes as he walked into the little kitchen, having finished his day's work. Already he began to count the pocket-money he would have in a fortnight's time, and speculated how best to spend it.

Deeply immersed in these pleasant contemplations, Len dozed off into a heavy sleep. Jim's deep voice seemed miles away when he shouted, 'Right you are, Len bach; come up and start chucking this coal back.'

Len came back to reality with a start and made his way up the coal-face he already hated with every fibre in his body. He worked in a semi-conscious state, only faintly aware of the three or four occasions when the haulier and his horse noisily changed the full tram of coal for an empty one. When the fireman came round and chatted with Jim he waited respectfully on his knees, wishing fervently that the man would stop there till the end of the shift. But he had ceased to take any interest in what was happening. His brain was numbed with the physical exhaustion that again consumed him even though his father had been careful to limit the amount of work to a mini-mum.

The poor lad, accustomed to the fresh air of the mountain, felt the foul atmosphere of the pit beginning to choke him. He thought again of his mother, and now wished he had listened to her advice and tried the examination for the secondary school. Young Mary, Ezra's daughter, had done so and passed successfully, although she was no better scholar than he. Too late now, he thought to himself, half weeping; now he had started in the pit he had to continue. He wondered if the rain had stopped up above; it seemed years since he had left its refreshing coolness. He was sorry now he had ever grumbled at the rain, and was willing for it to pour down for ever as long as he was on the surface to see it.

Tears involuntarily gushed to his eyes and he was on the point of bursting into sobs when a terrific crash shook the whole earth. For a moment he stood paralysed with fear, then he rushed headlong with a wild scream towards his father. Big Jim caught the terror-stricken, hysterical lad to him.

'Duw, duw, mun, don't ever let it be said that the son of Big Jim is frightened by a noise. That was only gas and squeeze busting inside the coal, mun. There, there, now, don't be 'fraid no more.'

It took Len some time to control his quivering flesh. The crash had sent the memory of the explosion flashing through his mind, and in a split second he had seen himself in the place of the bodies he had watched being buried on the day of the funeral.

Jim made the lad rest back on the roadway again until, some half-hour later, he took him down the roadway to fetch some timber. Here Len saw another lad with his adult mate engaged in the same task. The sight of someone his own age immediately restored his confidence. His natural taciturn unsociability evaporated with the new contact in the new environment. While the two men were chatting and selecting the timber they wanted, Len shyly asked the strange lad, 'How long you been working?'

'Oh,' was the casual, off-handed reply, 'a long time now, butty. More than six months, I believe, though I can't 'member 'xactly, because it be so long ago.' Saying which, he took a lump of chewing-gum from his mouth and spat noisily into an empty tram near him.

'Well, what do you think of the bloody hole?' patronisingly.

'Not so bad,' lied Len, trying to forget the torments of the day.

'Huh. I'm only sticking it till I'm old enough to get a horse.'

'Get a horse?' queried Len amazedly.

'Ay, ay, that's it. I'm going to be a haulier.'

'Oh, I see. Like that man who do bring the horse to fetch our full trams out?'

'You got it, butty. And, by Christ, can't I handle them!' warming to his subject. 'Take a tip from a old hand, butty, never take no bloody nonsense from them. When they turn twp or stupid, a sprag will always bring them to their senses.'

He accompanied these remarks with a clicking sound and a practical demonstration which left Len staring with admiration. The budding haulier put the chewing-gum back into his mouth with a grimace and remarked, 'This bloody stuff be getting too weak for me now; I will have to start chewing 'bacca soon.'

Len felt he would like to have a say: 'I only started to work today,' he said hesitantly.

'Be that so? Ah well never mind you'll soon get used to it when you have worked so long as me.'

Their conversation was interrupted by the man with Big Jim.

'What the hell be you blabbing 'bout by there?' he demanded. 'Why don't you come and give me a hand with this blasted timber?'

'All right, all right, keep your wool on,' the lad said casually, and turning to Len he hurriedly whispered: 'That's my butty. I 'spose I'd better go and give him a hand. Come out same time as me to-night — we be working next place to you. My name is Will Evans. So long.' With this he and his mate left, each with one end of a long nine-foot prop on his shoulder.

Shortly after this finishing time came and Len gathered all the tools together, his father showing him how to put them securely on the tool bar.

He dressed in quick time, the clothes sticking to his steaming body, and as he envisaged his triumphant entry into the house all his old pride began to surge through him again. To make sure his face was quite black he rubbed it vigorously with his dusty cap.

On the way out he told his father of the request made by Will, the lad in the next working place. Big Jim took him round to it and they both waited for the others to finish; then the two men and their boys went out together, the former in front.

Len felt elated as he retraced his steps along the roadway that in the morning had seemed like the pathway to hell. He chattered incessantly and already felt he was an old hand in the pit. His new-found mate let him ramble on for a while then broke in with the question: 'Do you know Sam Dangler?'

Len shook his head negatively.

'Huh, you have missed a treat. That's a haulier for you, mun. You ought to see him handling the rough 'uns.' He stopped half-way up the trip. This is how he do do it,' he remarked, catching hold of an imaginary rein. 'Whoa boy, whoa! Ah, bite you sod, would you?'

giving a sharp tug and pressing his body back as though he were pulling the non-existent rein. 'Take that, you bloody cow!' hitting the air with a short piece of timber. 'Whoa, boy. Steady now. Ah, that's got you. Come to your senses, have you?' He flung the sprag into the roadway triumphantly and remarked: 'That's how Sam Dangler do conquer him, see?' A moment's pause, then: 'He's a devil. All the horses do know him, and after a week he have very near got them talking. I'm going to be like him one day. He do have more trumps off the colliers than any haulier in the pit.'

He broke off here to take Len on the side and whisper in his ear: 'You want to watch your old man on pay day. Tell him straight from the beginning that if he want you to work he have got to give you trumps. Huh. Fathers be the worst butties going. They do think their own sons be bloody slaves and do never think of trumping 'em. Oh, no. They do pocket that their bloody selves and the old 'ooman don't have a smell of it. You listen to me,' he continued sagely. 'Don't let any butty make out of you unless he pay you for it, father or no father.'

A voice drifted down to the two lads from the top of the trip: 'Will-o! What the bloody hell be you hanging like a shirt behind there for?'

They hurriedly continued their way, and eventually over-took their mates on the pit bottom, where they had to wait a while in the queue before they were bundled into the cage.

The sound of the iron knocker, announcing to the men on the surface that all was ready, came to Len's ears like the chime of sweet-tolling bells. The cage sprang up the shaft like a projectile released from a mighty catapult, and in a matter of breathless minutes the roar of the air beating against the droppers drowned every other sound. There was a clamouring rush as the chains caught the covering and Len once more saw the light of day.

from *Cwmardy* (1937)

ALEXANDER CORDELL
Rhondda Doing Well

Spring had come to the land, and the Rhondda, when I entered it that sunny afternoon in April 1910, was as bright as a young girl out in her Easter clothes, with the wild flowers of the mountains a madness of colour in the sun. Dandy wet-a-beds grew in yellow carpets along the lanes; bluebells waved their heads off in the woodland as I strode into the Coal Country. And I thought, as I walked alone down from the mountain, of the generations of men who had come in before me, seeking new lives in the valleys of the Coal Rush.

I thought of my father; of how he had come here with a pack on his back, as I, to settle in the pits of Tonypandy. After a year or so, he had told me, he had hungered for a wife, so he took himself to Gilfach Goch where the women are known to be extra decent. There, at the Fair, he had sought out my mother; sweeping his bowler in the gutter, she related, while she curtsied back, but my wicked old Grandad showed him the door because she was Congregational and my father was Church of England.

But next morning he missed a shift, did my father, and was straight back over to Gilfach Goch, and what with Grandad shouting on the doorstep and my mother howling, it was a choice bit for the relatives, he said, with neighbours chipping in and children swinging on the gate. And up and down Glamorgan Terrace (they lived in Number Six) people were scandalised, apparently, because my Grandad was proving an awkward old sod. But, after a while my grandfather repented, and my father, dolled up posh in his new suit and funeral bowler, called and asked officially for her hand, but he had to go Congregational.

Within a month my mother had been pledged, banned and bedded in Tonypandy, and since my father never did things by halves, nine months to the day she brought forth me.

I sighed, smiling at my thoughts as I plodded down the mountain sheep track into Gilfach Goch. And I stopped for a bit outside Number Six, Glamorgan Terrace, and touched the gate that my people's hands had touched, until I saw curtains move.

Then, I was away to Penygraig, and along the valley road to Tonypandy.

God must have been in a good humour when he fashioned the towns of the Rhondda, and had a great time inventing some of the names.

He must, I think, have made a fork of two fingers and laid them on the land, pressing them into the rich soil so that the big dividing ridges of Maerdy and Tynewydd rose up in between. The mountains, upon which He breathed in His labours, grew green; the land of His touch became fertile. One valley He called Rhondda Fach, the other Rhondda Fawr, and down each green belt He ran a foaming river.

It was a big country, like its granite sister-land up north; in the rounded hills lay unbounded wealth — timber, limestone, coal, and Man smelled its riches from afar.

The Coal Rush of the nineteenth century began.

Begging for food and money, the immigrants flooded in. Speculation mushroomed, leader-barons rose, and the twin valleys, divided communities of alien habits and customs, began to prosper. In the lust for wealth, pit after pit was sunk by imported navvies called sinkers. Little townships sprang up haphazardly around individual pits, often named after their engineers or owners — roughly a town to the mile by the year 1900, some overlapping; all joined in the south by a common road; here was the confluence of the two rivers, Fach and Fawr. Communities like Maerdy and Ferndale rose in the Rhondda Fach; Treherbert, Treorchy and Trealaw darkened the sky of Rhondda Fawr.

Tonypandy, the town of my birth, lay near the end of the river confluence at Porth.

Now, with my bundle over my shoulder and whistling to have my teeth out, I strode through the Rhondda, past the two big Naval Pits and over the Adare incline and on to Tonypandy square.

It was a gorgeous April afternoon and a Saturday long-pay day, too, and the place was crowded with people going about their business; broughams and traps, pony and dog carts coming and going; melodeons playing in the gutters. Ragged tramps tugged at my sleeve for alms; wizened Irish, the refuse of the old Eastern Valley ironworks trudged in melancholy discontent among the poshed up, bowlered gentlemen bowing this way and that to hoop-skirted ladies: coloured parasols flourished, for the spring day was hot.

It was obvious to a stranger that the Rhondda, in the spring of 1910, despite its labour troubles, was doing well. With Glamorgan county sitting on a crock of gold, this was the end of the rainbow: over ten million tons of coal and coke were exported from Barry docks that year, and most of it came from the Rhondda pits.

On I went, pushing my way through the crowded pavements —

seeking lodgings first, then a job, and there was a new delight in me at being back among my father's people.

from *This Sweet and Bitter Earth* (1977)

The Courting of Esther

She was a true country girl. Anyone arriving in the Rhondda from the standstill rustic parts needed to wear a different pair of life's boots with us, and for a long time Esther pretended to be comfortable in hers. Except for a good sprinkling of Irish and Bristol-way invaders, nearly everybody of full stature had hailed from the Welsh arcadies, or their parents had, and most newcomers soon felt at home and ceased to sigh for the lost innocences of country places. Esther continued to talk of her native shire. Sometimes they had fierce seas there, but the weather was quite different in that clement spot which bordered the Atlantic, a patch or two of yellow corn waving in gentle pulsations under ever-blue skies, peaceful cattle keeping want unfailingly at bay for the lucky owners. Once or twice, however, she referred to the bad poverty that had brought her to us, for thirty shillings a month and her keep. Yet, after almost four years, she was to lose heart and return to the scenes she had left, though not before she struck her own private blow for our angry place.

Her cheeks were fuschia-red, and her sorrel hair filled an enamel bowl when she washed it every Wednesday, her half-day off. I first saw her as she was laying the tea-table in our living-room when I arrived from the elementary school just above Dai Morgan's slaughter-house on the mountain's lower slope. I was about nine then. Esther couldn't have been more than nineteen. Her brother had come to Clydach Vale to work in D.A. Thomas's Cambrian pit months before; he lodged with one of my father's customers and had sought a place for his sister. Esther arrived with a roped tin trunk and a 'transfer' letter from the minister of her Baptist chapel in Cardigan to a fellow minister in Clydach Vale. She had enough English words for the conveyance of such thoughts as she wished to disclose, and very soon — my own tutoring was of aid — picked up the more or less alien tongue profusely.

For some weeks she had refused to go out. On her afternoon off she would sit at one of the two windows of our front room upstairs and stare down at the main road as if foreseeing dire things happening there. The big Central pub opposite, open all day, especially held her attention. Her brother, who was not as good-looking as she, came to see her sometimes in a criss-crossed muffler and a cap, already a young collier well in with the boyos and not one to shun the Central; he would wink at me from the sofa as if we both must have patience with women. Of course I had quickly sensed Esther's inferior position and taken advantage of it in demands for services and attentions. She was not of truculent character, and we rapidly established amicable relations. Her habit of modestly keeping her eyelids down pleased me. In return for her stories of country life I educated her in arithmetic, English spelling and other simplicities during my school homework at our large table, while she ironed at one end. Lessons in her own school had been conducted in Welsh and she seemed to want to reapprehend even arithmetic through the English language....

It was a time when adult nerves were frayed in Clydach Vale. Another strike, of important dimensions on this occasion, lay in the wind. For me, strikes of the past were only talk — especially in connexion with my father's big ledger. Groups of Rhondda colliers idling all day on street corners had looked contented enough to me. (It was not in Clydach Vale that one week the men downed tools because they objected to a certain police-sergeant on the grounds that he had made a collier's wife into his fancy woman. The disliked sergeant was removed.) But this new strike was to become a bitter one. It lasted twelve months. It also drastically altered the disposition of our Esther, opened my own eyes a fraction, and caused my father to keep at the ready under his bed a gun he yearly took into the country for a few autumn days of pheasant and partridge shooting. It was the strike when nearly every shop down in Tonypandy was wrecked and looted by rioters and the cardinal error was made (by, it was long believed, Winston Churchill, the Home Secretary) of drafting armed troops into the Rhondda. While it happened it was little but enjoyable excitement for me; I learned all about its implications much later....

Months of the strike had passed when one night I woke before dawn and heard a distant bugle call. The bugle hadn't wakened me. My parents had come from their room into mine, the long front room overlooking the main road. I saw them standing at one of the dim windows. A curtain was pulled aside an inch or two. There was a whisper of softly tramping feet in the road below, where the gas lamps were always extinguished hours before dawn by a man with a long pole. The bugle sounded again, more faintly. I went back to sleep.

It was not a soldier's bugle. Our Clydach Vale men, led by their agent Noah Rees, had been signalled thus to assembly. They planned to wreck the colliery powerhouse. They did not succeed. Extra police had been drafted to the colliery — it was said there had been a betrayer — and attacked the men at the bridge which approached the vital powerhouse. Not a man got through. I learned what the bugle and tramping feet meant when I listened to talk in our shop next day; and coarse-mouthed, but not coarse-natured, Jim Reilly told me that his bastard of a father had been in the fight and had a lump on his head the size of an egg out of a gander's arse, which he didn't know was a male one until I told him. Jim hated his father and took pleasure in telling me of the mishap.... When the charity soup kitchens were opened in the schools for the strikers' children, and pea soup with chunks of beef in it was the most perpetual item, Jim said he hoped the bloody strike would last for ever. He had never eaten so well in his life.

I was not eligible for the feasts in our school. We had enough food at home and did not lack cake throughout the strike. But debts grew and grew in our Ledger of Old Accounts. Tidy old customers could spare a few shillings out of Federation strike pay. But orders had to be cut down, or it was bankruptcy for us. My mother looked more and more harassed. My father stayed at home in the evenings. Before this strike, I had enjoyed what could be called neglect, which wasn't that for me. I had the public life of the shop, where there was always something going on. My father would draw up important letters for ignorant customers, especially those who were not chapel-goers and therefore could not consult a minister. He gave advice on legal matters and witnessed wills. Almost as many men as women came to the shop, and all of them talked. My father was such a talker that I stopped listening. His verbosity filled my mother with foot-tapping impatience; she had a constant cry of anguish — 'Come to the point!' It had no lasting effect.

She volunteered for the roster of noon service in the charity soup kitchens, and, on returning to the shop, always kept her flowered or fruited hat on all the afternoon. She liked the handsome big hats of the time, had many, and saw no reason to lower this flag during our bad time, except for not buying new ones in Cardiff, or taking trips there. Life wasn't much changed at home. Esther would seldom venture out. Her brother, now that she was installed comfortably in her place, had stopped coming to see her, but once or twice she sent him half a crown at his lodgings. She was certain he would not take part in the rioting going on down in Tonypandy; he had been a chapel boy in Cardigan.

In all the twelve months our shop was not attacked and looted. But my father placed his gun under the bed. He put it there after Dai Morgan's slaughter-house below my school had been raided and set on fire one night. By that time the soldiers had come. Their holiday tents dotted a low mountain field above Llwynypia colliery, where another pitched battle with police had taken place; hundreds of rioters had attempted to storm the yard and reach the powerhouse, and were foiled again. Down in the pits of this colliery astute Sir Leonard Llewellyn, D.A.'s general manager, had left three hundred ponies, instead of bringing them up for strike-time grazing on the mountains, thus exciting great public sympathy for these forlorn animals alleged to be abandoned by the men; constant inquiries about their welfare from George V, fresh on the throne, added to the newspaper pity for them. In Tonypandy all the shops in long Dunraven Street were boarded up. Schoolchildren were forbidden to stray far, but roving towards Tonypandy with Jim Reilly one evening we saw a young man dashing through a back lane with a whole ham in his arms like a baby. We thought the police were in pursuit, would seize us too, and we sped in his wake until he threatened to kick our backsides if we didn't clear off. He must have thought we wanted a share of his ham.

Clydach Vale had remained comparatively quiet for a long time. The narrow, though long, cul-de-sac was not so easy for concealment or escape as the main valley. Our looters went down to Tonypandy. Then, as the second winter of the strike approached, we had our share of street battles. A tradesman suspected of revealing to the police a second plan for attacking the powerhouse of our colliery found his premises gutted. I saw his furniture and ledgers smouldering in the middle of the road. There was less looting now than retaliation against authority, especially against the soldiers, who in Tonypandy paraded the streets with fixed bayonets and were known to have given warning prods in a few scuffles with jeering gangs of men. The continued presence of soldiers brought bitter hatred and hardened the strikers.

Then, late one afternoon, came the battle that was to turn our Esther into a woman of full stature, brave and, after a time, faulty. I stood with her at one of our front windows upstairs. Below, in the locked shop, my father and mother remained on guard. A double row of policemen, two mounted sergeants at either end of them, had drawn up in the road outside the corner pub. An attack was expected. Marauding bands of rioters had been active for days in Clydach Vale, swooping on the police with taunting suddenness; they knew the lay-out of the back lanes better than these men drafted to the place from elsewhere. I was unaware then that my father had concealed in our stable the son of an old customer who was on the run after one of the brawls; it was not safe to tell schoolboys anything.

A mob was prowling in the near-by back lanes now. Fight was wanted, and nothing else. 'I can hear them,' Esther whispered, her hand gripping my shoulder. I couldn't. My first awareness of the quick attack was a huge noise of smashing glass. The window of Evans the butcher, only five numbers down on the corner of our side, had been stoned by men rushing from the sloped round at the opposite pub corner. They swarmed into view. *'Iesu Mawr!'* Esther breathed, gripping me tighter. I climbed on to the sill to get a better view, diagonally. We were safe from stones up here.

The road below mesmerized me. I was scarcely aware of Esther's grip and heavy breathing. Crammed with yelling strikers armed with sticks and mandrels, the road rose to my eyes. Policemen, far outnumbered, bounded among the rioters with batons drawn. The two horses reared. Their riders, one hand kept firmly on the reins, flayed long switches on to the rioters. I saw a helmet flying on to the porch steps of the pub, a rioter falling there, and a baton crashing down on his head as he attempted to rise. I heard a strange cry from Esther. Her grip left my shoulder.

She ran out of the road. Her flight down our back yard, then through the lane and round the corner into the main road, must have been done in record time. I saw her plunge into the mob, the only woman there. She whirled, ducked, fell to her knees, leapt up. I jumped from the sill and raced downstairs into the shop. My mother, arms folded, sat on a chair far away from the windows. The doorblind was down, my father peering from its side; he did not have the advantageous view of the corner battle that the upstairs window gave. 'Esther's fighting out there!' I shouted, and was not believed at once.

There was nothing to be done. It seemed only a minute later that Esther's hysterical cry came from our living-room calling for my mother. By then the rioters had retreated round the pub corner, though several lay in the road, and were to be borne off to the police-station cells. In our living-room Esther lay on the sofa, blood coming from her mouth and streaking her neck. Her bright hair had fled its many pins and the lost diamante back-comb my mother had given her at Christmas. Her frantic wailing was a revelation to me. It was my first experience of a woman demolished by emotional excess. I stood petrified until my mother, gathering the shining hair from the puffed face, told me to fill a bowl — 'lukewarm from the kettle', she commanded, wonderfully calm; 'a sponge and a towel'. My father hurried in. 'She saw her brother hit by a truncheon,' my mother said. I heard it in bewildered respect.

'I saw him falling down,' Esther sobbed, more coherent now. '*Iesu*, I thought he'd been killed.'

That was not the only shock for her. There had been the horror of discovering that her brother was among the wicked men at all. Another shame made her cower now: she'd brought disgrace on us. Would the police come for her? My father said no, and this turned out to be correct. My mother sent her to bed. Esther descended from it in an hour and said she wanted to do some ironing. She had lost a tooth and thought it had 'gone down'. Her lip was cut and a knee grazed. A different kind of injury took some time to manifest itself. But she did not really question or upbraid herself for her action. If her brother had been killed she would somehow have gathered up the stocky corpse and borne it to safe keeping. Actually he had got away round the corner, and he was not prosecuted, as over the months, some known rioters were. He scolded Esther for her interference. He said his pit butties would make fun of him.

Her decline began from this time. It obeyed the slow countrified rhythm natural to her, a contrast to her quickness of mind in picking up such essentials to living in the Rhondda as English speech and the wearing of frivolous clothes. For a long time I was not conscious that she had changed. Yet I reaped a new benefit from this different Esther who, when the strike was over heartlessly kept a well-behaved young collier dangling on a string — a courtship in which none the less she made a last valiant effort to adjust herself normally to such an abnormal place as Clydach Vale.

The Cambrian Combine men lost their long struggle. They gave in to D.A.'s terms for return to work. But everybody knew their endurance now and in the next strike they were to earn their reward. We had nearly two years of peace after the twelve-month dispute. And it was soon after our colliery began working that Esther allowed herself to be courted by a pit butty of her brother, a lodger needing to settle down in the usual way. His name was Gwilym. He had not taken part in any of the rioting, belonged to the Cambrian Male Voice Choir (eisteddfod winners in their day), and was afflicted with a patience which, had it not derived from the respected virtue love brings to some men, could be called wishy-washy.

To Esther his dogged wooing brought eighteen months of sombre procrastination, and if she did not really break a man's heart, this was because men's hearts in our heavily masculine world were not easily broken over baulked love. Silent about the courtship's preliminaries for some time, the whole affair bred an amount of strange humbug and evasions in her. I thought she spent her Wednesday evenings off at her brother's lodgings, where she was friendly with the landlady. Then one Wednesday she obtained my mother's permission to take me to the Empire Theatre in Tonypandy. I had not been there before; neither had Esther. In the street she whispered, 'You can keep your shilling for the seat. A friend will pay. But don't tell anyone, will you?' Her face had a hunted look under a straw hat decorated with flowers, and her person smelled of the carbolic soap which she believed had a safe-guarding property against nasty things — I came to realize presently that for her I possessed the same property on these occasions.

Outside the chemist's shop on Tonypandy Square, an area busy enough for the assignation not to be noticed, her young man viewed me with surprise. Esther gave no explanation to him, and he courteously accepted my presence. Wearing a stiff collar and tie instead of a criss-crossed muffler, he did not speak much, looking steadily ahead out of pale grey eyes. He asked my age before buying the Empire tickets, and I was allowed in for half-price. We sat on a long hard bench in the pit. Esther placed me between her and Gwilym. She kept her eyelids down as if they would never lift in such a place. The seats became packed. An attendant bawled 'Close up', and, tightly wedged between Esther's rigid thigh and Gwilym's warmly thick one, I was too excited to be bothered by the palpitating silence of the two courters. Great cerise curtains parted to reveal the only fairytale magic I knew in my upbringing. The play was called *A Royal Divorce*. I remember marble stairs in a garden and Napoleon's handsomely fat wife descending them in a trailing gown, real tears streaming down her pink cheeks, her crown off her head and dangling in a hand, so that there was no mistaking that her time was up.

It was the first of five or six such Wednesday treats. We saw the Carl Rosa Opera in *Rigoletto*, for which admission prices were doubled and no half-price. Gwilym did not jib; and I had extra pocket-money. We saw *The Bells*, *The Lights of London*, and *East Lynne*. One touring company distributed in the interval household utensils, baskets of groceries and toys to those who had lucky numbers on their admission tickets, which we hadn't. I always sat between the courters, and Esther's eyelids were always down, though she missed nothing. When we walked home, she told Gwilym outside our closed shop door, 'Next Wednesday,' nodded, and he stood there with a pinched smile until we vanished within. Proper courters went for their doting into the back lanes, where the mountain sheep wandered at night foraging for cabbage stalks and potato peelings. Allowing Gwilym to walk home with us after dark was Esther's only concession.

We were found out. A friend of my mother's had seen us twice in the Empire with the lovesick young man. Esther confessed, and my profitable chaperonage ceased. But my mother encouraged the courtship. She made it her responsibility to discover Gwilym's reputation. The report was sound. Esther, if inclined to choose a collier, couldn't do better. A first-class servant would be lost, but no doubt her married name would adorn a fresh double page of our black ledger; she and Gwilym would be trustworthy, teetotal and clean-minded.

Esther remained both inclined and not. Her Wednesday evenings became a privacy beyond my ken. But I was love's messenger for Gwilym, thus making some return for his Empire treats. He would hang about the colliers' gossiping corner opposite the Central for hours, waiting for me to appear and take a folded scrap of paper to Esther. She would read the notes with a frown, and, never putting anything in writing for anyone, give me a verbal message to take back — 'Tell him I wasn't in a temper,' or, 'Say I don't like menageries or concerts'. I found myself with a contempt of Gwilym's abject slavery to a girl familiar to me as the horse in our stable. Once or twice I avoided returning to him with her message. On some Saturday evenings, still waiting at the corner, he would hand me a quarter-pound bag of her favourite sweets, Rowntree's fruit gums. She would count the sweets and give me exactly half; if there was an odd number I had the extra one.

But at last she took to going into our back lane with him on Wednesday nights. This promising move began more than a year after my Empire treats. I knew about it because she came in that way, sharp at ten o'clock, instead of by the shop door. But nothing was said. The courtship went on for a further long while without incident. Once Gwilym handed me a brooch in a tiny box for her. Esther gave it a shrewd glance, said he must have won it at a hoopla stall in the fair, and later handed it to the woman who combed the gigantic Cambrian waste tip for saleable bits of coal. My contempt of Gwilym increased. However bad the winter weather he seemed to be waiting oftener at the corner, and I noticed his voice had become hoarse. Esther told me he had been missing choir practice. But he did not take to any drinking. This would have given her reason to arrive at the hard decision.

Her flat-iron, while I sat at the other end of the table on homework evenings, would plunge down with more force than she had supplied formerly, her gob of testing spit issue more virulently. She tended to talk of Gwilym oftener, and derogatively. 'He comes from North Wales,' she would say. Or, 'He plays quoits in that field down by the river.' Or even, 'He sings in the Male Voice Choir.' These criticisms seemed undeserved even to me. Months had gone by when she said, 'Your father says there's going to be another strike. The bums I might have in if I get married.' Few disgraces were more terrible than bailiffs removing household possessions. A crowd of sightseers would gather to view the dramatic act, news of it passing rapidly from street to street.

'We're always having strikes,' I pointed out, not displeased at the prospect of another. Esther shook out a rolled bodice with an impatient flapping, and I added, 'Gwilym can find someone else.' Our chapel was full of unmarried girls, most of them singing louder and sweeter than anyone else.

Esther drew herself up, her eyelids shooting up too. 'He wants *me!*'

The predicted strike came. It was a more orderly one this time, and, for a while, all our Cambrian men did not come out. Gwilym remained in work. Yet this promising sign was of no avail. One Wednesday night Esther returned as usual through the back lane. But this time she entered our living room with drama in her face. Her bared eyes looked distraught as eyes that have seen the supernatural. Panic lay in them, as it had when she returned from among the rioters. My mother was in the living-room. After a hard swallow and a jerking back of her shoulder, Esther announced at once, 'I must go back to the country now.' It was a month's notice. She had come to decision at last. I heard no explanation of it. I did not ask her for one. Time was changing our old association, and I was to look at her with a new curiosity.

My mother attempted to make Esther think more carefully over the miserable retreat from courage. Herself critical of the coalmining life, none the less she had a deep admiration for most colliers' wives, and also (when she forgot the Ledger of Old Accounts) for the men's important struggles for better conditions and rewards. Besides, Esther hailed from a very poor Cardigan home; her farm-labourer father earned only eighteen shillings a week. My mother reminded her that there were plenty of other young men to choose from. But Esther would not budge. Her brother came to see her and failed in persuasions; and she refused to go out during the month's notice. Somewhere far away in me I felt an oddly welcome acceptance of her going. She departed with her roped tin trunk while — to my relief — I was at morning school.

It was a long time before I stopped missing her. My mother found a Clydach Vale girl to come in daily; she stole cocoa and soap from the shop, putting them up her elastic-edged knickers. We had three or four girls in quick succession, but not one was of the order of Esther, and each tried to impose her will on me by the usual method of accusation, to attempt to reduce confidence by inducing guilt. Except for a silver-frosted Christmas card one Christmas, Esther did not write to us. When I thought of her I imagined her milking in some lonely green fastness where a policeman was rare as a butterfly on an iceberg. She wore a thick flannel skirt, checked shawl and stout boots as she trudged with two pails to the stone dairy of a whitewashed farmhouse tucked away on a hymn-pure hillside. She had forgotten all the English words picked up so nimbly with us. She would marry a farmhand who put an X to documents requiring his signature, as some country-born colliers did, asking my father to witness it.

I was wrong. It must have been three or four years later — the Kaiser's war had begun — when one September afternoon I arrived home from the intermediate school at Porth to which I had passed by then, and found a lady visitor seated at the tea-table with my mother. Under a wide hat containing a sharp-eyed bird with outspread wings, she sat with an erectness conveying not only the discipline of a lengthy corset but correct visitor's manners. She looked altogether dressily well-off. It was Esther. She had given a cry when I slouched in with my satchel hanging from a shoulder:

'He's grown!'

My adolescent embarrassment lasted throughout tea....

'Esther is married now,' my mother had said, and they soon resumed talk appropriate to their mutual status.

She had married into Insurance. Her husband, much older than herself, was district superintendent for one of the impressive companies, his area in West Wales extensive. They owned a bay-windowed house in a Cardiganshire coastal town, well away from the unbridled sea. The Welsh husband bore the astonishing Christian name of Alfonso. He went to London four times a year, but Esther had never gone with him there. Perhaps it was effort to be his contemporary — even to my furtive glance her clothes seemed too old for her — that made her look fifty or more to me, thus deepening my embarrassment. There was even a slight trace of compassionate patronage of my mother. As a married woman Esther was not only her equal but lived immune to the insecurities of such a place as the Rhondda, our everlasting strikes beyond the aid even of Insurance.

'Alfonso,' she said, 'is always praising my sponge cakes.' This was a salutation to my mother.

'Alfonso can't be a Cardigan name,' my mother remarked.

'No. Belonging to his family it is. He says there was a Spaniard long ago that was shipwrecked in Cardigan Bay and married his great-grandmother. A long, thin nose my Alfonso's got, and hair black and shiny as a beetle, forty-five though he was last birthday. A mop of hair he's got like you don't see anywhere in Cardigan.'

I stared hard at my plate, listening. I did not hear of any children. Esther had come to Clydach Vale that day to visit the brother she had once attempted to rescue from policemen's truncheons; he too had married, and a child had been born the week before. Gwilym was not mentioned while I sat at the table; but I already knew he had left Clydach Vale, to work in Cwmparc pits. I gladly escaped into the shop when my father came in for a quick cup of tea, and when he returned I went out for a walk. Esther had left by the time I returned. In the manner of visitors coming from the country, she had brought us a present. It was a plucked duck, and, since the weather was warm, she had stuffed it discriminately with sage leaves and a quartered onion.

from *Print of a Hare's Foot* (1969)

LEWIS JONES

Big Jim Leads the Riot

That night, as though by some inaudible command, most of the able-bodied strikers made their way in casual groups to the Square, but except for the more adventurous, the women remained at home. By midnight the Square was thronged with people. No one seemed to know what they were there for, yet every group of ten or so appeared to have a leader. There was complete absence of shouting and hilarity, but the night air quivered in the drone of five thousand whispering voices, and presently, without a command or a shouted order, the strikers slowly formed themselves into a procession which threaded its way like smoke towards the pits.

Every voice was now silent, even the drone of whispered talking had ceased, and the only sound that disturbed the peaceful air was the shuffle of heavy-booted feet and the sharp clang of iron hobnails on the stony road. Suddenly, when the head of the procession was already a quarter of a mile on the way to the pit, there was a rush from those in the rear who had not yet left the Square. Hearing shouts and screams, the strikers in front turned to see what had happened behind them. The scurry of their twisting feet sounded above the din, but the darkness was too heavy to permit sight and the only news was spread by the deepening moans and the wild undulations that swept along the ranks like waves.

As the foremost strikers, pressing back upon each other, tried to force their way back to the rear, the tumult and trampling became wilder and more desperate until the pressure was eased as sections of the men broke from the main body and turned up the little side lane that circled round to the Square. Only those in the immediate vicinity saw them go, and before anyone had time to conjecture about the manoeuvre, a whistle pierced the air with three distinct blasts, which were immediately followed by a roar from the front and the wild clamour of galloping horses.

For a second the men in the procession froze into immobility. They did not know what was happening. Nothing could be seen. Nothing could be felt but the increasing undulations that marked the fighting at the rear. The world at that moment seemed to be dominated by the horrifying trample of unseen horses' hoofs bearing down on the front ranks of strikers, and as the hoofs tore into their flesh the air was filled with screams. Above the moans and thuds an anguished cry, 'We are trapped', swelled to a hysterical roar, and in a moment everything had become mad tumult as clubs swished down on unprotected heads. In the hearts of all the strikers there was one overwhelming desire — for light. Light to see what was actually happening. Light to fight back. Light to see the enemy.

The horses had torn through to the centre of the procession, leaving behind them a trail of bleeding bodies, and it seemed that the one-sided fight was already over when a soft red glow, deepening in intensity, dissolved the darkness. It came from the pit. It grew wider and brighter, spreading its crimson wings over the valley like a red glare from hell, and at once the men realised that someone had set the power-house on fire. They paid no attention to the fellows lying on the ground, but concentrated on the column of horses rearing and plunging in the roadway, that was bounded on one side by a high stone wall, on the other by a stout wooden fence separating the road from the pit and the burning power-house. As the glow quickly grew to a flame that showed up everything in crimson relief, the panting men and frightened horses in the centre of the procession could be seen, mixed together like dough in which the yeast was fermenting. But there was no sight or sound of the men who had turned up the little side-lane. Their existence was forgotten.

In the houses of the village lights that had been extinguished suddenly flared into new life. Women, already dressed, came tumbling out of their doorways and rushed screaming and cursing towards the Square. Above the tumult could be heard the voice of Big Jim booming instructions to tear up the fences, and in a matter of seconds every man had dashed across the road and provided himself with an improvised weapon.

Again the commanding voice rang out: 'Pick your man and bring him down.'

Big Jim had now assumed command, and as the strikers instinctively rallied their forces and rushed headlong down the narrow roadway towards their separate objectives, the tumult rose to even greater volume. Shouts and curses mingled with groans and cries, while cracking thuds joined in the chorus. Horses driven mad by ripping spurs reared their forefeet into the air like hammers that methodically broke down the barrier of human bodies before them. Here and there bleeding men tore a rider from his mount and his screams would end abruptly.

The pressure of the horses was too great for the strikers, and they slowly beat a track for themselves over the heads and bodies of the men. The eyes of the mounted police were anxiously fixed on the

Square, and they gradually drew nearer, ready to join the ranks of the foot-police who were already in possession. If they succeeded in this manoeuvre it meant that the strikers were trapped in a *cul de sac* with the police concentrated in the only outlet.

The strikers fought desperately to prevent this fusion of forces but the sticks they had torn from the fence were too short to make effective weapons against the mounted men and each minute the battle lasted made the trap more secure. Suddenly, however, as they were on the point of giving up hope, they heard a mad roar from the hill that led to the opposite side of the square. They looked anxiously in the direction of the sound and saw a compact body of men rushing down the hill to fling itself with wild impetuosity upon the surprised police. The horses screamed horribly as the sharpened points of long broomhandles were plunged into their soft sides and they kicked out frantically in all directions, dislodging their riders who became easy victims of those who were waiting to get them on the ground. This reinforcing body of strikers was that which had slipped up the side-lane when the first charge took place. They had gathered all the children's marbles they could lay hands on and now scattered these under the feet of the horses, bringing them crashing to the ground.

The sweeping suddenness of the attack disorganised the police, who ran like rabbits for refuge in the neighbouring side-streets. But here women were waiting for them with buckets of water and slops which they emptied on to them from the bedroom windows. Gradually the police were driven from the Square which was left in the possession of the strikers.

Ezra at once climbed up to a precarious platform on the Fountain, where he stood supported by the great arms of Big Jim, and surveyed the scene. Jim's face was streaming with blood, but he paid no heed to the wound from which it flowed, being much more concerned about the absence of Len, whom he had not seen since the fight began. A deep silence that contrasted eerily with the previous clamour fell over the Square as the strikers waited for Ezra.

Clearing his throat, he began to speak, warning them that the battle was not yet over and that unless they stood firm it would be lost. The police were reforming their ranks, cutting them off from their own wounded. They could not allow this, and he suggested that a message should be sent to the chief of police asking that the wounded of both sides might be collected and brought to the surgery. Twenty men would be enough to bring them all in, he said, and then, raising his voice, concluded:

'If he agrees, well and good. lf not, we must fight for it. Is it agreed we send a message to the chief?'

A roar of assent swept the air like a tidal wave.

'Will anyone volunteer?'

'Ay, I be just the man for that,' shouted Big Jim above all the other voices.

Ezra hurriedly wrote a note and with this in one hand and a blood-stained handkerchief in the other, Big Jim made his way to the spot where the police were regathering and concentrating their forces. But he had only gone about two hundred yards when he was suddenly surrounded by police, who sprang upon him from the darkness of a side lane. 'Hold on, boys,' roared Jim waving his handkerchief wildly as he saw their threatening demeanour and the loosely twirling truncheons that seemed to itch with desire to land on his head.

'I have got a special message for your chief if you will be good enough to take me to him.'

After some muttering among themselves the police, with apparent disappointment, hemmed him in and curtly ordered him to 'Get going'. They led him to where the main body of police was concentrated, and as the little group approached a tall, military-looking man stepped forward.

'Who are you?'" he asked harshly.

'My name is Mishter Roberts, known to everybody as Big Jim. Old soldier. Served through the Boer War with the old 41st and proud of it. I have got a letter here from our leader.'

The police chief silently held out his hand for the message. A slow smile crept across his face as he read it. As an old soldier he appreciated Jim's courage and also the request made by the strikers, and turning to one of his subordinates he remarked: 'Evidently these men regard this as a war and expect the mutual courtesies of such.' Then, turning to Big Jim, 'So you are an old soldier, eh?'

'Ay, sir, and a reservist. Seven years with the old 41st, the best line regiment in the British Army and most battle honours.'

He drew himself up smartly to the full height of his magnificent body and saluted.

The chief acknowledged the salute.

'Tell your leader that the request is granted. I hope to see you again in better times, Mr Roberts.'

With another salute Big Jim turned sharply on his heel and marched back through the open ranks of police.

His old war days had risen vividly to his mind. Everything that had happened during the night had assisted in reviving habits and memories of his old life, and when he reached the Square he gave a gasp of pleasured surprise as the strikers made a clear path for him to the Fountain, where he saw Len and his mate, Will, chatting excitedly to Ezra.

Both young men were black with mud and coal-dust and their clothing was in tatters, but Ezra seemed pleased with what they were telling him.

Jim strolled up, still in his military mood, coughed and smartly saluted before reporting: 'Your request is granted, sir.' The strikers around looked at him in amazement and Len stared at him with open mouth.

from *Cwmardy* (1937)

ALEXANDER CORDELL
The Police Charge

The colliers were organised by the time we got back.

Columns were being formed by the Federation stewards; tempers were regained. They even raised a cheer for us as we took our place in the Ely Lodge ranks.

Urchins and pit boys were handing out Tom Mann pamphlets and colliers' newspapers like *Justice* and *Labour Leader*; a brass band came from nowhere and formed up at our head.

Women and children were running out of their doors, pent with excitement, the wives black-shawled and capped, hopping about us like frock-coated undertakers. Bang, bang, on a big bass drum, and we were off up the hill to Clydach. And we were but one such mass meeting.

All over the Rhondda the colliers were answering the Union's call; snake after snake of men marching in the mountain towns in search of blacklegs and imported labour — the old, old stick which was used to thrash miners.

Up past River View we went to the colliery, bringing families to their doors, waving to Patsy Pearl who was feeding her Madog on her doorstep (and I saw Ricardo, the ice-cream man, fashioned on the bedroom window) and on to the colliery where we chased out the blacklegs and hosed out the engine fires, stopping the cage.

One blackleg we caught, wrapped him in a bedsheet, and marched him like a ghost at the head of the band; another we hoisted to the top of the pit-head, leaving him swinging there, yelling for a pig-sticking.

Down the valley road then, and along the railway to the Nantgwyn Naval colliery; here we did the same, then marched on to the hated Ely through Penygraig, making sure it was shut. Back down Amos Hill we went, singing and cheering, with half the population following us now, some said twelve thousand. To the two Pandy pits and the Anthony we went — all of the Cambrian Combine, with whom we were in dispute. Here we gave the blacklegs a run, sending the women and children after them, and Primrose Culpepper and Rachel Odd in the van, had a field day, hitting the daylight out of them.

It was nearing dusk and we were tired by the time we got back to Pandy Square, leaving behind us a trail of wet fires and halted cages; the wheels of shunting engines jammed, trucks derailed.

The police, mainly Glamorgan Constabulary, watched at the entrances to colliery offices or agents' houses, arms folded, and did not move against us. 'What of the county police now, then?' called some-one.

'And what of the big Metropolitans?' asked somebody else. 'Skulking behind the curtains of the Thistle Hotel, are they?'

'They'll stop skulking when we go down there tomorrow,' I replied. 'Big trouble will arrive when we tackle the Scotch.'

'You can say that again,' said Bron, when I got back to the Hut...

We had been asleep for about an hour, I suppose, when I was aware of a gathering of people in the Square. Bron awoke, too, sitting up beside me. 'What's happening?'

'It's the Glamorgan pit — hell's setting alight.'

'But you're drowning the Scotch fires in the morning!'

'Earlier, it seems,' I said, getting out on to the boards and peering through the frosted window.

Men were thronging to and fro on the Square under the light of the fountain; I heard bass shouts and the high voices of women. And just then the door nearly came off its hinges under Heinie's fist. He entered on a rush of words: 'The Cambrian management have taken over the Scotch,' he cried. 'Word's just come out.'

'But what about our pickets?'

'Flung out by the police. There's three outside with split heads — one's a hospital case.'

'And Lindsay's occupied the colliery?'

'That's it,' said Heinie. 'And Llewellyn, the Combine manager, has gone underground with eighty blacklegs.'

'We'll soon dig them out.'

'But there's a hundred policemen guarding the top — they're all over the yard, and in the power station.'

I was dressing hastily. 'If there is there'll be trouble!'

'There's trouble already — it never really stopped. A lot of the lads are at Llwynypia now. And another fifty Cardiff bobbies have come in overnight to the Thistle Hotel.'

'So they're making the Glamorgan Scotch a show-down, eh ?'

'That's the size of it,' said Heinie. 'A gang of our boys tried to talk to the blacklegs, but the police drove them off.'

'I'm comin', too,' said Bron. She was pulling on her drawers, unconcerned about Heinie.

'You're not. You're staying here,' I said.

Heinie said, 'The Management's taken the scabs underground, they say, to save the ponies.'

'Yet they took those horses down themselves especially?'

'But it works,' cried Mattie, appearing at the door. 'Now there'll he talk about the brutal miners, though Manager Llewellyn don't give a sod if all four hundred ponies drown.'

'You're dealing wi' some lovely people,' said Bron.

'If he isn't careful he'll drown his eighty blacklegs,' and I flung open the door.

Bugles were blowing in strident blasts as I ran out on to the Square.

Word had gone around like a prairie fire blazing. The Combine Management had got control of the Big Glamorgan colliery, known as the Scotch. Blacklegs were working the engines underground. Chief Constable Lindsay had thrown out our pickets and a force of constables were now guarding the colliery pits.

The colliers were infuriated.

Out of their beds rolled the children, out of the doors poured the men, grabbing their tools as they went — mandrels, axe-handles, shovel hafts, brooms.

Followed by their shrieking women, they came pell-mell on to Pandy Square, raising the roof, and even the dear departed in the cemetery must have cocked their dusty ears to listen, said Bron.

From Court Street to Chapel Street they came; up from afar as The Golden Age in Williamstown; rushing in streams from Gilfach, Maddox, Primrose and the Bush, and they packed the Square — the centre of all Town activity — like sprats in a cask.

Moses Culpepper and his Primrose were there, also Rachel and her Bill. The McCarthys came in force, led by Etta, wielding a poker and shrieking like a Sioux Indian. All the Arses came, save Rosie and child; I saw Dai Parcel, Gwilym and Owen; also John Haley and Will Shanklyn with the O'Learys. Diving into the mêlée of the swaying mob, they joined the chorus of yells and threats, for the Town was maddened by the management's occupation of the Scotch.

Where, earlier, there had been organisation and purpose, now it was anarchy, without a Union leader in sight. All the thick-eared fraternity turned out this time, too, with famous people like Tom Thomas and Martin Fury crowding in with the likes of Dai Rush and Snookey Boxer, their blood up at the prospect of battle.

Mr Duck, lately returned from exchange work over in Senghenydd, fought his way into the crowd beside me.

'Toby, this is madness!' he cried, cultured.

'Try telling them that,' I shouted back.

'Where's Mabon at a time like this?'

'Or Noah Rees, Mainwaring — Watts Morgan — where's anyone?'

The men were swaying in a body, shoulder to shoulder, across the length and breadth of the Square, chanting, amid cat-calls, 'The Scotch, the Scotch, the *Scotch!*'

I yelled to Mattie and Heinie, 'Raise me, get me up!' and they swung me high on their shoulders, turning me in the crush of men.

I shouted, my hands flung up, 'Listen, *listen*! Don't act like a mob. Wait for Mabon!'

A man yelled above the rest, 'We're always waiting for bloody Mabon — we don't need the Union to dig out bloody Llewellyn.'

'Pelt out the scabs — run them out of Town!'

I shouted, 'The police are waiting for us, remember?'

'Bloody bad luck for them!'

From my swaying perch, I saw the face of Bron among the infuriated men, with John Haley beside her, barging and shoving for room, trying to protect her.

'*Bron!*' I fought myself down and ploughed through the men towards her, but the sheer weight of their numbers swept me away.

'Bron, *go back!*'

The falling of a leaf will start an avalanche.

In hundreds we started the march on Llwynypia. Meeting other columns coming down from Clydach Vale, Dinas, Penygraig and Trealaw, we marched up the Llwynypia Road and on to the Big Glamorgan colliery. Some lit torches, and from these other firebrands blazed. The pale moon was rolling on billowy, wash-day clouds, her light dimmed with the redness of the waving torches.

Now that we were committed to drown out the Scotch by force, there came upon the marching men an unearthly quiet.

'My gran's milk,' said Heinie, beside me, 'I've never heard colliers as quiet as this.'

Doors were coming open along the road; whole families standing there, their faces pale with apprehension. The torch-light shot shadows into the eyes of the women. This move spelled more hunger: some, like the Ely people, had been eating skint for three months already; their bellies gnawed.

'How are you, Toby?' asked John Haley, pushing into the ranks with Tommy Arse.

'No better for asking,' I answered. 'This business stinks.'

'But time we stopped the Scotch isn't it? She's on the list.'

'We should have done it this morning, before the police made it into a fortress.'

'Time comes when you've got to fight, man,' said he, tersely, and his eyes were shining. 'Like loving when you've got to love.'

'Ye don't usually get your skull fractured, just for loving,' said Duck behind me.

'The women don't hold with it,' said Mattie. 'My wife's playin' Hamlet, first act.'

'She ain't usual,' replied Ben Block. 'My missus is behind us — she says give 'em hell.'

'Time'll come when we'll be behind the women,' grumbled Dai Parcel, over to my left. 'Under their skirts, me, when the batons come out — Toby's right, this business stinks.'

'Then why are ye here?' shouted Tommy Arse, and I chanced a look at him in the tramping of the boots; big and handsome he looked, a boy made into a man.

'Because colliers stick together,' I replied.

'And fall together likewise,' said Heinie. 'It won't be the first time I've had a baton on me nut.'

Lock and Company, the grocers, had barricaded their doors and windows to protect their hams, for the best money hangs from ceilings. Studley's Fruit Shop, in the process of getting out the apples and pears, hung a drape over the photograph of the late lamented Queen Victoria, since loyal subjects appeared few and far between. Watkins the Flannel had got his bales inside; the Monument Chemist slammed shut, with Tailor Jones going demented to save his Union boss frock coats, and the roars that came up from the Square that night eased the slates off the workhouse roof, according to Solly Freedman, the pawnbroker, raising dust up Zion Hill with his trunk on wheels.

We marched on.

There grew an accompaniment to the stamping thunder; a low chanting in the ranks, like cattle lowing; by the time we neared the Big Glamorgan we numbered thousands.

We of the Ely were in the van. Behind us, I saw a massive column now, snaking back to Tonypandy, a great wedge of torch-light. The chanting rose higher as we spilled along the railings of the Scotch.

Many women had joined us, their faces wild, their shawls scragged back over their hair; many armed with pokers, for women fight to kill.

Urchins were darting through the ranks of men, their shrill cries sparking the growing of shouts and bawls.

Before us the road lamps were bright; the pit-wheels of the six pits of the Big Glamorgan stood black against the stars.

A man in the crowd yelled, 'Pull up the railings as weapons. If we get the power house we'll stop the Scotch!' and the men about me spilling out of the ranks and began to tear up the wooden fencing surrounding the colliery. Stone-throwing began; glass clashed and tinkled as windows shattered. Then came quiet.

Before us on the road the police began to mass. Led by a mounted figure, Chief Constable Lindsay, the 'Roman Centurion', they formed up out of the shadows silently, without command; no sound came but the clattering hooves of the horses and their slithering hobnails.

And they stood like a black barrier between us and the power station.

Big bastards, these; we feared them. They might have been ordinary Welsh policemen, but they were hand-picked in anti-riot, from Cardiff and Swansea mainly, and no bloody truck with the black-faced yobs of the Rhondda.

The silence grew in strength and power.

Stock still these policemen stood, and it was clever. Even Lindsay's horse was motionless, with Lindsay astride him, his sabre stiffly upwards.

As black marble statues, they were motionless: the night was as shifty as a monastery in Lent.

'Christ,' said Heinie beside me, 'now we're goin' to blutty 'ave it.'

We hesitated.

From within the colliery came shouted commands. More police poured out, breaking the tension; others were forming up on the east of the colliery, also behind us, boots clattering in the eerie silence.

Then a new leader swept to the fore of us, John Haley, and he shouted, wielding a fencing post, 'Right, follow me! Come on — get the power house, stop the pumps!"

Bedlam came loose in a chorus of cat-calls and shouts; men lacking courage.

'Dig out the manager!'

'Beat up the blacklegs!'

'Bring up the ponies!'

A new chanting began, *Scabs, scabs, scabs!*

Stones began whistling overhead; the windows of the power house clashed as urchins got the range. Ed Masumbala I saw, his black face shining with sweat, as the rush at the police began. Hair down, fighting to be free of men who tried to hold her, Rachel Odd was like a mad thing, swinging her fire-tongs; behind her came Primrose Culpepper and half her brood, darting forward from the crush, baiting the wedge of policemen barring our way.

But, though I joined John Haley and reviled them, the mass of colliers did not shift.

'Wait till they charge, then,' I shouted. 'And pull out these damned women!'

Stones were hissing over us now; empty windows, stab-toothed, were grinning at the moon, truck buffers ringing as the stones pelted down. The grass slope above the road was thronged with children and ruffians, but the police, so far, were out of their range.

Men hauled the women and children out of it: the road was clear for a charge.

But the police charged first.

I have never seen anything like it.

They came in a solid box of blue. Tense, gripping our weapons, we awaited them.

They came in a phalanx, the centurion attack of another age; stamping upright, like automatons, faces lifted, expressionless; knees bobbing up, with mechanical precision; approaching slowly, short, hardwood truncheons held upright at their belts, big fists gripping white. Wide-shouldered and burly, their domed helmets made them gigantic.

Their pace quickened to a rasped command as the distance closed.

Seventy yards.

A collier bawled. 'Come on, then, Bobbies, and God help ye!'

Fifty yards.

'Christ!' whispered a man beside me.

In the front rank, I crouched, waiting. Mattie was one side of me, Heinie on the other.

Twenty yards.

I could see their big faces now; jaws thrust out; some split wide in joyful anticipation. Some of these Bristol bastards were just delighted by the Welsh.

Ten yards.

Gleaming red, on a command, the batons flew up.

'Charge!'

In dervish yells, they leaped at us.

Our front ranks bulged upward to the impact: the mandrels high, the truncheons smashed down.

Instantly, as pole-axed, men fell sprawling; the colliers stayed down, but all the policemen rose, as if commanded. And their truncheons rose and fell again and again in smashes of pain.

Men about me were howling, clutching their red faces; others were crawling among the stamping boots, yelling from bloody mouths. Heinie was down, pulling a policeman with him; Mattie was flailing away at bobbing heads. Helmets were being tipped off, chin-straps torn away; amid a sea of struggling, cursing colliers and policemen, the palings and batons, mandrels and axe-handles rose and fell in flailing, crunching thuds.

Men with broken limbs reeled out of the fight with disjointed cries. A face loomed up before me as John Haley struck out; I elbowed him for room and hit blindly, and the punch caught a policeman square. Instantly, he slipped down the front of me and I lowered him to the ground; next moment the bugger was on my legs. Dull blows were thudding all over me now as my companions thinned out around me; two policemen at me, now three, and their weapons were thudding down on my arms, an old trick of the anti-riot: a baton actually splintered on my shoulder as I ducked and brought down my fencing post on to an unprotected head, which disappeared, as if by magic. It was a bawling mêlée of a fight: Tommy Arse leaped to my side, hooking with his fists and shouting madly, and I had to fight to save him from a six foot Bobby; then Haley grabbed his collar and dragged him out, a moment after somebody felled the boy from behind.

'Get him out!'

We fought for room in a chorus of yells and screams, taking the stabbing blows on the fleshy parts of our bodies, blows that brought a numbing pain.

I saw the furious, snarling faces, yet knew no anger.

Strangely, I fought in a comradeship that embraced even the police. The agony of it all seemed to stitch us together; it was neither my fight, nor theirs. Removed in time and space, in reality I was not there. Amid the cries, the blood, there was an astonishing cleanness ... until I saw the truncheon come down that felled Moses Culpepper. On top of Sam Rays he fell, soundlessly: men trampling on the mounding bodies now.

I saw another baton coming and hooked my fist into the body of a constable; he grunted and doubled up; I felt my knuckles crack on the big buckle of his belt. Another baton descended, a weapon in slow motion; step by step towards Heinie's unprotected face it came. I saw it, but could do nothing: it hit Heinie on the cheek, breaking the bone, spinning him sideways.

'Collar him!' shouted Mattie.

'Haul him out,' I gasped, and barged into them with Mattie Kelly and Bill Odd beside me.

One-handed, shouting to the pain of my broken hand, my desperation drove them before me.

Will Parry was near me: there was Albert Arse, Shanklyn, O'Leary. Ed Masumbala was with us, pulling policemen aside, clubbing them down with his fist; there was Dai Parcel, Gwilym, Owen and Duck; also Snookey Boxer and Ben Block, gasping fat, but fighting like a demon beside the McCarthy lads (though Dano was down). Moses was on his feet again, his face a mask of blood. And then somebody bellowed:

'Look out, lads — look out, behind you!' and we swung to a new enemy.

Rhondda policemen were coming over the Taff Railway at our rear. They came in a tearing, swaying clutch, arms reaching for us — their capes streaming out behind them like flying witches.

'These sods are real Welsh mind,' yelled Mattie, and head down, clutching his face, he bolted.

I paused in my flight to grab Tommy with my good hand while John Haley helped me; together, dragging him between us, we ran, while Ben Block, Albert Arse and Bill Odd fought off the police like a rear party.

from *This Sweet and Bitter Earth* (1977)

Nightgown

She had married Walt after a summer courtship during which they had walked together in a silence like aversion.

Coming of a family of colliers, too, the smell of the hulking young man tramping to her when she stepped out of an evening was the sole smell of men. He would have the faintly scowling look which presently she, too, acquired. He half resented having to go about this business, but still his feet impelled him to her street corner and made him wait until, closed-faced and glancing sideways threateningly, she came out of her father's house. They walked wordless on the grit beside the railway track, his mouth open as though in a perpetual yawn. For courting she had always worn a new lilac dress out of a proper draper's shop. This dress was her last fling in that line.

She got married in it, and they took one of the seven-and-six-penny slices of the long blocks of concreted stone whipping round a slope and called Bryn Hyfryd — that is, Pleasant Hill. Like her father, Walt was a pub collier, not chapel.

The big sons had arrived with unchanged regularity, each of the same heavy poundage. When the sex of the fifth was told her, she turned her face sullenly to the wall and did not look at him for some time. And he was her last. She was to have no companionable daughter after all, to dote on when the men were in the pit. As the sons grew, the house became so obstreperously male that she began to lose nearly all feminine attributes and was apt to wear a man's cap and her sons' shoes, socks, and mufflers to run out to the shop. Her expression became tight as a fist, her jaw jutted out like her men's, and like them she only used her voice when it was necessary, though sometimes she would clang out at them with a criticism they did not understand. They would only scowl the family scowl.

For a while she had turned in her shut-up way to Trevor, her last-born. She wanted him to be small and delicate — she had imagined he was of a different mould from his brothers — and she had dim ideas of his putting his hand to something more elegant than a pick in the pits. He grew into the tall, gruff image of his brothers. Yet still, when the time came for him to leave school at fourteen, she had bestirred herself, cornering him and speaking in her sullen way:

'Trevor, you don't want to go to that dirty old pit, do you? Plenty of other things to do. One white face let me have coming home to me now.'

He had set up a hostile bellow at once. 'I'm going to the pit. Dad's going to ask his haulier for me.' He stared at her in fear. 'To the pits I'm going. You let me alone.' He dreaded her hard but seeking approaches; his brothers would poke jeering fun at him, asking him if his napkins were pinned on all right, it was as if they tried to destroy her need of him, snatching him away.

She had even attempted to wring help from her husband: 'Walt, why can't Trevor be something else? What do I want with six men in the pit? One collier's more work in the house than four cleanjob men.'

'Give me a shilling, 'ooman,' he said, crossing his red-spotted white muffler, 'and don't talk daft.' And off he went to The Miskin Arms.

So one bitter January morning she had seen her last-born leave the house with her other men, pit trousers on his lengthening legs and a gleaming new jack and food tin under his arm. From that day he had ranged up inextricably with his brothers, sitting down with them at four o'clock to bacon and potatoes, even the same quantity of everything, and never derided by them again. She accepted his loss, as she was bound to do, though her jutting jaw seemed more bony, thrust out like a lonely hand into the world's air.

They were all on the day's shift in the pits, and in a way she had good luck, for not one met with any accidents to speak of, they worked regular, and had no fancies to stay at home because of a pain in big toe or ear lobe, like some lazybones. So there ought to have been good money in the house. But there wasn't.

They ate most of it, with the rest for drinking. Bacon was their chief passion, and it must be of the best cut. In the shop, where she was never free of debt, nearly every day she would ask for three pounds of thick rashers when others would ask for one, and Mr Griffiths would drop a hint, looking significantly at his thick ledger, saying: 'Three pounds, Mrs Rees, *again*?' her reply was always: 'I've got big men to feed.' As if that was sufficient explanation for all debt and she could do nothing about it; there were big, strapping men in the world and they had to be fed.

Except with one neighbour, she made no kind of real contact with anyone outside her home. And not much inside it. Of the middle height and bonily skimped of body, she seemed extinguished by the assembly of big males she had put into the world of her big husband. Peering out surly from under the poke of her man's cap, she never went beyond the main street of the village, though as a child she had been once to the seaside, in a buff straw hat ringed with daisies.

Gathered in their pit-dirt for the important four-o'clock meal, with bath pans and hot foods steaming in the fireplace, the little kitchen was crowded as the Black Hole of Calcutta. None of the sons, not even the eldest, looked like marrying, though sometimes, like a shoving parent bird, she would try to push them out of the nest. One or two of them set up brief associations with girls which never seemed to come properly to anything. They were of the kind that never marry until the entertainments of youth, such as football, whippet-racing, and beer, have palled at last. She would complain to her next-door-up neighbour that she had no room to put down even a thimble.

This neighbour, Mrs Lewis — the other neighbours set her bristling — was her only friend in the place, though the two never entered each other's house. In low voices they conversed over the back wall, exchanging all the eternal woes of women in words of cold, knowledgeable judgement that God Himself could have learnt from. To Mrs Lewis' remark that Trevor, her last, going to work in the pits ought to set her on her feet now, she said automatically, but sighing for once: 'I've got big men to feed.'

That fact was the core of her world. Trevor's money, even when he began to earn a man's wage, was of no advantage. Still she was in debt at the shop. The six men were profitless; the demands of their insides made them white elephants.

So now, at fifty, still she could not sit down soft for an hour and dream of a day by the seaside with herself in a clean new dress at last and a draper's-shop hat fresh as a rose.

But often in the morning she skulked to London House, the draper's on the corner of the main road, and stopped for a moment to peer sideways into the window where two wax women, one fair and one dark, stood dressed in all the latest and smiling a pink, healthy smile. Looking beautiful beyond compare, these two ladies were now more living to her than her old dream of a loving daughter. They had no big men to feed and, poised in their eternal shade, smiled leisurely above their furs and silk blouses. It was her treat to see them, as she stood glancing out from under Enoch's throw-away cap, her toe-sprouting shoes unlaced and her skirt of drab flannel hanging scarecrow. Every other week they wore something new. The days when Mr Roberts the draper changed their outfits, the sight of the new wonders remained in her eyes until the men arrived home from the pit.

Then one morning she was startled to find the fair wax lady attired in a wonderful white silk nightgown, flowing down over the legs most richly and trimmed with lace at bosom and cuffs. That anyone could wear such luxuriance in bed struck her at first like a blow in the face. Besides, it was a shock to see the grand lady standing there undressed, as you might say in public. But, staring into the window, she was suddenly thrilled.

She went home feeling this new luxury round her like a sweet, clean silence. Where no men were.

At four o'clock they all clattered in, Walt and her five big swart sons, flinging down food tins and jacks. The piled heaps of bacon and potatoes were ready. On the scrubbed table were six large plates, cutlery, mugs and a loaf; a handful of lumpy salt chucked down in the middle. They ate their meal before washing, in their pit-dirt, and the six black faces, red mouths and white eyes gleaming, could be differentiated only by a mother.

Jaw stuck out, she worked about the table, shifting on to each plate four thick slices of bacon, a stream of sizzling fat, ladles of potatoes and tinned tomatoes They poked their knives into the heap of salt, scattered it over the plate, and began. Lap of tongue around food was their only noise for a while She poured the thick black tea out of a battered enamel pot big enough for a palace or a workhouse.

At last a football match was mentioned, and what somebody said last night in The Miskin taproom about that little whippet. She got the tarts ready, full-sized plates of them, and they slogged at these; the six plates were left naked in a trice. Oddments followed: cheese, cake, and jams. They only stopped eating when she stopped producing.

She said, unexpectedly: 'Shouldn't be surprised if you'd all sit there till doomsday, 'long as I went on bringing food without stoppage.'

'Aye,' said Ivor. 'What about a tin of peaches?'

Yet not one of them, not even her middle-aged husband, had a protuberant belly or any other signs of large eating. Work in the pit kept them sinewy and their sizes as nature intended. Similarly, they could have drunk beer from buckets, like horses, without looking it. Everything three or four times the nice quantities eaten by most people, but no luxuries except that the sons never spread jam thinly on bread like millionaires' sons but in fat dabs, and sometimes they demanded pineapple chunks for breakfast as if they were kings or something. She wondered sometimes that they did not grind up the jam pots, too, in their strong white shiny teeth; but Trevor, the youngest, had the right to lick the pots, and thrust down his tongue almost to the bottom.

At once, after the meal, the table was shoved back. She dragged in

the wooden tub before the fire. The pans were simmering on hobs
and fire. Her husband always washed first, taking the clean water. He
slung his pit clothes to the corner, belched and stepped into the tub.
He did not seem in a hurry this afternoon. He stood and rubbed up
his curls — still black and crisp after fifty years — and bulged the
muscle of his black right arm. 'Look there,' he said, 'you pups, if a
muscle like that you got at my age, men you can call yourselves .'

Ranged about the kitchen, waiting for their bath turn with cigarette
stuck to red-licked lower lip, the five sons looked variously derisive,
secure in their own bone and muscle. But they said nothing; the
father had a certain power, lordly in his maturity. He stood there
naked, handsome and well-endowed; he stood musing for a bit, lik-
ing the hot water round his feet and calves. But his wife, out and in
with towels, shirts, and buckets, had heard his remark. With the impatience that had seemed to writhe about her ever since they had
clattered in, she cried: 'What are you standing there for showing off,
you big ram! Wash yourself, man, and get away with you.'

He took no notice. One after the other the sons stripped; after the
third bath the water was changed, being then thick and heavy as
mud. They washed each other's back, and she scuttled in and out like
a dark, irritated crab this afternoon, her angry voice nipping at them.
When Ieuan, the eldest and six foot two, from where he was standing
in the tub spat across into a pan of fresh water on the fire, in a sudden
fury she snatched up the dirty coal-shovel and gave him a ringing
smack on his washed behind. Yet the water was only intended for the
dirt-crusted tub. He scowled; she shouted: 'You blackguard, you keep
your spit for public-house floors.'

After she had gone into the scullery, Trevor, waiting his turn,
grunted: 'What's the matter with the old woman today?' Ieuan
stepped out of the tub. The shovel blow might have been the tickle of
a feather but Trevor advised him: 'Better wash your best face again;
that shovel's left marks.'

From six o'clock onwards one by one they left the house, all, including Walt, in a navy-blue serge suit, muffler, cap, and yellowish-brown
shoes, their faces glistening pale from soap. They strutted away on
their long, easy legs to their various entertainments, though with
their heads somehow down in a kind of ducking. Their tallness made
it a bit awkward for themselves in some of the places down in the
pits.

Left alone with the piles of crusted pit clothes, all waiting to be
washed or dried of their sweat, she stood taking a cup of tea and

nibbling a piece of bread, looking out of the window. Except on Sundays her men seldom saw her take a meal, though even on Sunday she never ate bacon. There was a month or two of summer when she appeared to enjoy a real plate of something, for she liked kidney beans and would eat a whole plateful, standing with her back to the room and looking out of the window towards the distant mountain brows under the sky, as if she was thinking of heaven. Her fourth son Emlyn said to her once: 'Your Sunday feed lasts you all the week, does it? Or a good guzzle you have when we're in the pit?'

She stood thinking till her head hurt. The day died on the mountain-tops. Where was the money coming from, with them everlastingly pushing expensive bacon into their red mouths? The clock ticked.

Suddenly, taking a coin from a secret place and pulling on a cap, she hurried out. A spot burning in her cheeks, she shot into the corner draper's just as he was about to close, and, putting out her jaw, panted to old Roberts: 'What's the price of that silk nightgown on the lady in the window?'

After a glance at the collier's wife in man's cap and skirt rough as an old mat, Roberts said crossly: 'A price you can't afford, so there!' But when she seemed to mean business he told her it was seventy bob and elevenpence and he hoped that the pit manager's wife or the doctor's would fancy it.

She said defiantly: 'You sell it to me. A bob or more a week I'll pay you, and you keep it till I've finished the amount. Take it out of the window now at once and lay it by. Go on now, fetch it out.'

'What's the matter with you!' he shouted testily, as though he was enraged as well as astonished at her wanting a silk night-gown. 'What d'you want it for?'

'Fetch it out,' she threatened, 'or my husband Walt Rees I'll send to you quick.' The family of big, fighting males was well known in the streets. After some more palaver Roberts agreed to accept her instalments and, appeased, she insisted on waiting until he had undraped the wax lady in the window. With a bony, trembling finger she felt the soft white silk for a second and hurried out of the shop.

How she managed to pay for the nightgown in less than a year was a mystery, for she had never a penny to spare, and a silver coin in the house in the middle of the week was rare as a Christian in England. But regularly she shot into the draper's and opened her grey fist to Roberts. Sometimes she demanded to see the nightgown, frightened that he might have sold it for quick money to someone else, though Roberts would shout at her: 'What's the matter with you? Packed up safe it is.'

One day she braved his wrath and asked if she could take it away, promising faithful to keep up the payments. But he exclaimed: 'Be off! I wouldn't give credit to Moses's wife or the concubines of King Solomon. Enough tradesmen here been ruined by credit. Buying silk nightgowns indeed! What next?'

She wanted the nightgown in the house; she was fearful it would never be hers in time. Her instinct told her to be swift. So she hastened, robbing still further her own stomach and in tiny lots even trying to rob the men's, though they would scowl and grumble if even the rind was off their bacon. But at last, when March winds blew down off the mountains so that she had to wrap round here scraggy chest the gaunt shawl in which her five lusty babies had been nursed, she paid the last instalment. Her chin and cheeks blue in excitement, she took the parcel home when the men were in the pit.

Locking the door, she washed her hands, opened the parcel, and sat with the silk delicately in her hands, sitting quiet for half an hour at last, her eyes come out in a gleam from her dark face, brilliant. Then she hid the parcel down under household things in a drawer which the men never used.

A week or two later, when she was asking for the usual three pounds of bacon at the shop, Mr Griffith said to her, stern: 'What about the old debts, now then? Pity you don't pay up, instead of buying silk nightgowns. Cotton is good enough for my missus to sleep in, and you lolling in silk, and don't pay for all your bacon and other things. Pineapple chunks every day. Hoo!' And he glared.

'Nightgown isn't for *my* back,' she snapped. 'A wedding present for a relation it is.' But she was a bit winded that the draper had betrayed her secret to his fellow tradesman.

He grumbled: 'Don't know what you do with all you take out of my shop. Bacon every day enough to feed a funeral, and tins of fruit and salmons by the dozen. Eat for fun, do you?'

'I've got big men to feed.' She scowled, as usual.

Yet she seemed less saturnine as she sweated over the fireplace and now never once exclaimed in irritation at some clumsiness of the men. Even when, nearly at Easter, she began to go bad, no complaint came from her, and of course the men did not notice, for their bacon was always ready and the tarts as many, their bath water hot, and evening shirts ironed.

On Easter Bank Holiday, when she stopped working for a while because the men had gone to whippet races over in Maerdy Valley, she had time to think of her pains. She felt as if the wheels of several coal wagons had gone over her body, though there were no feeling at all in her legs. When the men arrived home at midnight, boozed up, there were hot faggots for them, basting pans savoury full, and their pit clothes were ready for the morning. She attended on them in a slower fashion, her face closed and her body shorter, because her legs had gone bowed. But they never noticed, jabbering of the whippets.

Mrs Lewis next door said she ought to stay in bed for a week. She replied that the men had to be fed.

A fortnight later, just before they arrived home from the pit and the kitchen was hot as a furnace, her legs kicked themselves in the air, the full frying pan in her hand went flying, and when they came in they found her black-faced on the floor with the rashers of bacon all about her. She died in the night as the district nurse was wetting her lips with water. Walt, who was sleeping in a chair downstairs, went up too late to say farewell.

Because the house was upside down as a result, with the men not fed properly, none of them went to work in the morning. At nine o'clock Mrs Lewis next door, for the first time after thirty years of back-wall friendship with the deceased, stepped momentously into the house. But she had received her instructions weeks ago. After a while she called down from upstairs to the men sitting uneasily in the kitchen: 'Come up; she is ready now.'

They slunk up in procession, six big men, with their heads ducked, disturbed out of the rhythm of their daily life of work, food, and pub. And entering the room for the last view, they stared in surprise.

A stranger lay on the bed ready for her coffin. A splended, shiny white silk nightgown flowing down over her feet, with rich lace frilling bosom and hands, she lay like a lady taking a rest, clean and comfortable. So much they stared, it might have been an angel shining there. But her face jutted stern, bidding no approach to the contented peace she had found.

The father said, cocking his head respectfully: 'There's a fine 'ooman she looks. Better than when I married her!'

'A grand nightshirt,' mumbled Enoch. 'That nurse brought it in her bag?'

'A shroud they call it,' said Emlyn.

'In with the medical benefits it is,' said the father soberly. 'Don't they dock us enough every week from our wages?'

After gazing for a minute longer at the white apparition, lying there so majestically unknown, they filed downstairs. There Mrs Lewis awaited them. 'Haven't you got no 'ooman relation to come in and look after you?' she demanded.

The father shook his head, scowling in effort to concentrate on a new problem. Big, black-curled, and still vigorous, he sat among his five strapping sons who, like him, smelt of the warm, dark energy of life. He said: 'A new missus I shall have to be looking for. Who is there about, Mrs Lewis, that is respectable and can cook for us and see to our washings? My boys I got to think about. A nice little widow or something you know of that would marry a steady working chap? A good home is waiting for her by here, though a long day it will be before I find one that can feed and clean us like the one above; *she* worked regular as a clock, fair play to her.'

'I don't know as I would recommend any 'ooman,' said Mrs Lewis with rising colour.

'Pity you're not a widow! Ah well, I must ask the landlady of The Miskin if she knows of one,' he said, concentrated.

from *A Finger in Every Pie* (1942)

J.O. FRANCIS
Conversation in a Train

If any impartial inquirer wishes to test the assertion that Englishmen are English and Welshmen Welsh, he has but to make the journey from Paddington to, say, Ystrad Rhondda. Then, if he has eyes to see and ears to hear, he will not be seduced by any of these heretics of race who go about the country behaving like glorified phrenologists.

The man who goes aboard the Fishguard express with a carriage full of Englishmen knows exactly what to expect. They will be stiff, reserved, and silent. They will put up their newspapers as a fortification against familiarity....

When the train pulls up at Newport the atmosphere grows a little warmer. One feels that the glacial period is done. If a Western Valley train is in the bay the world takes on a new verdure of cheeriness, and man is heard to hail his brother man. Newport Station evokes a little thrill of sympathy in the Celtic heart. If it dared, Newport would like to linger and chat and ask about the people at home. But, as there are many silent Saxons on its platforms, in the courtesy of its compassion it assumes an unbending attitude which is not native to it. To the Welshman, however, it gives a little hospitable smile and whispers to him that he is now within the Cymric border. He knows at once that the new-comers on the train are of his kindred. The icicles begin to melt, and he can now summon up courage enough to ask a neighbour if he may look at the Newport *Argus* or the *Western Mail*.

It would be vain effort to try to compress the Great Western Railway Station at Cardiff into a paragraph. Such a gathering ground for all classes, creeds, and clans demands either a full-length treatment or else a respectful silence.

The reader must straightway put himself into a third-class compartment of a Taff Vale Railway train bound for the Rhondda Valley. Then, passing Castell Coch, he swings through the gates of Glamorgan and up towards Pontypridd — that Mecca of the Valley Pilgrims — and there, if he be a true-blue South Walian, he has but to look through the window to see an uncle, or a cousin, or an aunt upon the platform....

Moving up the valley of the Rhondda, the traveller finds a sharp contrast to those cold companions of Paddington. In spite of measured heads and cephalic indexes, he knows full well that there is still a mystery of race at work in the souls of men. Conversation flows easily through the carriage. It deals with everything and with nothing. The terms of address are altered. In place of the frigid 'sir' of the Great Western comes the friendly 'Well, no mun,' of the Taff Vale Railway. The former is a barrier to easy conversation; the latter is a bridge.

Imagine yourself, in such circumstances, face to face with some hard-bitten old collier, who sits before you with a pungent cloud of 'Ringer' or 'Franklin' trailing across the pallor of a blue-scarred visage. He must, of course, be one of the real old Valley breed, who remembers the 'Glorans' — not a member of the new invading hosts of anywhere. He has been down to Pontypridd, and is now returning, dressed in his 'evening clothes' ('*dillad dwetydd*'). Soon, whether you will or not, you will be deep in some such dialogue as this:

He: 'Nice weather for the time of year we're having.' (Or seasonable equivalent.)

You: 'Yes, very!'

He: 'Going far?'

You (knowing he would despise an easy victory): 'Just up the Valley.'

He: 'Oh, aay!'

(A pause. Do you think he has abandoned the attack? It is the silence of the strategist.)

He: 'Coming up from Cardiff, I suppose?'

You: 'Well, I changed there.'

He: 'Oh, aay! Busy place Cardiff, too. I haven't been there now this long time.' (With sudden suspicion, politely veiled.) 'Down from North Wales you are, p'r'aps?'

You (swift in denial): 'Oh no! I've just come from London.'

He (accepting the lesser of the two evils): 'Oh, aay! I was up in the Crystal Palace once to a brass band competition. Abertillery pretty near won, too. The 'Beer and 'Bacco Band' people used to call it. Going up to Treherbert you are, I dare say?'

You: 'No, only as far as Ystrad.'

He (with renewed enthusiasm): 'Ystrad? Jawch, mun, that's where I'm living. There aren't many people I don't know in Ystrad. On business, I suppose?'

You: 'Well, no. I'm going to see a relation.'

He: 'Oh, aay! Tidy people in Ystrad, too. P'r'aps you're belonging to Mr Rees Price up there? You're both the same stamp, however.'

You: 'No, I'm afraid I don't know Mr Rees Price.'

He: 'That's strange! Aay, as I was saying, I know pretty near everybody in Ystrad. I shouldn't be surprised if I'd known your relations there for years.'

Sooner or later you reach a point when you feel it would be impolite to maintain your defence any longer. Having given him good sport, not allowing too swift a victory, you yield and gratify him with the name he seeks.

On a railway line in England a traveller would resent these queries because they would violate a taciturn tradition. Amongst the friendly South Welsh he would, if he knew his anthropology, expect and revel in this deep concern for other people's destinies. And, remembering those easy gossiping moments of the Taff Vale Railway, he will maintain that, in despite of all the measuring of heads, there is a great gulf fixed between the spirit of Paddington and the spirit of the Valleys that converge on Pontypridd.

from *The Legend of the Welsh* (1924)

GWYN THOMAS
The Jazz Bands

Somewhere outside my window a child is whistling. He is walking fast down the hill and whistling. The tune on his lips is 'Swanee'. I go to the window and watch him. He is moving through a fan of light from a street lamp. His head is thrown back, his lips protrude strongly and his body moves briskly. 'D.I.X.I.—Even Mamee, How I love you, how I love you, my dear old Swanee....' The Mississippi and the Taff kiss with dark humming lubricity under an ashen hood of years. Swanee, my dear old Swanee.

The sound of it promotes a roaring life inside my ears. Whenever I hear it, brave ghosts, in endless procession, march again. My eyes are full of the wonder they knew in the months of that long, idle, beautifully lit summer of 1926.

By the beginning of June the hills were bulging with a clearer loveliness than they had ever known before. No smoke rose from the great chimneys to write messages on the sky that puzzled and saddened the minds of the young. The endless journeys of coal trams on the incline, loaded on the upward run, empty and terrifyingly fast on the down, ceased to rattle through the night and mark our dreams. The parade of nailed boots on the pavements at dawn fell silent. Day after glorious day came up over the hills that had been restored by a quirk of social conflict to the calm they lost a hundred years before.

When the school holidays came we took to the mountain tops, joining the liberated pit-ponies among the ferns on the broad plateaux. That was the picture for us who were young. For our fathers and mothers there was the inclosing fence of hinted fears, fear of hunger, fear of defeat.

And then, out of the quietness and the golden light, partly to ease their fret, a new excitement was born. The carnivals and the jazz bands.

Rapture can sprout in the oddest places and it certainly sprouted then and there. We formed bands by the dozen, great lumps of beauty and precision, a hundred men and more in each, blowing out their songs as they marched up and down the valleys, amazing and deafening us all. Their instruments were gazookas, with a thunderous bringing up of drums in the rear. Gazookas: small tin zeppelins through which you hummed the tune as loudly as possible. Each band was done up in the uniform of some remote character never before seen in Meadow Prospect. Foreign Legionaries, Chinamen,

Carabinieri, Grenadiers, Gauchos, Sultans, Pearl-divers, or what we thought these performers looked like, and there were some very myopic voters among the designers. There was even one group of lads living up on the colder slopes of Mynydd Coch, and eager to put in a word from the world's freezing fringes who did themselves up as Eskimos, but they were liquidated because even Mathew Sewell the Sotto, our leading maestro and musical adviser, could not think up a suitable theme song for boys dressed up as delegates from the Arctic and chronically out of touch with the carnival spirit....

At the carnival's end Gomer and Cynlais said we would go back over the mountain path, for the macadamed roads would be too hard after the disappointments of the day. Up the mountain we went. Everything was plain because the moon was full. The path was narrow and we walked single file, women, children, Matadors, Sons of Dixie and Britannias. We reached the mountaintop. We reached the straight green path that leads past Llangysgod on down to Meadow Prospect. And across the lovely deep-ferned plateau we walked slowly, like a little army, most of the men with children hanging on to their arms, the women walking as best they could in the rear. Then they all fell quiet. We stood still, I and two or three others, and watched them pass, listening to the curious quietness that had fallen upon them. Far away we heard a high crazy laugh from Cynlais Coleman, who was trying to comfort Moira Hallam in their defeat. Some kind of sadness seemed to have come down on us. It was not a miserable sadness, for we could all feel some kind of contentment enriching its dark root. It may have been the moon making the mountain seem so secure and serene. We were like an army that had nothing left to cheer about or cry about, not sure if it was advancing or retreating and not caring. We had lost. As we watched the weird disguises, the strange yet utterly familiar faces, of Britannias, Matadors and Africans, shuffle past, we knew that the bubble of frivolity, blown with such pathetic care, had burst for ever and that new and colder winds of danger would come from all the world's corners to find us on the morrow. But for that moment we were touched by the moon and the magic of longing. We sensed some friendliness and forgiveness in the loved and loving earth we walked on. For minutes the silence must have gone on. Just the sound of many feet swishing through the summer grass. Then somebody started playing a gazooka. The tune he played was one of those sweet, deep things that form as simply as dew upon a mood like ours. It must have been 'All Through the Night' scored for a million talking tears and a basic disbelief in the dawn. It had all the golden softness of an age-long hunger to be at rest. The player, distant from us now, at the head of the long and formless procession, played it very quietly, as if he were thinking rather than playing. Thinking about the night, conflict, beauty, the intricate labour of living and the dark little dish of thinking self in which they were all compounded. Then the others joined in and the children began to sing.

from *Gazooka* (1957)

J. KITCHENER DAVIES
Against Goliath

You went down to Tonypandy for the Strike and the General Strike,
for the jazz carnival, and the football of strikers and police,
to the soup-kitchens and the cobbling,
the jumble-sales for sore-ridden Lazarus,
helping to sweep the spare crumbs from the boards for the dogs
            under the tables,
pouring alms like rubble on the tips
or sowing basic slag on allotment gardens of ashes
to cheat the arid earth into synthetic fertility.
There the hedges had fallen and the gaps were gaping
and the narrow streets were like funnels for the whirlwind's pouring,
            blast upon blast,
to whip the corners and raise the house-tops
whirling wretches like empty chip-bags
from wall to post, from gutter to gutter;
the cloudbursts and the hailstones choking every grating
splitting the pavements and flooding through the houses,
and clanging like a death-rattle in the windowless cellars;
and famine like a stiff broom sweeping through the homes
from front to back and over the steep garden-steps,
down the back-lane to the river's floods, —
the wrack and black water pouring from the valley,
to be battered and spewed to the level land's hollow banks,
rubbish abandoned to rot.
 And there you were like Canute on the shore,
or like Atlas in a coal pit
with your shoulder under the rocks holding back a fall,
or with your arms outstretched between the crag and the sea
shouting 'Hey! Hey!'
in the path of the crazed Gadarene swine.
 O yes, you challenged the whirlwind's teeth
and climbed to the top of the tree bent in half
by the tempest's shocks, until you needed
to sink your nails in the bark and close your eyes
to keep from becoming drunk with the sway of your mast.
Remember,
there was no need for you, more than the rest of your fellows,
to scream your guts out on a soap-box

on the street-corners and the town-squares:
that was the sort of thing expected in a muffler-and-cap,
not nice in a collar-and-tie.
No call for you to march in the ranks of the jobless,
your dragon-rampant hobnobbing with the hammer-and-sickle,
up to the square of Y Petrys, down Ynyscynon and across
            Y Brithweunydd,
past Y Llethr-ddu to Porth and Dinas
and back over Tylacelyn and through Coed y Meibion
to the field of the Square, and the waggons, the megaphone,
            the open-mouthed thousands.

No!
there was no need for you
to dare the Empire and the Hippodrome packed on Sunday evening,
— you a dandy bantam on the dung-heap of the spurred cocks
of the Federation and the Exchange —
but you ventured,
and ventured in elections for the Town Council and the County
and Parliament presently
against Goliath in a day that knows no miracle, —
the giant with picks of posts as a sweetener on your bread,
while you reached out your slice and begged like a clever slave.
Well no, I am not ashamed to admit
that the garden near the house has been turned over through
            the years
and diligently weeded, till the back was near breaking;
but the soil is stronger than I, the convolvulus
like cancer twisting itself through the bowels
squeezing life to the ground, inch by relentless inch.
The deeper I dug, the swifter would wind
the snake-like convolvulus through the loose soil,
climbing each stake and bush beneath my hands
and strangling the roses and the beans in their flowering
and raising their pure white bells like banners,
or like girls with petal-like lips
baring their teeth to smile whitely
with no laughter reaching their eyes, nothing but rancour
            in those pools.
I wanted to save Cwm Rhondda for the nation
and the nation itself as a garden that had fertility.

'How often I desired to gather your chicks but you did not desire it.'
But it was a boost to the heart to hear passers-by over the garden wall
begging me — 'Stop killing yourself, simpleton;
you're working too hard from morning to evening,
from spring to autumn, and your garden's soil will not pay you.'
Then as they turned to their strolling I heard:
'There he is, doubled over, so foolish, so foolish.'
And the furtive weeds stealing bed after bed
so that only a single bed was clear of their ravening,
my home, my wife, and three little lasses, —
Welsh-speaking Welsh and proud as princesses.
 Yes, I confess that I tried to hurl myself
into the whirlwind's teeth to be raised on its wings
and be blown by its thrust where it willed
as a hero to save my land.
Since it not only blows where it will, the tempest,
but blows what it will before it where it will;
'Who at its birth knows its growth,' I said.

O shut your mouth with your lying self-pity
and your false unctuous boasting.
You know it was a giddy game with squirrels
to slip from bough to bough;
and a more reckless game to hover in the wind
like a paper kite, a string tying you safe to the ground,
where the crowd gathered to marvel at your feats
on the pantomime trapeze and your clowning in the circus.
Not riding the whirlwind, but hanging to the mane
of a little roundabout horse, that was your valour,
a child's wooden-horse in a nursery,
and the sound of the wind no more to you than the crackle of
                  recorded music from vanity fair's screeching machine.
You suffered not so much as a scratch on your skin
by following the squirrels — the soup-kitchen and the cobbling —
when your alms were pus in the septic wound,
inflamed sores, on the wretched souls of the Means Test.
The flag-waving marching, the eloquence and electioneering
were nothing but stunting your plane in wayward loops
instead of flying straight on your journey to your hangar,
like fliers of the authorized parties.
'If he,' they said, 'would fly straight for the mark, like us,

stopping his flourishes, he would go quite far, —
there would be offices and honour and a seat in Parliament
and a chance to work wisely for Wales
within the only Party that matters.'
'And as it is,' said others, 'they will shut his mouth with offices soon,
and buy him off like the rest with ribbons.'
Of your own free will you provoked the whirlwinds
dangling humorously to amuse the open-mouthed rabble.
Your shovelling with a sand spade and a seaside bucket
in the garden, chopping the convolvulus
— the cancer of Englishness that is twining through Wales —
that was nothing at all but a chance to listen closely round the hedge
to the unconcerned passers-by so gentle in calling you simple;
but you never heard their words after they turned away, —
the Welsh are too courteous to speak the truth to your face, —
'the stupid fool, the half-wit, the idiot,' they said,
'it will be more than he can do to keep a single bed free
from the convolvulus, — his home will turn English in time
like all our homes when the children reach school age.'
And so it would, very likely,
had the Welsh School not come to sustain your home in your stead.
The tempest's roar in the distance is music
to your ears when its sound is blowing.
But who at its birth knows its growth, you said.
Well, not you, despite your boast and your false and deceitful
            pitying...
but it is another thing to answer it.

translated by Joseph P. Clancy
from 'Sŵn y Gwynt sy'n Chwythu' (1953)

IDRIS DAVIES

One Day by the Sea

Let's go to Barry Island, Maggie fach,
And give all the kids one day by the sea,
And sherbert and buns and paper hats,
And a rattling ride on the Figure Eight;
We'll have tea on the sands, and rides on the donkeys,
And sit in the evening with the folk of Cwm Rhondda,
Singing the sweet old hymns of Pantycelyn
When the sun goes down beyond the rocky islands.
Come on, Maggie fach, or the train will be gone
Then the kids will be howling at home all day,
Sticky with dirt and gooseberry jam.
Leave the washing alone for today, Maggie fach,
And put on your best and come out to the sun
And down to the holiday sea.
We'll carry the sandwiches in a big brown bag
And leave our troubles behind for a day
With the chickens and the big black tips
And the rival soup-kitchens, quarrelling like hell.
Come, Maggie fach, with a rose on your breast
And an old Welsh tune on your little red lips,
And we'll all sing together in the Cardiff train
Down to the holiday sea.

from *The Angry Summer* (1943)

/

JACK JONES
A Political Dogfight

But for 'them old Communists' the Rhondda would have been as dead as mutton during the General Election campaign of 1931, when the Rhondda was rightly regarded as one of the very few places which was safe from the political avalanche which almost completely buried the Labour Party. 'Though', as Councillor W. Rees, J.P., put it at the Rhondda Divisional Labour Party conference, 'National candidates are to be had at a penny a bunch, yet none of 'em will dare show their faces in either of the Rhondda divisions.'

And Councillor W. Rees, J.P., was quite right, and it looked like two unopposed returns for our two Labour candidates until the Communists rushed in where others feared to tread.

'Well, well, well, well,' said Councillor W. Rees, J.P., on hearing that the Communists were putting up a candidate in both the Rhondda divisions, 'and they haven't a dog's chance against us, and here they are putting us to the expense of a fight. Well, well, well, well.'

The scores of thousands of Rhondda unemployed said to each other on hearing the news: 'Well, we're going to have a bit of fun after all.'

And they certainly did 'have a bit of fun', for the Communist speakers and hecklers were as colourful as they were unscrupulous. Oh, the things they said, and the charges they made, on pitches near the labour exchanges, on street-corners and in the Rhondda's many Workmen's Halls. Actually accused our two Labour members of having agreed to the cut in unemployment pay which they said would affect four hundred thousand unemployed miners. Fancy saying a thing like that. But that was nothing. And they kept on saying such outrageous things until our Labour people, in one of the divisions especially, began to be afraid, and an S.O.S. was sent out to all respectable people, irrespective of party, to rally to our support. And many, who had years previously gone about the Rhondda saying 'We must at all costs stop these old Labour people from getting in', now went about saying 'We must at all costs stop these old Communist people from getting in'. And they were stopped. Some of our ministers of religion worked very hard. They did, and stood firm in face of Communist attacks. For the Communists — and Dai Hippo, who went about with yards of red ribbon hanging from him, saying he was sub-agent or something of the sort, was one of the worst in this respect — were fond of asking our ministers of religion such questions as: 'What's the difference between a party of militant rationalism and a party of militant atheism?' One of our ministers told Dai Hippo that he, Dai Hippo, didn't know what he was talking about, and that in any case such a question·was a purely theological question, and that he was not under any circumstances prepared to discuss theology with a member of a party which in Russia had deprived every one connected with religion of all rights. He was loudly cheered for that. But the Communists kept on heckling. Of course, they were annoyed because some of our chapels, which they were always referring to as 'God-boxes', had been thrown open to the Labour candidates and their supporting speakers, who had spoken from the pulpits more in sorrow than in anger against their godless Communist opponents.

During the campaign there were three meetings held at Beulah, two in the Chapel and one in the vestry; Dan was not present at either of them, though Councillor W. Rees, J.P., and others had wanted him to take the chair as other ministers had at other places. Dan said he intended keeping clear of politics.

'Then why didn't he, that's what I'd like to know?' one of his deacons who was a strong Labour supporter had cried on hearing of the scene Dan had got himself mixed up in. 'After refusing to have anything to do with us he goes and makes a fool of himself at a Communist open-air meeting.'

And it has to be admitted that Dan was foolish, extremely so, though he hasn't admitted it to this day. No more has old Evans the draper, who was with him that night, the eve of the poll it was, when, instead of being at the Labour meeting which was then in progress at Beulah, they were standing on the edge of the big crowd which had gathered to listen to the relay Communist meeting which had been in progress for some hours on the large open space just off the Square.

Dai Hippo was acting as chairman, and speaker after speaker, local, national and international, came and mounted the lorry in turn as they were released from other meetings, and came 'to do a turn' at Pandy's great open-air eve-of-the-poll rally before going on to somewhere else.

Dan had walked up through the crowded main street and on to the crowded Square with old Evans the draper, more with the intention of mixing with the Rhondda crowd and studying it whilst under the influence of demagogues, than of listening to the speakers; for he knew but little as yet of the nature of that majority of Rhondda's young people who were seldom, if ever, to be found in church or chapel, but who were this eve-of-the-poll night roaming the streets and standing around speakers in their thousands, 'having a bit of fun on the cheap', as he heard more than one of them put it.

So, lending but one indifferent ear to the speakers, and the other attentive ear to what was being said by those about him, Dan stood with old Evans the draper and nearly two thousand other Rhondda people, mostly young people, at the Communist open-air meeting. The youngsters were enjoying themselves.

'That's the stuff to give 'em,' they cried as speaker after speaker attacked Labour.

'Let the buggers have it.'

'They won't have to live on fifteen bob a week.'

'No, more like fifteen bloody quid.'

'Up the Reds.'

'Damned fine speaker, wasn't 'e?' said one to another as the Scottish comrade made way for 'one of our London comrades'.

'Yes, he went for 'em bald-headed. I wonder what this chap's like.'

'Bloody great. I heard him in the Workmen's Hall last night. And didn't he slash 'em. Oh, you ought to hear him going for the Chapel people too. You'll hear him now.'

'Our London comrade' had been speaking for about five minutes when old Evans the draper, who had been listening attentively, pulled Dan's sleeve and whispered: 'Have you been listening to this chap?'

'No, not particularly. Same as the rest, I suppose.'

'Just listen to him.'

Dan listened to a sharp voice which pierced the air like a poisoned arrow. He stood on tiptoe to get a glimpse of the speaker, but it was too dark to make out his features. Just the figure standing on the lorry, and the keen voice dripping with contempt. When Dan began listening to him he was whipping, not capitalism, nor the Labour candidates, but, to Dan's surprise, the listening crowd.

'And we have to appeal for your support after ten years of depression and unemployment, and after two Labour governments have openly betrayed you. But isn't there something about three tries for a Welshman?' he sneered. 'Humph! Revolutionary Rhondda, do you call it, Comrade Chairman? Why, these people wouldn't revolute if they saw their kiddies starving before their very eyes. No, don't tell me they would. If they had any revolutionary spirit in 'em they'd have returned the Communist candidate at the last General Election. Well, you've been let down again since then, and now you've got another chance to show what you're made of. We told you then —

and we're telling you now — that the Communist Party is your only hope. Are you again going to return the reactionary, treacherous Labour candidates? Are you again going to listen to your spiritual guides, to the bible-punching, hymn-singing, pie-in-the-sky promisers? Are you? Huh, Marx was right. Religion is the opium for the people. That's what you Rhondda people have been doped with. Religion. Yes, Marx was right —'

'Marx was wrong if he said that!' Dan heard himself shout. 'Now what have I done?' he thought.

'Boy,' gasped old Evans the draper as those standing about them turned to look at Dan.

'Who the hell is he, then?'some of the crowd growled.

Dan, white and trembling, was asking himself 'How did I come to say that?' and whilst one inner voice was telling him to run away from the crowd, another was urging him to stand his ground.

Again that cold, contemptuous, piercing voice: 'I don't know whether the comrade who interjected has read Marx and Lenin on religion — but he can't have, for, if he had, he'd know that I was right in saying that religion is the opium for the people —'

'You were wrong!' cried Dan, almost hysterically this time.

'Shut up!' growled a section of the crowd. Dai Hippo rose from where he was seated on the end of the lorry and said to the speaker: 'Just a minute, comrade. I'll squash this bugger whoever he is.' Then he tried the gag which had proved successful in driving away troublesome interjectors on previous occasions. 'As chairman of this meeting,' he roared into the night, 'I want to tell the comrade back there — whoever he is — that being as he seems to know so much he'd better come up here on to this lorry and try to prove to this crowd that our comrade here is wrong. Either that — or shut his mouth.'

'Up you come!' roared the crowd, smacking its lips in anticipation of an additional juicy 'bit of fun'.

'That's squashed him all right,' said Dai Hippo to 'our London comrade. No, I'm damned if it has,' he added on seeing the crowd part to make way for two men, one young, the other old.

'What, have you brought your father with you?' he sneered as Dan and old Evans the draper came up to the lorry.

Those around the lorry laughed and one cried: 'P'r'aps it's the old feller's going to do the talking, Dai.'

'Well, which of you is it?' snapped Dai Hippo.

'I — I —' was all Dan could say. His heart was beating violently and his breath was coming and going as though he had just finished running a mile uphill. He hadn't wanted to come through that crowd. Then why had he come? Why was he standing there?'

'Come on, up you get,' commanded Dai Hippo.

'Ay, get up!' roared the crowd.

And there he was, standing up on the lorry by the side of Dai Hippo, who was shouting: 'I'm going to give this comrade ten minutes to say what he's got to say — though judging by the look of him I don't think he'll need that long.'

'Looks as if he's blotted his bloody copy-book,' shouts one from the crowd, and gets a huge laugh.

Dan prayed silently.

'Ten minutes. Get at it,' said Dai Hippo.

'Friends of — er — my Rhondda friends — I — er —'

'Speak up!' from the back of the crowd.

'Come on, spit it out,' said Dai Hippo.

But he had nothing to 'spit out', or if he had he couldn't do so. 'Our London comrade' stood looking contemptuously at him as he struggled to say something. The impatient crowd began to jeer and to make the disconcerting noise flattered with the name of 'raspberry'. From all parts of the crowd he got 'the raspberry' as he stood trembling like a leaf and as dumb as an oyster up on the lorry. 'The boys' thought it great fun and didn't they let him have it. The din was terrific. Old Evans the draper looked up at Dan anxiously and tugged at the left leg of his trousers, but Dan by now appeared to be in that kind of trance he was afflicted by, and his eyes were fixed on the star-studded curtain of night which hung, sloping outwards, to where it appeared to be pegged to the skyline. Then, just as he was struck in the face by a well-aimed dab of filth thrown by someone in the crowd, it came. His unchained voice silenced the jeering crowd.

'Friends, my dear Rhondda friends, I am not a politician, and I do not stand here in the name of any political party. I stand here as the humble servant of our Father —"

'Ay, how is the old chap these days?' cried one standing near the lorry in a tone of mock solicitude, and there was laughter loud and long.

'— to defend His Holy name against scoffers and blasphemers, and our belief in Him against those who seek to ridicule it. My friend here —'

'I'm no friend of yours,' snarled our London comrade.

'— though why he thought it necessary to drag religion into this —

this political dog-fight is beyond me. What right has he — Marx, Lenin or any one else to sneer at my religion, to call it dope, to describe it as the opium for the people? If he had attempted to live in accordance with the teachings of Christ he would know that religion is not such as he has described it, would know that it is a living, a burning faith which is daily subjected to many severe trials. And the religious soul dares not indulge in pipe-dreams, for it has to be always on the alert in case this vanity fair of a world overwhelms and destroys it. Real religion means a stern, never-ending fight to keep one's soul unspotted by the world. In their journey through this world Christians are accompanied by that inward monitor Who sees to it —'

'Tripe!' interjected 'our London comrade'.

'Oh, my comrades, don't, I beseech you, let any one turn you from God. Go Labour, Liberal, Communist or Conservative, but stick to God. "Labour has betrayed you," says my friend here. Of that I know nothing, but what I do know is that God has never failed you — He never will fail us. Of that I am certain. So let us —'

'Your time's up!' shouted Dai Hippo, placing himself between Dan and the crowd, which he then proceeded to address: 'Comrades, I'm now able to tell you that we've been listening to one of our Rhondda preachers. Had I known that he wouldn't have had the chance to speak from our platform. Why the hell should he? I bet he wouldn't let our comrade here put the case against religion from his pulpit, the cowards' castles that he and his sort stand up in every Sunday. Not he. Come on, get down off this lorry so as we can get on with our meeting,' he told Dan.

'May God bless you all!' cried Dan before getting down on the ground.

In exchange for the blessing a few gave him 'the raspberry' again. But Dan didn't hear them, neither did he hear 'our London comrade' start slamming him and his religion, for he was being assisted out of the crowd in something approaching a state of collapse by old Evans the draper, who insisted on seeing him home. Dan rested in the doorway of the Bon Marché as the Communist demonstration, about two thousand strong, which had been parading the streets all the evening, passed by with Comrades Ike Matson, Lily Hopkins and Rose Morris at its head.

'Feel better now, boy?' asked old Evans.

'Yes, thank you, Mr Evans. I'm quite all right now.'

'Don't say lies, boy. Come on, take my arm.'

'But, really —'
'Shut up, boy, and do as you're told.'
'I'm sorry I made such a — such a —'
'Shut up. If you were going to apologize for having made an exhibition of yourself, then don't — now or in the future. There'll be plenty to tell you that, but I think it's more such exhibitions we want. Now, take it easy.' Supported by the old man Dan slowly made his way home.

from *Rhondda Roundabout* (1934)

HUW MENAI
Spring in the Rhondda

(written in a child's book)

Daisies have reached our Valley — O!
    And Miner's Row is sprayed with green
And none but lonely God I know
    Had heart to sow the wonder seen.

Down to the doorstep of Despair
    To banish care the Spring has come,
With spirit blithe that would not spare
    The lair of lost hope in the slum.

Above the noises may be heard
    The singing bird, to song reborn;
And days of warmth will pass the word
    To gird the roses round the thorn.

And of these blessings we are proud,
    That help to make the cloud less clear —
We who in children's laughter, loud
    Hosannas of the Angels hear!

from *The Simple Vision* (1945)

JACK JONES

Say a Word for the Rhondda

May-day in the Rhondda, and a lovely morning it was, though Dan had forgotten all about the Miners' May-day Demonstration, and was only reminded of it by finding his uncle Shoni at breakfast in the kitchen when he went down to his.

Shoni was eating with the morning paper before him.

'Hullo, Dan,' he cried. 'What do you think?'

'Of what?'

'Bandy's matched for the championship.'

'What do Dan want to know about that, do you think?' said Emily.

'Why shouldn't he want to know, woman? Bandy's a Rhondda boy, and he's putting the Rhondda on the map, isn't he?'

'On the map, indeed. Bit more porridge, Dan?'

'Please.'

'Though I'll say this for him,' grudgingly admitted Emily, 'he's looked after his mother, though what he wanted to take her to that big old house for is beyond me, for she told me herself she'd rather ten times be back down here with us. That little house was plenty big enough for them two.'

'So it's your May-day Demonstration day, Uncle Shoni?'' said Dan.

'Yes, taking a shift off to go to a meeting,' grumbled Emily. 'Humph! As if they wasn't having enough shifts off as it is.'

'Oh, woman — Though maybe you're right for once in a while, for our May-day demonstrations are not by a long way what they used to be, Dan. We used to have processions, bands, sports — a good day out. Now we only get a couple of speeches in the Workmen's Hall, and — napoo. But there'll be a procession here to-day — not ours, though. Not the Miners' Federation procession, but a Communist procession. They're having a May-day of their own. Rotten, that is, for we're all Rhondda chaps, see, Dan. So why can't we get together, that's what I'd like to know.'

'It's too late to ask that now,' Emily said. 'Oh, Dan, there was a letter for you. I put it in your room. Shall I go and get it?'

'No, it doesn't matter. I shall be going in soon.'

'But you're not stopping there to read,' Shoni told him, 'for I'm marching you out before me to get yourself a bellyful of fresh air. Why don't you slip in to our meeting at the Workmen's Hall and hear Lansbury —'

'Is that fresh air?' said Emily.

'Let's have another cup of tea, you.'

'Can't you say please?'

'No, I'm damned if I will. Oh, all right, then, *please*, will that do you?'

'Another cup for you, Dan?'

'Please.'

'There. That's the way to say please, Shoni.'

'Ay, you're very polite, I know. Will I have a bit of a scrape?' he asked no one in particular as he ran his fingers over his chin. 'No, I think I'll do. What do you think, Dan?'

'I should shave if I were you.'

'P'raps I'd better.' He rose and stretched himself. 'Ay, that's great news about Bandy. He can thank Big Mog for bringing that off; and Mog'll back him for anything up to a thousand.'

'What, a thousand pounds?' cried Emily.

'Yes, and more if it's wanted, for Mog's not spending much these days. He's been practically on the tack since the Captain's gone.'

'A thousand pounds,' repeated Emily. 'I didn't know that there was that much left in the Rhondda. Well, shave if you're going to, and get out so as I can get on with my work.'

Shoni went into the scullery to shave as Dan went into his room for the letter his aunt had put there. On opening it he was surprised to find that it was a 'call' from a new and flourishing chapel in the comparatively prosperous anthracite-mining area, a chapel at which he had preached in the autumn of the previous year. Dan sat with the letter in his hand trying to recall the place, for he had preached away in many places, well, about once a month, during his pastorship of Beulah. A countryfied sort of place it was, he remembered, with two new pits well away from the pleasant and well-planned township, a township where the prospects were good — this was mentioned in the letter. Nothing in the letter about salary, though enough was said about the chapel's freedom from debt and its income to indicate that the salary would be substantially higher than that he was in receipt of at Beulah. He went on trying to recall the people of the place whom he had, judging from the letter, so much impressed. They were, if he remembered aright, people less easy to move than the Rhondda people, more — would 'canny' be the word? he asked himself, then rejected it in favour of 'close'. Yes, that was it, 'close'. And he remembered that they looked altogether more prosperous than the Rhondda people in every way. Hadn't he been shown large gardens, small-holdings, which the miners of that open and more fruitful area cultivated in their spare time? Of course he had, and that was what he had been trying to think of. There was something of the old Welsh peasant about them, not so industrialized as the people of the Rhondda. There were apple trees, pigs, cows... Yes, one of the pleasantest of mining areas, whereas the Rhondda — well, the Rhondda was not pleasant in that sense! And they wanted him to leave the Rhondda, dear old rowdy Rhondda, to go to them. But why him? he humbly asked himself. Surely such a chapel — still, there was the letter. What a surprise! After barely three years' ministry. Well, well.

He rose from his chair with the intention of informing his aunt and uncle of the nature of the letter, but thought better of it before he got to the door of the kitchen. Old Evans the draper, he thought. Yes, old Evans.

On his way up to the Bon Marché he was held up by the long and strong procession of Communists and unemployed which was marching to the meeting-place in the open air which was not a stone's-throw from the Workmen's Hall, where, at the same hour, the Miners' Federation and Rhondda Labour Party May-day meeting was to be held.

The Communist procession was headed by a 'Revolutionaries' Jazz Band' which was something more than merely funny; it was, at times, inspiring; and its bandmaster was none other than our old comrade Mordecai Rees, by this time also the leader of the Red Rebels Dance Band which was drawing young Rhondda to dance to Mordecai's class-conscious numbers at the Ambulance Hall on Monday, Thursday and Saturday each week, Admission 6d (ladies and unemployed half-price). His last two numbers, the 'Rostov Rag' and the 'Trotsky Trot', were being whistled by the young people in all parts of the Rhondda, and there was about this time a strong rumour to the effect that Mordecai and his Red Rebels were likely to receive an invitation from the Comintern to tour Russia under the auspices of the All-Russian Central Council of Culture Disseminators.

Close up to the band, under the red banner on which was inscribed 'Workers of the World, Unite', marched the redoubtable Dai Hippo, with the two speakers for the demonstration one on either side. One of the speakers was far gone in years, but the flashing eyes were the eyes of a youth. With fifty-five years of trade-union and revolutionary activity behind him, he marched like a well-trained soldier, commanding the respect of all who lined the streets — irrespective of party — for, whatever might be said of him, he had been a fighter, and a great one, all his days. The other speaker, also a fighter, was about half the size and age of his colleague and was well worth listening to even though he were not worth following.

Close on the heels of the speakers came the local leaders, Comrades Ike Matson, Lily Hopkins, Councillor Rose Morris who had got back on to the Rhondda Council at the March elections, Trevor Short, Jerry Dando, and others too numerous to mention.

Stretched out in fours for about a quarter of a mile behind the leaders were the rank and file of Rhondda Communism, many carrying banners on which could be read 'Down With the Means Test', and 'Down' with many other things besides. A platoon here and there sang, and there were many women carrying babies who marched at their husbands' sides. A few of those lining the street tittered now and then as the procession marched by, but Dan saw nothing to laugh at. What he saw were rows of careworn faces, faces which had looked in many directions for help and guidance before becoming bitter and turning to Communism as the last hope.

'Please, God, help them,' he murmured as the last section of fours marched by him, and it may have been that it was then that he decided to continue serving God in the Rhondda. However, he went on his way towards the Bon Marché with the intention of discussing the letter he had received with old Evans.

He found Lucy standing in the doorway looking after the procession.

'Good morning. Mr. Evans in?'

'Come in.' He followed her in. 'Mr. Evans was taken ill — very ill, I'm afraid — last night.'

'But —'

'I've wired for his son and daughter: they should be here this evening. My mother's seeing to him until they arrive. I do hope they'll arrive in time.'

'As bad as that?'

'I'm afraid so. Sit down a minute.'

He sat down, feeling he wanted to.

'It was Dr. Thomas told me to wire for his son and daughter —'

'But I must see him,' said Dan, rising. 'Is he conscious?'

'He is — off and on — or he was when I left the house — but how he is now —'

But Dan was gone with his breath in his fist, as they say in the Rhondda, praying as he went that he might be allowed to see his old friend alive. His prayer was answered, granted rather.

In reply to his knock, Mrs Meredith, Lucy's mother, came to the door. When she saw him she cried: 'Well, I've just this minute sent down to the house for you.'

'I called at the shop,' Dan explained as he followed her into the house. 'How is he?'

Mrs Meredith sighed. 'All but, I'm afraid. He's been asking for you. I'll ask Dr Thomas if I can bring you in.'

Dr Thomas came out to him.

'How is he, doctor?'

The doctor lit a Gold Flake, and held out his case to Dan. 'Oh, I quite forgot, you don't smoke. Well, I give him an hour at the most,' he bluntly said as he seated himself. 'You can go in — he's expecting you. Now, Mr Price, pull yourself together, please, for you'll find him much the same as ever in himself. Well, you know what I mean. Prepared, calm — almost happy — ready to go. I'm staying until — well, in case.'

The able and hard-hit Rhondda doctor went on smoking with a slightly contemptuous look in his eyes as he watched the young pastor struggling with his emotion. The doctor was on familiar terms with old Death, too much so to feel very much moved on finding him settling himself near the bedside of an aged person. Dr Thomas had fought old Death on battlefields, in dressing-stations, hospitals, down in the depths and darkness of Rhondda pits, in distressed Rhondda homes. He was but one of Rhondda's many panel and colliery doctors, one of the devoted band of medical men whose care is the body of the Rhondda, whilst Dan was a member of that other devoted band whose care is its soul. Body and soul of the Rhondda, thought the tired, dry-eyed and rather world-weary doctor as he sat looking at Dan, whose eyes were filled with tears.

'That's right,' said the doctor, as Dan forced a smile. 'In you go.'

Old Evans greeted him with a smile from where he was lying in bed, and Mrs Meredith rose from where she was sitting and went out of the room as Dan entered.

'Well, boy, here I am — causing a lot of fuss. Sit down, boy.'

'Why, you look — well, not so bad,' said Dan as he sat in the chair near the head of the bed and smiled into the eyes of his old friend, whose time was nearly ended.

'I don't feel so bad, my boy. It's not going to be so hard, after all. I'm glad you've come. I was going to talk to you ever so many times about it, but I kept on saying "Plenty of time". Then — last night. Now I know that there isn't plenty. There's very little time. Listen, my boy. You and Lucy. Hurting each other you are, and you're being hurt most. You need her more than she needs you, and you'll need her more still as time goes on — here in the Rhondda...'

'But you mustn't tire yourself now, for we can discuss this some other time when you're —'

'Please, my boy. That's what I thought. "Some other time." Now I know it must be now or never. I've willed this house to you; the furniture and all that's in it to Lucy. I hope you'll marry — soon after I've gone — gone to join my dear wife. She and I were happy in this house, and I'd like if you and Lucy — You like her, don't you, my boy?'

'I've loved her from the moment when I first saw her.'

'And she loves you, my boy. Give me a drop of that stuff in the glass there.'

Dan tilted up his head and held the glass to his lips, and the old man drained the glass of its contents.

'Yes,' wheezed the old man as Dan lowered his head on to the pillow again, 'I know she does. Found her crying one night, crying because you'd been keeping away from the shop. She's a good gel, my boy, and she'll make you a good wife. For you'll marry her?'

'If she'll have me, yes, with all my heart.'

'She'll have you. And may God bless you in every way. There, that's off my mind. P'raps I'll sleep a bit now. But don't go away. Sit — sit there.'

Dan sat for a time, maybe ten minutes, then the old man opened his eyes and said faintly: 'Will you just say a word, my boy?'

Dan slipped down on to his knees, and the old man's right hand moved until it came to rest on the young pastor's head. Dan started praying for the restoration of health to his old friend, who interrupted with: 'No, no, never mind me, my boy. I'm all right. My troubles are nearly over. Say — say a word for the Rhondda, please.'

So Dan went on praying for the Rhondda and its people until Dr Thomas came into the room and lifted the dead man's hand from off Dan's head.

Lucy, who had closed the shop for the lunch-hour and had rushed up to see how things were with the old man, met Dan as, blinded with tears, he came out of the room where his old friend lay dead, and where Dr Thomas and Mrs Meredith were discussing in whispers some of the things which will have to be done for all of us as our time comes.

'Dan bach,' she cried lovingly.

'Lucy.'

They clung to each other for a while.

They are to be married on the Saturday before August Bank Holi-day, the very day on which Bandy Bowen is having a smack at the British Lightweight champion in the open air on the Cardiff City ground. Let's hope it keeps fine for them.

from *Rhondda Roundabout* (1934)

HUW MENAI
Beyond the Slag Heaps

The lights go out; the day is done
For all save haunting ghosts,
The windows darken one by one
Upon the stellar hosts.

Quiet the valley is and back
A thousand years ago
Before adventure broke a track
Leaving what ruts of woe!

Time then was like a happy elf
Not an all-fateful mood
And man had room to stretch himself
Knowing that life was good.

Nothing to win a child's sweet praise
Has here been brought about
Since those nymph-haunted halcyon days
Of heron, otter, trout.

from *The Simple Vision* (1945)

RHYS DAVIES
The Dark World

'Where can we go tonight?' Jim asked. Once again it was raining. The rows of houses in the valley bed were huddled in cold grey mist. Beyond them the mountains prowled unseen. The iron street-lamps spurted feeble jets of light. There were three weeks to go before Christmas. They stood in a chapel doorway and idly talked, their feet splashed by the rain.

Thomas said: 'There's someone dead up in Calfaria Terrace.'

'Shall we go to see him?' Jim suggested immediately.

They had not seen any corpses for some weeks. One evening they had seen five, and so for a while the visits had lost their interest. When on these expeditions, they would search through the endless rows of houses for windows covered with white sheets, the sign that death was within, and when a house was found thus, they would knock at the door and respectfully ask if they might see the dead. Only once they were denied, and this had been at a villa, not a common house. Everywhere else they had been taken to the parlour or bedroom where the corpse lay, sometimes in a coffin, and allowed a few seconds' stare. Sometimes the woman of the house, or maybe a daughter, would whisper: 'You knew him, did you?' Or, if the deceased was a child: 'You were in the same school?' They would nod gravely. Often they had walked three or four miles through the valley searching out these dramatic houses. It was Jim who always knocked at the door and said, his cap in his hand: 'We've come to pay our respects, mum.'

At the house in Calfaria Terrace they were two in a crowd. The dead had been dead only a day and neighbours were also paying their respects, as was the custom: there was quite a procession to the upstairs room. The corpse was only a very old man, and his family seemed quite cheerful about it. Thomas heard the woman of the house whisper busily on the landing to a neighbour in a shawl: 'That black blouse you had on the line, Jinny, it'll be a help. The 'surance won't cover the funeral, and you know Emlyn lost four days in the pit last week. Still, gone he is now, and there'll be room for a lodger.' And, entreatingly: 'You'll breadcrumb the ham for me, Jinny?... I 'on't forget you when you're in trouble of your own.' The dead old man lay under a patchwork quilt. His face was set in an expression of mild surprise. Thomas noticed dried soapsuds in his ear. Four more people came into the bedroom and the two boys were almost hustled out. No one had taken any particular notice of them. Downstairs they asked a skinny, cruel-looking young woman for a glass of water and to their pleased astonishment she gave them each a glass of small beer.

'It didn't seem as though he was dead at all,' Jim said, as if cheated. 'Let's look for more. In November there's lot of them. They get bronchitis and consumption.'

'It was like a wedding,' Thomas said. Again they stood in a doorway and looked with vacant boredom through the black curtains of rain sweeping the valley.

'My mother had a new baby last night,' Jim suddenly blurted out, frowning. But when Thomas asked what kind it was, Jim said he didn't know yet. But he knew that there were nine of them now, beside his father and mother and two lodgers. He did not complain. But of late he had been expressing an ambition to go to sea when he left school, instead of going to the colliery.

Jim, in the evenings, was often pushed out of home by his mother, a bitter black-browed woman who was never without a noisy baby. Jim's father was Irish, a collier of drunken reputation in the place, and the whole family was common as a clump of dock. Thomas's mother sometimes made one or two surprised remarks at his association with Jim. They shared a double desk in school. Occasionally Thomas expressed disgust at Jim's unwashed condition.

Again they set out down the streets, keeping a sharp look-out for white sheets in the windows. After a while they found a house so arrayed, yellow blobs of candle-light like sunflowers shining through the white of the window. Jim knocked and respectfully made his request to a big creaking woman in black. But she said gently: 'Too late you are. The coffin was screwed down after tea today. Funeral is tomorrow. The wreaths you would like to see?'

Jim hesitated, looking back enquiringly over his shoulder at Thomas. Without speaking, both rejected the invitation and with mumbled thanks they backed away. 'No luck tonight,' Jim muttered.

'There was the small beer,' Thomas reminded him. A wind had jumped down from the mountains and as they scurried on it unhooked a faulty door of a street-lamp and blew out the wispy light. When they had reached the bottom of the vale the night was black and rough and moaning, the rain stinging hot on cheeks and hands like whips. Here was a jumbled mass of swarthy and bedraggled dwellings. A spaniel, dragging her swollen belly, whined out to them from under a bony bush. She sounded lost and confused and exhausted with the burden that weighted her to earth. In the dark alleyways they found a white sheet. A winter silence was here, the black houses were glossy in the rain. No one was about.

'Let's go back,' whispered Thomas. 'It's wet and late.'

'There's one here,' Jim protested. 'After coming all this way!' And he tapped at the door, which had no knocker.

The door was opened and in a shaft of lamplight stood a man's shape, behind him a warm fire-coloured interior, for the door opened on to the living room. Jim made his polite request, and the man silently stood aside. They walked into the glow.

But the taste of death was in the house, true and raw. A very bent old woman in a black cardigan, clasped at her stringy throat with a geranium brooch, sat nodding before the fire. Thomas was staring at the man, who had cried out: 'It's Thomas!' He sat down heavily on a chair. 'Oh, Thomas!' he said in a wounded voice. His stricken face was as though he were struggling to repudiate a new pain. A tall, handsome man, known to Thomas as Elias, his face had the grey, tough pallor of the underground worker.

The boy stood silent in the shock of the recognition and the suspicion prowling about his mind. He could not speak, he dare not ask. Then fearfully the man said:

'You've come to see Gwen, have you? All this way. Only yesterday I was wondering if your mother had heard. You've come to see her?'

'Yes,' Thomas muttered, his head bent. Jim stood waiting, shifting his feet. The old woman kept on nodding her head. Her son said to her loudly, his voice sounding out in suffering, not having conquered this new reminder of the past years: 'Mam, this is Thomas, Mrs Morgan's boy. You remember? That Gwen was so fond of.'

The old woman dreadfully began to weep. Her face, crumpled and brown, winced and shook out slow, difficult tears. 'Me it ought to have been,' she said with a thin obsession. 'No sense in it, no sense at all.'

Thomas glanced secretly at Elias, to see if his emotion had abated. Three years ago he used to carry notes from Elias to Gwen, who had been the servant at home. It seemed to him that Elias and Gwen were always quarrelling. Elias used to stand for hours on the street corner until he came past, hurry up to him and say hoarsely: 'Thomas, please will you take this to Gwen.' In the kitchen at home, Gwen would always toss her head on the receipt of a note, and sometimes she indignantly threw them on the fire without reading them... But Gwen used to be nice. She always kept back for him, after her evening out, some of Elias's chocolates. Once or twice she had obtained permission to take him to the music-hall and gloriously he had sat between her and Elias, watching the marvellous conjurors and the women in tights who heaved their bejewelled bosoms as they sang funny songs. But Elias, he had felt, had not welcomed those intrusions. After a long time, Gwen had married him. But before she left to do this, she had wept every day for a week, her strong, kind face wet and gloomy. His mother had given her a handsome parlour clock, and Gwen had tearfully said she would never wind it as it would last longer if unused. Then gradually she had disappeared, gone into her new married life down the other end of the valley.

Elias looked older, older and thinner. Thomas kept his gaze away from him as much as possible. He felt shy at being drawn into the intimacy of all this grief. The old woman kept on quavering. At last Elias said, quietly now: 'You will come upstairs to see her, Thomas. And your friend.' He opened a door at the staircase and, tall and gaunt, waited for them to pass. Thomas walked past him unwillingly, his stomach gone cold. He did not want to go upstairs. But he thought that Elias would take a refusal hardly. Jim, silent and impassive, followed with politely quiet steps.

In a small, small bedroom with a low ceiling two candles were burning. A bunch of snowy chrysanthemums stood on a table beside a pink covered bed. Elias had preceded them and now he lifted a starched white square of cloth from off the head and shoulders of the dead.

She was lying tucked in the bed as if quietly asleep. The bedroom was so small there was nowhere else to look. Thomas looked, and started with a terrified surprise. The sheets were folded back, low under Gwen's chest, and cradled in her arm was a pale waxen doll swathed in white. A doll! His amazement passed into terror. He could not move, and the scalp of his head contracted as though an icy wind passed over it. Surely that wasn't a baby, that pale stiff thing Gwen was nursing against her quiet breast? Elias was speaking in a hoarse whisper, and while he spoke he stroked a fold of the bedclothes with a grey hand.

'Very hard it was, Thomas, Gwen going like this. The two of them. I was in the pit, and they sent for me. But she had gone before I was here, though old Watkins let me come in his car.... I didn't see her, Thomas, and she asked for me —' His voice broke, and Thomas, in his bout of terror, saw him drop beside the bed and bury his face in the bed.

It was too much. Thomas wanted to get away; he wanted to run, away from the close narrow room, from the man beside the bed, from the figure in the bed that had been the warm Gwen, from the strange creature in her arms that looked as though it had never been warm. The terror became a nightmare menace coming nearer... Unconsciously he jerked his way out to the landing. Jim followed; he looked oppressed.

'Let's clear off,' he whispered nervously.

They went downstairs. The old woman was brewing tea, and in the labour seemed to forget her grief. 'You will have a cup,' she enquired, 'and a piece of nice cake?'

At this Jim was not unwilling to stay, but Thomas plucked his sleeve. Elias's heavy step could be heard on the stairs. Then he came in, quiet and remote-looking. He laid his hand on Thomas's shoulder for a second.

'Do you remember when we used to go to the Empire, Thomas? You and Gwen used to like that Chinaman that made a white pigeon come out of an empty box.'

But Thomas saw that he was not the same Elias who, though he would wait hours for the indifferent Gwen like a faithful dog, had been a strutting young man with a determined eye. He was changed now, his shoulders were slackened. She had defeated him after all. Thomas sipped half a cup of tea, but did not touch the cake. He scarcely spoke. Elias kept on reminding him of various happy incidents in the past. That picnic in the mountains when Elias had scaled the face of a quarry to fetch a blue flower Gwen had fancied. 'Didn't she dare me to get it!' he added, with a strange chuckle in his throat. 'And then she gave it to you!' He sat brooding for a while, his face turned away. Then, to Thomas's renewed terror, he began to weep again, quietly.

The mother, hobbling across to her son, whispered to the two boys. Perhaps they would go now. It was only yesterday her daughter-in-law had died, and the blow was still heavy on her son. She had stiffened herself out of her own abandonment to grief. The boys went to the door in silence. Jim looked reserved and uncommenting.

Outside, in the dark alley, he said: 'I wonder how she came to chuck the bucket! The baby was it?' Receiving no reply, he added with something like pride now: 'My mother's always having them, but she's only abed for three days, she don't die nor nothing near it.' Thomas still stumbling silently by his side, he went on: 'Perhaps he'll marry again; he's only a young bloke... I never seen a man cry before,' he added in a voice of contempt.

But for Thomas all the night was weeping. The dark alley was an avenue of the dead, the close-shuttered houses were tombs. He heard the wind howling, he could feel the cold ghostly prowling of the clouds. Drops of icy rain stung his cheeks. He was shivering. Gwen's face, bound in its white stillness, moved before him like a lost, dead moon. It frightened him, he wanted to have no connection with it; he felt his inside sicken.

'Shall we look for more?' Jim said. A roused, unappeased appetite was in his voice.

Thomas leaned against the wet wall of a house. Something broke in him. He put up his arm, buried his head in it, and cried. He cried in terror, in fear and in grief. There was something horrible in the dark world. A soft, howling whine came out of his throat. Jim, ashamed, passed from wonder into contempt.

'What's up with you!' he jeered. 'You seen plenty of 'em before, haven't you?... Shut up,' he hissed angrily. 'There's someone coming.' And he gave Thomas a push.

Thomas hit out. All the world was threatening and hostile. The back of his hand caught Jim sharply on the cheekbone. Immediately there was a scuffle. But it was short-lived. They had rolled into a pool of liquidly thin mud, and both were surprised and frightened by the mess they were in.

'Jesus,' exclaimed Jim, 'I'll cop it for this.'

Thomas lurched away. He stalked into the rough night. All about him was a new kingdom. Desperately he tried to think of something else. Of holidays by the sea, of Christmas, of the nut trees in a vale over the mountains, where, too, thrushes' nests could be found in the spring, marvellously coloured eggs in them. Jim, who had seen him weep, he thought of with anger and dislike.

At the top of the hill leading to his home he paused in fear. The bare high place was open to the hostile heavens, a lump of earth open like a helpless face to the blows of the wind and the rain. He heard derision in the howls of the wind, he felt anger in the stings of the rain.

from *A Finger in Every Pie* (1942)

IDRIS DAVIES
In Gardens in the Rhondda

In gardens in the Rhondda
The daffodils dance and shine
When tired men trudge homeward
From factory and mine.

The daffodils dance in gardens
Behind the grim brown row
Built among the slagheaps
In a hurry long ago.

They dance as though in passion
To shame and to indict
The brutes who built so basely
In the long Victorian night.

from *Tonypandy and Other Poems* (1945)

T. ROWLAND HUGHES
It's the People Make the Place

William Jones was nearing the end of his journey; another quarter of an hour and he would be in Bryn Glo. He hoped Crad had got the wire he had sent from Chester and that somebody would be at the station to meet him.

The train stopped at a little station at the bottom of the valley, and William Jones gazed rather apprehensively at the village that climbed the hillside close by, with its straight streets of houses of grey stone, all exactly alike, hanging below a huge coal-tip. Two men of middle age got into the compartment.

''Ow are you?' one of them greeted him.

'Pretty well, indeed, thanks.'

'Oh, Northman, is it?'

'Aye, from Llan-y-graig … Caernarvonshire.'

''Ow'r things lookin' up in those quarries now?'

'Uh?'

''Ow're things goin' in the quarries up there?'

'Oh, pretty well, indeed.'

'Good, mun. 'S warm today.'

'Uh?'

''Ot sun?'

'Yes, indeed.' William Jones hoped he'd given the right answer.

The collier sank back into his seat, mopping his brow: his companion pushed out his lips as he tried to light a discoloured, diminutive fag-end of a cigarette.

'Come for a little spell?'

'No, to stay. Thinking to go to work in the pits.'

The man with the cigarette stub burnt his lip. ''Ellfire!' he exclaimed. But the other man nodded quietly and understandingly.

'Where?' he enquired.

'Bryn Glo.'

''Ellfire! Is 'e goin' to sink a new pit there, Tom?' And the stub-smoker stared at William Jones as though he were a being from another world.

'Bryn Glo is on stop, you see,' Tom explained.

'Stop tap for a year,' corroborated his companion.

'Been what, did you say?' William Jones enquired.

'Finished, stopped, shut. The two pits, Number One and Small Pit. Small Pit has finished over two years.'

'Nearer three, boy,' the smoker remarked hostilely. 'And 'e's got a mansion by Cardiff, a 'ouse in London and a 'ouse on the Riviera.'

'Lord Stub, the owner, you see.' Tom nodded towards his companion. 'Jenk's a Communist,' he added, by way of explanation.

Jenk spat out the morsel of cigarette and felt vainly in his pocket for another one. "*E* don't smoke stumps,' he observed.

'*Diar annwl*, since three years!' marvelled William Jones, in an effort to keep the conversation going. 'Three years.'

Jenk stared at him in amazement. Had the man been living under a tub? If he had come from Africa or America one could have understood the thing, but this man hailed from Caernarvonshire and yet didn't know that Small Pit was shut down! "Ellfire!' he ejaculated once more.

'Got any people down here?' Tom enquired.

'Uh?'

'Got a brother or a sister in Bryn Glo?'

'A sister. Mary Williams.'

'Mary Williams... Mary Williams... D'you know Mary Williams, Jenk?'

'No. Where's she live?'

'Nelson Street — number seven.'

'Jenk 'ere lives in Nelson Street. 'Oo's in number seven, Jenk?'

'Dai Morgan's in number five, then Crad Williams in number six, then...'

'Crad is my brother-in-law.'

'Aye, thass it. Crad's in number seven. Every other 'ouse they number, you see Tom. Crad!' And Jenk wagged his head and grinned.

'Crad's a lad,' said Tom.

'Crad's a scream,' Jenk agreed. The epithet he used meant something very different in William Jones' Northern idiom, but he felt instinctively that there must be a mistake somewhere.

The train puffed slowly and noisily up the valley. On their left the tower of an ancient church rose from a green belt of woodland.

'Ynys-y-gog,' said Tom. 'Very old they say. An' d'you see that farm over by there?'

'Above the church?'

'Aye. Its walls are a foot thick. Ynys-y-gog farm. The squire used to live there long time ago.'

'*Tewch!*'

'Uh?'

But William Jones didn't try to explain to Tom that he wasn't asking him to shut up.

The view on their right was very different. A dozen or so streets with one or two large, square chapels nosed their way towards the pit with its lofty, black winding-gear. Rust had eaten into the stationary wheels, and William Jones noticed that grass was springing up again between the rails at the pithead.

'Aber pit,' said Jenk, nodding in its direction. 'Lord Stub,' he added before spitting through the window. 'There were five 'undred workin' in the Aber. But now...' Jenk spat again and groped inside his breast pocket in case a cigarette stump might be lurking there unseen. William Jones proffered his tobacco box, but Jenk, a fag-smoker, declined the offer.

'What right as 'e got to close the pit and go off to the Riviera? And 'undreds of 'is workmen on the dole. Uh?'

William Jones did not know.

The train jerked itself into the little station of Ynys-y-gog. A greyhound leapt into their carriage, followed by a merry corpulent man with a stentorian voice.

''Ullo, boiss, 'ullo! *Jawch*, it's 'ot today. But Jenk's not 'ot, Tom. Too thin to sweat in 'ell, boy! What about runnin' a race for me, Jenk? Fifty to one on Jenk, ain't it, Tom?' And the fat man roared with laughter for a full half-minute.

'Where're you goin', Jim?' Tom asked.

'Tre Glo. Mick's a sure thing there today, boiss. Yes, sure thing. Cigarette, Jenk?'

'Ta.' He offered one to William as well, but the latter shook his head and pointed to his pipe. Tom was not a smoker.

'What 'appened Wednesday in Pontypridd, Jim?' asked Jenk, holding out a lighted match to the greyhound's owner. 'You said *that* race was a sure thing.'

'*Jiw*, the old woman, my mother, boy.'

'What?'

'Fed 'im on the sly, boiss. Faggots, *myn yffarn i*, Tom! 'E wasn't able to stir. Shop Bracchi's chip potato cart would 'ave passed him. But he's in trim today, aren't you, Mick *bach*? No dog in Tre Glo'll be able to sniff 'im tonight, Jenk. The race'll be over before they raise their ears. *Jiw*, if you'd seen 'im on the mountain this mornin'.'

The next five minutes were spent in going over the career of Mick, the most promising greyhound in the world despite the fact that a host of calamities had prevented him from being a winner yet. But his hour of triumph was at hand.

As he was no judge of dogs William Jones leaned back in his corner and studied these three, to him, unusual men. All three were short of stature; all were rather shabbily dressed. It would be difficult to find two types in more striking contrast than Jenk and Jim, the one thin, austere and highly strung, the other corpulent, noisy and happy-go-lucky. Jim chattered incessantly without removing his cigarette from his mouth, while the other held his in his fingers, drawing deeply on it whenever he put it to his lips. Jenk did not join in the laughter, contenting himself with an occasional toss of the head and a rather grim smile. Never had William Jones seen so fine-drawn a face: 'just like a razor' he told himself. Jim, at first sight, with a ring on his little finger and a brightly-coloured tie hanging over his waistcoat, gave the impression of being fairly prosperous; but his boots, ragged trouser-ends and frayed coat-sleeves gave the lie to his ring and necktie. Tom, too, inclined to stoutness, had a breezy manner and the rapid chatter of the longdog's owner was kept going by his prompting. William Jones thought his flannel trousers were a shade too light in colour and too loose-fitting for a man past fifty whose hair, under his shapeless grey hat, was nearly white. He could hardly imagine Bob Griffith or even Dick Trombone wearing such a garment, but there was always a lot of swagger about the Southman, wasn't there? He didn't know that the posh trousers were a gift from some Relief organisation.

After the discussion about Mick's brilliant record had begun to pall Tom explained that their 'furriner' companion was from North Wales.

''E's come to look for work in Number One, Jim,' said Jenk in his dry, quiet way.

Jim laughed loud and long yet again. There's a boy Jenk was! he exclaimed. The longdog looked up and smiled too, or so William Jones thought.

'I'm not jokin', boy.' said Jenk.''E's come all the way from Caernarvonshire to look for a job in Bryn Glo. Fact.'

Jim looked doubtfully at William Jones and Jenk alternately. The quarryman felt very uncomfortable, not knowing whether to frown or nod and smile. He chose the latter alternative.

''Ave you got good dogs up there?' queried Jim, intent on reverting to his pet topic.

William Jones didn't know, having never seen a dog-race. He explained that his hobby was gardening. Tom, greatly interested, turned from looking out of the window.

"Lotment, maybe?' he enquired.

'No, a bit of garden at the back of the house.'

The train was now nearing Bryn Glo, and Tom pointed out the allotments on the hillside below the tip. Jenk and he spent most of their time there, he told William Jones, and they had been down to the market-town that afternoon looking for cabbage-seedlings to replace their crop of early potatoes. These had all been sold out, but they had been promised some the following week. Had William Jones tried growing tomatoes at all? How had he done with peas and beans that year? Had he begun picking his kidney-beans? The three men agreed solemnly that rain was badly needed.

The train clanked into Bryn Glo station. Heavens, here's a place! thought William Jones, gazing at the coal-tips looming dark over the narrow valley. He got up to lift the basket down from the rack but Jenk pushed him aside, telling him that *he* would carry it.

Crad, accompanied by his son Arfon and daughter Eleri, was waiting to greet William Jones at the station... They went down the steps and out into the street. William Jones noticed several men, some of them collarless, hanging round a shop bearing the name Bracchi in large letters. The sound of raucous singing came from a machine inside, and the quarryman caught a glimpse of a number of youths, some clustered around oval gaming-tables and others drinking coloured liquids out of long glasses. The shop was like a fair and he stared in astonishment at the scene. They came to a bridge spanning a broad river. A river? William Jones gazed down at the inky-black water slipping by with oily patches on its surface. He saw a little group of barefooted children standing in the water and groping about for flat stones.

'Very different from Llan-y-graig, William?' remarked Crad, noticing his brother-in-law's look of astonishment.

'Aye indeed, boy.'

'The Workmen's Hall,' Arfon said, nodding in the direction of a large red-brick Hall on their right.

'Oh?'

A little knot of men engaged in wordy argument was standing in front of it, one of them — possibly a fellow-comrade of Jenk — was shaking his fist at the other three. William Jones caught the two words 'Means Test' before the yells of an audience of children enjoying a film fell on his ears from the upper windows of the Hall.

'Aye indeed, boy,' he repeated as he noticed men of all ages loafing about the street. The place almost scared him.

They passed a Club from which came the sound of loud laughter, talking, and voices raised in song; and then William Jones noticed two bedraggled sheep roaming the street and nosing about everywhere. Never had he seen sheep coming from the mountain and into the streets of Llan-y-graig in search of food. The wonder was that neither the people about, nor the dogs, took the slightest notice of them.

As they went along Crad and Arfon kept up a constant exchange of greetings with passers-by, making William Jones think his brother-in-law and the boy had adopted the roistering habits of the inhabitants of this barbarous spot.Then they began to climb the slope, and he didn't at all care for the mean, unfinished streets branching off to right and left. They walked slowly, and he noticed that Crad was breathing rather heavily. They turned right soon after and he saw they were in Nelson Street. An ice-cream cart with children and dogs clustering round it stood by the kerb, and a large, untidy, loquacious woman was loitering on the pavement, nursing a squalling infant wrapped in a shawl, and wearing her husband's cap. She grinned at William Jones, and then nodded meaningly to a neighbour who had come out of a house across the street.

'A stranger from off, I s'pose!' she remarked. 'If I 'ad a couple of coppers in my pocket I'd be off to Barry Island for a week instead of stoppin' in this 'ole.' Crad winked broadly at William Jones, who also tried to appreciate the joke.

All the houses, of grey stone blackened by coal dust, were exactly alike; each had a large fernpot in the parlour window and all the window frames and doors badly needed a coat of paint. William Jones noticed, nevertheless, that the windows were spotlessly clean; every doorstep, as well as a half circle of pavement in front, was scrubbed white; while all the doorhandles shone bright in the sunlight. How strange, he reflected, that cleanliness like this should flourish amid all this hideousness. Perhaps it was just for show.

He was thankful when they arrived at the house, where he saw at once that a royal welcome awaited him — the kitchen shone like a new pin and a tempting meal was laid in readiness on the table...

'Brought these things from the 'lotment for you, Mrs Williams,' came a deep, musical voice from the scullery, and a short man over sixty came in with a basketful of garden produce — beans, peas, potatoes, and lettuce — which he set down on the dresser.

'I won't take them, indeed, David Morgan,' said Mary. 'You need them enough yourself.'

'Don't talk stupid nonsense, gel. We've got more'n we want. 'Ow are you, Crad?'

Crad introduced his brother-in-law to the visitor.

'David Morgan,' he told William Jones, 'conductor of the Bryn Glo choir. The best mixed choir in the world, isn't it, Dai?'

"As been, boy, 'as been. *Jawch*, there's lucky you are!' he told William Jones.

'What?'

'Comin' down 'ere today. We've got a Sacred Concert tomorrow night. Pendyrus Choir. Eight o'clock — after the meeting.'

'After chapel,' Crad explained, in case his brother-in-law didn't know what was meant by 'Meeting'. 'A male-voice choir from the Rhondda Fach, Pendyrus is, and they are trying to get money to go to up to the 'Steddfod in Caernarvon. Most of them on the dole, you see, William.'

'What d'you think of this place?' the musician asked.

'Well, indeed, a place ... a place very different to Llan-y-graig.'

'Doesn't look much of a place, does it?'

'Uh?'

'Rather an ugly-looking place to look at,' Mary translated.

'Well ... I don't know ... No, p'raps it isn't very beautiful.'

'Beautiful?' David Morgan gave a quiet laugh and, moving to the window, stood looking down at the village and the valley below. 'I've been to every part of England and in 'Merica — with the choir you understand — and I've seen plenty of prettier places. But you'd 'ave to look far for people to beat in this valley.'

'For people better than these,' interpreted Crad.

'They're not to be found anywhere, say what you like.' He gazed at the vale beneath. 'But Bryn Glo was a pretty place once, sure to be. Green pasture everywhere and that river clean and pure, curlin' white round the stones, and trees growin' on the banks. I don' remember the place like that, of course, because I came 'ere as a young man, but old Daniel Rees, conductor of the Male Voice Choir when I came 'ere, used to catch trout with 'is 'ands by the bridge over there, when 'e was a little boy. But there it is; it's the people make the place, ain't it?'

translated by Richard Ruck
from *William Jones* (1953)

RHYS DAVIES

The Last Struggle

Grief for the newly dead is natural in the living and thought of legacies and insurance money to be drawn from them comes second in most persons. Megan Pugh, wife of Sam Two Fingers, thought of the insurance on her husband first, that day when the pit under-manager came to her in person and sat in her kitchen telling her that all hope of rescuing Sam and the other two entombed miners had been abandoned. Megan managed to pull a face. But already her mind was wandering in speculation. A pity she would have to wear black for a time. There was a cerise dress in the window of Lewis Paris House that she madly coveted.

'The water it is,' mourned Mr Rowlands; 'they must have been drowned.' He avoided even thinking that the three men were very likely more horribly obliterated; drowning sounded ordinary. 'Can't get at them,' he mumbled, 'for weeks, p'raps never. Blocks of stone nearly as big as a house and water running under all the time; might cause a flood of the mine if we blast the stone.' There had been a big collapse of roof four days before; four days the men had been entombed.

Fifty pounds Sam was insured for, with the Globe and Atlas people, whose New Year gift calendar was on the wall; and of course there would be the compensation money from the pit too. She could go to the seaside; she could even live away from the valley at last. And why should she wear black! Black made her look sallow.

Perhaps, in a way, it was only natural that Megan should be so unnatural. Sam had always kept her short of money; you couldn't hold him off the dogs, though much of a drinker he was not and he had never hit her. He was known as Sam Two Fingers because after a previous accident in the pit one hand was left with the other fingers gone. The strange thing was those two fingers developed a peculiar iron grip.

Only a few months after she had married him — a couple of years ago it was they had hurried to the chapel — she felt it was a mistake; a false alarm the wedding had been. As a courter he had strutted cockily at her side and she took it as pleasure in being in her company. As a married man he had got bossy at once and, when she complained that he was never in the house, answered: 'You can't bring a dog race to the house, can you? Don't I sleep tidy at home every night? What more you want?'

She wanted to be taken about by him, she wanted clothes and train journeys; she did not want to become like the dumpy women of the valley, who only left their doors to go to the shops and the chapel. They had quarrelled like hell. But even in those two years she had been defeated. The valley was a man's valley, with pubs, clubs, dog tracks and football grounds for men only. Perhaps this would change if women went down to work in the pits. But not yet.

'The Company will give you compensation, I dare say,' Mr Rowlands mumbled in embarrassment, thinking her far-away look meant shock or worry.

'How much?' she asked.

Mr Rowlands shook his head. 'An inquest and an enquiry there'll have to be before anything is settled.' He was tired and grey from the worry, but tough from long experience of these incidents. Thank goodness, though, Sam Two Fingers' wife didn't make a scene, as some wives did, especially the young ones. He heaved himself up to make the other two calls with the sad news. In their black tomb the men were lying beyond the fret of the living, sealed away for ever from the numerous details and costs of this world. Megan Pugh had sense. She did not cry out for the remains to be found and re-buried in a proper funeral.

Megan locked her front door after him. She did not want neighbours coming in to condole. There were many things to plan. She was tied in no way. Not a child to delay her. The empty days were over. Next morning she was up early and by half-past nine was sitting in a tram car which linked the districts, colliery by colliery, of the long crab-coloured valley. The July sun shone. It would be nice by the sea if this weather kept.

At the valley's end, in a cottage overlooking the railway, she knocked at a door. It belonged to her Uncle Dai, a greaser on the railway and a private bookie. Dai was no fool with his money but could be persuaded. His wife made a cup of tea when she heard the news and, taking her cue from Megan's lack of tearful display, asked: 'What your plans now?' For Megan still had a gloss on her, knew how to wear a hat, and was a good-looker with skin and teeth still fresh as daisies.

'A little rest straight away,' Megan replied; 'a little rest by myself in Weston-super-Mare, to think things out.'

'Get married more careful next time,' Dai's wife said shrewdly.

'I've been locked up!' Megan said with violence.

'Aye, a regular old Tory your Sam was. A wife was set final for him and couldn't be broke away.'

Dai came in for his dinner at twelve. He made more money as a quiet bookie than as a greaser and did not dislike his niece. Megan produced the insurance book out of her bag and all the weekly payments for Sam were down regular.

'And there's the compensation from the pit too,' she added. 'Mrs. Bevan near me had a couple of hundred pounds when her Emlyn got killed.'

She was asking her uncle for an immediate loan of fifty pounds, since very likely, what with inquests and fusses, it would be a week or more before the insurance people paid out. For this favour she was willing to pay him two pounds interest. He could keep the insurance book for security and she would see the insurance agent and tell him that her Uncle Dai was handling her affairs. She wanted to go to Weston-super-Mare without delay; her nerves were upset from the shock.

The chance of making a couple of pounds on such a certain deal made even Dai joke: 'A fancy piece of goods in trousers you got in Weston-super-Mare, Megan? Well, well —'

So, bad though it looked, she skulked off the next day. She took train to the seaside town the other side of the Bristol Channel, did not jib at the high charge in a boarding-house, and then went at once to the drapers' shops and spent ten pounds in an hour. Her most daring purchases, owing to their colour, were a scarlet frock with handbag to match. For three days she lived in the shops and began to believe in happiness again. It was not until the Sunday that she felt appeased and, examining the beach and pier, began to wonder if she had come to the English town to look at men who did not work down under. For she would never marry another miner, coming home black and bellicose from dirty pits. Weston-super-Mare, in the season, is bright. She sat eating striped ice-cream and one afternoon she went to Cheddar to visit the famous caves. She kept herself to herself but noticed a man looking at her instead of at the crystal grottoes and stalactites. And in the coach going back there he was sitting next to her! They got talking. He said he was from Birmingham, but he belittled the caves and said there were much finer ones in India.

A quiet-looking chap he was, chatting quite sedate. Malaria had sent him back from India. He was an electrician and had a job in a Birmingham factory now. His lean, lonely appearance was of one who wants looking after, but he ushered her out of the high plush coach with polite confidence. She accepted his invitation to take a glass of something in the lounge of a hotel on the front.

At the end of the second week she told him, grandly: 'I am a widow. Husband killed in the pits at home. But I got a bit of property. Independent.' She wished to be respected and she sounded short.

'Well,' Ted Cricks said, 'that's fine. Look here, I got to go back on Monday. But I dare say I could do a week-end soon as you get home, ·if asked. Is there a pub I could stay at there?'

She got a bit flustered, thinking of the neighbours. But, sitting on a golden beach with the sky blue and music coming from the pier, the world seemed easy. The tide was rolling in, moving with dark but careless force. She gave him her address and invited him for a week-end. He could sleep at her Uncle Dai's. He said he would wire her from Birmingham.

'Back soon, lovely weather,' was all she had said on the post-card she had sent to Uncle Dai. Forty pounds had been spent and her new suitcase was full. She stayed a few more days. After all, there was the compensation money to come, and she had a houseful of furniture, to say nothing of a promising courter from Birmingham.

On the way back she stopped in Cardiff for an hour and drank three ruby ports in farewell of the triumphant holiday. Wearing the red dress she arrived in the valley at dusk with three pounds in the handbag. But she tossed her head at the valley and admired herself for the flaunting display she was making. It was time some woman showed a respect for her own wants in this place. She did not care what the neighbours, stern guardians of the inexorable laws of the hearth, would think of the gay clothes. Sam wasn't worth mourning, the way he had treated her. She had a good mind to march into a pub there and then and scandalise those entirely male haunts.

As it happened there was no one about in her street. Preened and sunburnt, she unlocked her door. In the dusky passageway she paused just behind the door. Was that the sound of mice? Then her head hung forward and she dropped her red handbag.

The kitchen door at the end of the passage was slowly opening. A two-fingered hand came round it. She could see it distinctly in the twilight. But she could not scream. Her knees like water, she went squatting to the floor. But her face was stretched up, stiffly gazing. The door had been pushed wide open and the ghost of Sam, grey and silent, stood looking at her.

Just the same as when he sat before the fire for a while after his evening bath, before going off to the dogs, he wore trousers and sleeve-rolled shirt, a loose belt round his middle. But his cheeks were hollow and his eyes burned. It was Sam and it wasn't. And from the look of those smouldering eyes she could not move. They stood looking at each other for an age. Suddenly the ghost breathed, far away: 'You get up from there!'

'Sam....' she whimpered at last.

'I'll Sam you!' he panted now. 'I'll give you Weston-super-Mare....' But she had fainted.

To her dying day Megan thought she would never forget those two fingers coming round the door. It had burned into her mind. She found herself lying on the kitchen sofa. The strange thing was that he did not attack her either with tongue or hand. He only looked at her now and again. But for her it was a dead man looking at her. He was still grey from his burial, and thinner, and in his eyes lurked that stagnant glow of one not yet fully back in the world.

'You...' she whispered, 'you were rescued?'

'Aye, I was rescued,' he replied, stern. 'The only one.'

For, when the cracks had sounded in the roofing, he had leapt to a manhole in the facing, a pick-axe in his hand. Two huge blocks of stone from the falling roof had sealed him in there neatly as in an upright coffin. He heard the rush of water and waited to be choked. But the water found a channel away from the manhole and it had faded to a trickling sound. And then time too had faded. The pick's wooden handle had been caught by the edge of the stone and he could not budge it in the narrow space. He had gnawed it through with his teeth, but how long this had taken he did not know, for he had slept, waking again and again to resume the gnawing. He swallowed the chewed-off wood. On the floor was a puddle of gritty water which he managed to scoop up with his hand. At last he could wrench away a stump of the handle. He had thumped with it against the stone for hours, for days, waking from sleep. The miracle had happened at last: they heard the ghostly tapping. By the time they reached him he was unconscious. But after attention he came to with a grunt. Sam Two Fingers was tough as a mule.

She did not ask for the history of his return. She only whimpered from the sofa: 'I want to go to bed.'

'Aye,' he said briefly, 'go on.'

She rose, swayed, but huddled herself to the door. He stood, looking taller in his leanness, and watched her from those resurrected eyes.

'A red dress!' was all he said. 'No mourning for me!'

He lay at her side in bed like a stranger, not moving. Even his breathing was different; soft it was, as a cat breathes. If only he would touch her she thought her fear would break; once more he would be an alive man. Yet she dreaded that he would touch her with that two-fingered hand. She forced her tongue to say: 'You are sleeping?' He did not answer but she knew he was awake. That night she went down to the last depths of the world. She slept at last and woke to find him gone from her side. And the house felt empty, as a house from which a dead person has been removed.

Yet he was downstairs and she smelt something burning. She went down in her nightgown. He had kindled the kitchen fire and was burning her red dress. Under his arm was the hand-bag. She whispered: 'There's three pound notes in that bag.'

'Not now,' he said. 'Three pounds towards the fifty you got to save.' And he thrust the bag into the fire's core.

Her new suitcase would come up with the station lorry that morning. She went pale. Thought of the suitcase brought that Birmingham man back to her mind. What was his name?... Had that holiday been? She ran upstairs and threw herself on the bed in fright. She did not know his address. But perhaps he would not come, perhaps he had only been playing with her, like they did on holiday. Very likely he was married.

She crept about the house, mechanical at tasks. Sam took very little notice of her, calm in his new power. His only move from the house was to the back lane, where he gossiped with such night-shift men as were hanging about. She had to go to the shops. Women looked at her curiously but no one spoke to her; she kept her eyes down. When she arrived back he was smashing up her suitcase, a look of calm but terrible deliberation in his face.

'Well,' she panted, 'there's foolish!'

'You shut up,' he said. He glanced at her shopping basket. 'You better start saving. Fifty quid you owe your uncle.'

Three days passed just the same, Sam silent but watching her like a cat that seems not to be watching. He never touched her, day or night. Was it that, though physically he was not harmed by his entombment, the shock had unhinged his mind? From him came that new shut-in strength. He had always been bossy and a talkative strutter, but now a deeper and more tenacious power surrounded him so that she felt he was following her even when she went out alone. She wanted to run away, to plead for sanctuary at her Uncle Dai's, screaming that Sam was contemplating some awful punishment, perhaps murder. He showed no signs of returning to work and sat reading a newspaper or book for hours. If only he went to a dog race!

Several times she walked as far as the tram-car stop but always turned back. And there he was still, grey by the fireside, his thick neck bent over a newspaper. If she said something he told her to shut up. But once again he warned her to start saving; he wasn't going to have her beholden to her tyke of an uncle.

'How can I save all that?' she whimpered, but a bit rebellious too.

'Starve yourself,' he barked. 'And if you buy any clothes I'll knock you into the middle of next week.'

Bad luck follows the damned. Sam it was who, when she was out, took in the telegram and opened it. She found the slip of paper on the kitchen table — 'Arriving tomorrow afternoon. Ted.' Sam sat laboriously reading the book of Dickens lent him by a neighbour. He said nothing and she knew by his shoulders that no word could be dragged out of him. She went upstairs and lay on the bed; her stomach was plunging. But presently a new thought came to her and she sat up with a vindictive expression. Now was her chance!

Next day she dressed herself carefully, made up her face, and took several aspirins. She told Sam: 'I've got a visitor coming to tea.'

'Aye,' he said, 'I'll be here.' And turned a page of that maddening book.

'When are you going back to work?' she forced herself to ask.

'You'll know when.... But I'm not working for you to bloody well pay your uncle fifty quid, see! You got to pay him off your own belly and back, if it takes you ten years.'

'You ... you devil!' she breathed. But her inside was plunging again. He read on calmly.

There was only one train in the afternoon. She could have met it. But, her face set, she stayed in the house. She did not want Ted to turn back at the station. The kettle was beginning to boil on the fire when the knocker went. Sam still read, sitting in old trousers and shirt-sleeves rolled up; with him a book had to be finished once begun. Her neck throbbing, she closed the kitchen door behind her. Ted stood on the front step with an attaché-case, a new soft hat, and a raincoat neatly folded over his arm. Quite smartly dressed he was, and a man who would make such a long journey to see a holiday pick-up is clearly much attracted. Her confidence grew. 'Hello, Megan,' he said with a kind of nervous jauntiness. 'You never thought I'd come, I bet?'

She smiled gently and quiveringly, the whole appeal of an ill-used woman in it. Her eyes had both hurt and begging. And in the passage she clutched his arm, whimpered a little against his shoulder and let him smell her hair, shampooed that morning. He said, unsteadily: 'Why, what's the matter?... There, there now. Have you missed me?'

'Something has happened,' she whispered. 'My husband is here.'

He stiffened. 'But you told me he was dead.'

'It was a mistake. He was rescued after being buried a whole week in the pit.... Oh, Ted, so cruel he's been to me. I've been going mad. I can't stand it any longer, no indeed I can't.' She clung to his arm.

A call made to a man's gallantry — unless he is of exceptional quality — is rarely left unanswered. Though still bewildered, Ted's face became stern. Having travelled to India he looked upon himself as a man of the world. This dour, ugly coal-mining valley with its harsh look and frowning mountains had depressed him as he walked up from the station. And here was a dainty, tragical little woman chained in it by some ruffian of a husband who was ill-treating her.

All the same, he mumbled cautiously enough: 'Well, do you want me to see him?'

'Yes,' she whispered, in a weak little voice.

'And you want to come away with me?' he asked, a trifle uneasily.

Again she laid her head in trust on his shoulder and breathed: 'Yes.'

Sam looked up from his book when they walked in. The table was laid for tea, very bright and clean, though there was not much food. Sam looked thick, squat and working-man beside Ted's slim but half-wavering height. Megan, standing with her eyes suddenly flashing, said to her husband, who had nodded briefly to the stranger: 'A friend that I met in Weston-super-Mare.'

'Your fancy man, you mean,' Sam grunted, and gave Ted another hard but not dangerous look.

'Will you sit down, Ted?' she asked in an ignoring way, and went to pour water into the teapot.

'You stop that!' barked Sam to her. 'There's no fancy man of my wife going to drink tea in my house.'

'Don't be so silly,' she said unsteadily, and went on pouring water.

He lifted his foot and neatly kicked the pot out of her hand. It smashed on the hearth. Ted involuntarily jumped up, his hat falling from his knee. Megan began whimpering; perhaps her hand was scalded. 'Here!' exclaimed Ted in a peculiar way. Sam sat back in his chair and looked at him squarely. 'What you going to do about it?' he asked, but quite polite.

'He's taking me away!' shouted Megan, enraged. Her face had become twisted and mottled, lips thin as a viper's, eyes hard and menacing. But only for a moment — for she had caught Ted's glance at her. She threw herself whimpering into the sofa, her head lolling woebegone.

Sam, quite calm, told Ted to sit down again. He then addressed the visitor exclusively and with concentration, paying no attention to Megan's sobs: 'Look here now, Mr What's-your-name, you listen to me.... You're welcome to her, if you like. She's a bitch but got good points and only wants training — ever had anything to do with grey-hounds?' Ted, pale at the gills, shook his head. 'Well,' Sam resumed, 'you don't know how they got to be trained, then, and what I'm meaning is that everybody's got to be trained in the same way. Every-body's got to knuckle under some way or another. I got to knuckle under to a lot of sods in the pits, and as I see it a woman's got to knuckle under to a boss of a husband.... She,' he jerked a thumb towards Megan, 'don't want to and thinks she can break this bloody world's rules and go kicking around with no respect for anything.... Know what she did soon as she thought I wasn't coming out of that pit alive? Raised fifty quid on my insurance and ran off to Weston-super-Mare without as much as buying a black blouse in mourning of me! That's the sort of woman she is. The old blooming place is talking about it. Why did she do it? All because I go off to the dogs when I've had a day's bellyful of the pits and don't hang around her neck of evenings like a suckling pig.' His eyes seemed to shoot together in a righteous ferocity. 'She's one of those women that want to make a chap go wobbly at the knees before her, see? Or treat him like a concertina ready for her to play a tune on when she feels like it. She's got to be cured of it, and that's my warning to you.' He slewed a cunning little eye over the startled visitor. 'All the same, she's mar-ried to me and I'm not divorcing her, see! But if you want her, there she is and you won't be hearing from me any more.'

Ted had listened to this recital with astonishment and perhaps a bit of fear in his narrow, orderly face. He opened his mouth but closed it again. It was the decisive moment. Suddenly Megan jumped wildly off the sofa.

'You're a bully and a brute,' she flared at Sam. Her fists doubled, she heaved towards him. 'If I was a man I'd knock you down. I don't care if *he* takes me away or not. I'm going to leave you.' Glitteringly she advanced a step further towards him. He looked at her unswerv-ingly but his eyes began to dance. 'You've never been anything else but a mean ruffian, and I hate you. I wish you were rotting now in the pit!' Their gaze was entwined like two flames. She screamed: 'I'm going, I'm going now.'

As if to ward off a blow, he lifted his hand. It was the stumpy two-fingered hand. And she stared at those fingers like someone gone daft. The shadow of a little grin seemed to lurk on his face. But all he said, coolly, was: 'Don't forget your Uncle Dai wants fifty quid off you, and if I know the tyke he'll track you down to the end of the earth for fifty bob!'

Shrinking back, she broke into sobbing and fell once more on to the sofa. 'Why wasn't you killed, why wasn't you killed!' she wept.

Sam turned to the visitor: 'Well, what you going to do? Make up your mind, man. Women don't like mild guts. If you want her, she's there.'

Ted shifted his new hat uneasily from one knee to the other. But he mumbled: 'It can't be done if you won't divorce her."

'I see you got a respect for the wedding ring,' Sam said approvingly. He added largely: 'Seeing that you thought I was dead I'm not blaming you for chasing a skirt to where you got no business.... Well,' he raised his voice to the still sobbing Megan, 'seems that your fancy bloke don't want you. Perhaps he thinks you'd do him in for the sake of insurance on him. So you're left on the seashore properly, eh?'

Megan wept: 'I won't be bandied about. Devils of men. I'll kill myself —' She jumped up again.

'You've brought it on your own head,' Sam barked, very severe. 'What about me, coming back after seven days in my grave and finding my wife gallivanting to the seaside on the insurance money? Expect me to sit down and eat a pork pie as if nothing had happened? By Christ, what about me! I been dead and come alive again and I find the world gone rotten because a woman haven't got even the bit of decency to pull down the blinds and sit wearing a bit of black for me.'

She gazed at him in fear. But for the first time since her return he looked more the old Sam, more alive, as if he was smashing his way through from wherever he had been, that place of stern and ghostly silence. Yet there was something new in him too, something less cocky and more mature. She shrank back from him, and at the same time her body slackened. Her face looked dwindled and older. She leaned against the dresser, hanging her head.

The visitor rose awkwardly. The room had suddenly filled with a new private tension in which he was cancelled out. He did not know what to say. Sam helped him. 'They'll give you a meal in the Tuberville Arms. Beer there is all right. So long.' Ted went out with a quick sidling movement; even his slim hips, going round the door, looked relieved.

'Done for proper, aren't you!' Sam remarked. 'Fancy man gone, fifty quid in debt, and a cruel husband back from the grave. Well, there's the door. It's a free country.'

'He wasn't ever my fancy man,' she burst out. 'Everything was respectful. We were only interested in each other.... How was I to know they'd rescue you,' she wailed, 'after Mr Rowlands told me there wasn't any hope!'

'You should have stayed here and gone into mourning properly,' he insisted, severe as a chapel minister. 'Coming back here dressed up in red like a Christmas doll....' His voice began to boil again.

She leaned her head on the dresser shelf and wept again. Hearing him approach she lifted her head and cried out in hysteria, a long irritating howl. It was her last struggle. He gave her a crack on the jaw, not heavy but sufficient to send her against the wall, where she slumped down more in submission than because of the blow. She stopped howling. She saw him not as Sam but as some huge force not to be escaped. He picked her up. His two fingers dug into her back. His mouth caught hers like flame obliterating a piece of paper. She writhed and twisted for a few moments. But she went under, and came to life again.

from *The Trip to London* (1946)

GARETH ALBAN DAVIES
A Son of the Manse

'What would W.P. have said?' The question rises to the surface inevitably as you ponder the destruction of Noddfa Chapel, Treorci. Perhaps a sense of nemesis creeps in as well: an avenging angel breathed his revenge in the shattered organ, and the graffiti on the walls. Nemesis for having confused the might of the Ocean Coal Company with the mighty power of God. Nemesis too — a warning this to all male voice choirs, big and small — for having made regular attendance in the chapel's choir rehearsals a condition of employment. W.P., as a considerable coal magnate, probably supposed that he was doing God's work for Him.

Such negative perceptions of chapel life — often more the product of legend than reality — go far towards explaining the closed doors of Noddfa, since, for a majority perhaps of people in the twenties and thirties, especially the men-folk, Welsh Nonconformity had betrayed the working class, giving succour to their enemies, administering a soothing balm where it should have provided a lash, and some astringent medicine. There were other reasons too, such as the ebbing of the Welsh language, and the full tide of exodus, to Luton, or Birmingham; the effects also of the Second World War, and an increasingly secularized community.

As a result Cwm Rhondda has tended to forget, or ignore, the enriching effects that the chapels had. Indeed, before the advent of television, the motor-car, and the clubs, they were the focus of people's lives. Not just the drawing power of God's star performers, like Philip Jones, or Jubilee Young, but the quiet round of piety and prayer, the excitement of oratorio or operetta, the intellectual sustenance of lectures and Young People's meetings. Indeed, in quality of life the valleys have suffered a tragic dimunition since the religion of the Con supplanted the con of religion.

But I do not want to paint in glowing tones what proved to be the sunset of Welsh Nonconformity. I simply want to paint myself into one corner of it, for as a son of the manse, I was both part of that older and fast disappearing order, and a critical observer of it. To begin with, I was born into a bastion of privilege. To have been spoon-fed by one's house-master at Eton bears no comparison with being brought up in one of those echoing mausoleums, where damp usually rose higher than ambition, and where gentility still sometimes passed for Godliness. Of course, the awful pretensions were there in the names given to some of these residences: Llys-myfyr, the Court of Contemplation; Bugeilfod, Shepherd's Rest, and so on. Nevertheless, I can think of no childhood or youth fuller of blessing, not only my own, but that of many other 'plant y Mans'.

For one thing, there were the books, by the shelf and roomful. Not just on religion and theology, but on history and politics. Cheap volumes of the Left Book Club mingled with the smaller format of the Thinkers' Library, or the greenbacks of the Benn Educational series. There were a few score volumes of fiction, history, and philosophy, in the marvellous Everyman's Library. And our house held a special place for books about Wales, her history and religious tradition, her literature too, for my father was a great, if indigent, patron of Welsh writers and scholars. On a lordly salary of £226 per year he bought books by the hundred. My mother dreaded his return from Evans' Bookshop in one of the Cardiff arcades, or from the more leisurely procuring afforded by his regular trips to the family town of Carmarthen, where Williams Curio's bookshop in King Street offered a temptation to curious flesh no less libidinous than a night out in Soho.

It was not just the quantity of books, however, but the respect they engendered. Respect for scholarship, and for pure intellect. Respect for education, and for tradition. In my father's case, I came to feel that he put books and book learning too high on his list: his first question to me, after an absence, was usually 'What have you been reading? ' as though enlightenment, or self-improvement, or experience of life, could hardly have come in any other way. Nevertheless, the example of his reverence for learning marked me indelibly, and it is a mark in all except those few that rebelled intemperately against the values of the Manse.

There was a place for learning too in the physical sense, a sanctuary where its rites were practised. The word itself says it: the study! Here also pretentiousness reigned at times, and a high seriousness that would not admit self-mockery. My mother was no prude, but I recall her anger when she discovered that some visiting divine, after the exertions of the morning service and a hearty meal, had retired to bed not to rest (as we had been assured), but in order to read a novel by P.G. Woodhouse. For her the action personified the *trahison des clercs*, even perhaps the sin against the Holy Ghost!

Respect for the study might take an extreme form, such as the case of the minister's wife, who was forbidden even to enter the sanctum, lest she disturb the musings of the pastor. More common was the banishment of children, as though their prattling, and their curious fingers, might get in the way of communication with the On-high. But the high seriousness was useful at times. The magic formula 'He's in the study' could prove sufficient to substitute reverence for anger in the breast of a testy deacon. And the minister himself occasionally needed, one should not forget, a place to experience a self-respect so easily undermined in those difficult years by questioning from without, as well as from within.

Something of the magic rubbed off on me. To sit there in the seclusion, surrounded by calm and books, enjoying a dozing reverie broken only by the call to a meal! To read a book with head tilted backwards on the mahogany (and inscribed) swivel-armchair, and feet on top of the anthracite stove! In such a place you enjoyed wall-to-wall carpeting within, if not without. Fortunately too, the heat of the stove kept the dampness from stripping the wall-paper, and the fungus from entirely engulfing the cement floor.

But it would be quite wrong to conclude that the manse was by nature a place that kept out the world. Rather the reverse, for the world brought its problems to you. Chapel members came with intractable difficulties — rent that could not be paid or mortgages covered, parents whose sacrifice for their children's education meant skimping and going skint, families torn by exile, others where independence and self-respect were ravaged by the need to 'eat your house' before you could qualify for public assistance.

The same problems had to be confronted also on a broader front. Ministers had to search their conscience long, before deciding whether accepting membership of the panel that arbitrated in cases of need would mean entering into a pact with the devil, or could be a way towards alleviating the misery and hardship of the poor. On the other hand, no heart-searching was required when a scheme got under way, with the help of the people of Bristol if I remember right-ly, to purchase and distribute boots and shoes to the Rhondda unemployed. I have a vague memory still of boxes piled up in a corner of the study.

My father was fortunate in getting what must have appeared at the time a more positive role. He was twice member of a deputation to Downing Street to see two Prime Ministers, Ramsay Macdonald and Neville Chamberlain. Both left a deep bitterness, but Ramsay Mac was the greater disappointment to him as they left empty-handed: 'You could see that the only thing he had on his mind was his trip to an international conference in Stresa on the following day.' Those fruitless flirtations in the corridors of power were what finally impelled my father's decision that Wales must look to herself if she was to begin to solve her problems.

Not all Rhondda ministers became, as he did, a keen supporter of *Plaid Cymru*; indeed, there was in some a reluctance to enter the political debate. But many, in their differing ways, were political radicals. To be fair, I cannot recall hearing any visiting preacher protest with the vehemence of a Peter Price in Merthyr Tydfil, bawling out his local steelmasters by name, 'Mr Guest, and Mr Keen, and Mr Nettlefold,' before delivering them to the bar of judgment; or of a Bryn Thomas in the Cynon Valley, who became an active supporter of the Communist Party. But one of our neighbouring Congregationalist ministers, Llew Williams, became a Labour MP for the Llanelli constituency. We gave welcome also, on many an evening, to one of the most outspoken critics of capitalism, who was forced to give up his ministry in a respectable Southport church, because his congregation refused to pay him his salary. This was D.R. Davies, who later wrote *On to Orthodoxy*, one of the most remarkable acts of recantation in the history of modern radicalism.

I daresay that Rhondda ministers too were in some measure subject to restraints. Certainly the voices of radicalism and protest were often to be heard in our house, but inevitably they were more guarded in their pulpit utterances, for a minister's independence was not beyond challenge, and he was obliged to maintain a fractious unity between local employer and employed in the life of the church. On the other hand, my father took great pride in the fact that Bethesda, Ton, had always offered him a 'free pulpit', a compliment gratefully given by someone whose pacifist views were well known to his congregation during the Second World War.

Whatever the clash of opinions, the manse was a great centre of conversation and debate. Ministers drifted in and out — a morning call bringing new returns of *Y Ddeiseb*, the referendum in favour of an independent Wales; someone stopping off on the way to the monthly meetings of local clergy of all denominations; gatherings at the manse of three or four ministers engaged in a joint venture, perhaps a commentary on one of the Gospels. And there were the set occasions: tea on the Sundays of the Big Meetings, when other ministers and laymen had a chance to meet the preacher of the day; and the regular Sunday evening fixtures, when ministers preaching elsewhere in the locality would look in, and often stay for supper.

On all these occasions conversation was the thing, and if I had my place at the table, it was because I liked being there. A cliché representation portrays the Welsh Nonconformist minister as the bigoted and bestarched upholder of an unyielding ethic, one of those 'black Parchs' that Dylan Thomas mentioned, or a Bern-Dafydd plucked from one of Caradoc Evans' short-stories. I am not denying that the likes of these existed, nor indeed that they would sometimes sit at our table like black-suited dinosaurs, inveighing against strong drink and the desecration of the Sabbath in between mouthfuls.

Yet these were in my experience very untypical. The conversation was usually amusing and light-hearted, interspersed with ribald comment, and above all a fund of good stories, told with the rhetorical mastery that years in the pulpit had fashioned. Naturally too, these preachers brought stories from their workplace to be told without embarrassment, because we were *en famille*. Here I first heard the word *Crem.*, tossed off as naturally as a miner would refer to his mandrel; I can recall too the shock it produced in me, convinced as I was that death was not to be treated lightly. In fact, funerals were often a source of comic relief. For instance, Mansel Thomas, Hebron, Ton, officiating at the funeral of a Nothing-arian (to use the language of the trade), who had neither family nor friends, nor the kind of respectable social contacts that guaranteed a packed house:

> In fact, when I got there, there was only one mourner, an old friend, and once he realized that nobody else was going to come, and that we had all that long march in front of us, from Ystrad up to Treorci cemetery, he put his hand on my arm, and said, 'Walk back by here with me, will you, so they'll think it's a bloody *private*.'

Then there was Morley Lewis, Bodringallt's story about another funeral, when my father and he found themselves burying someone that neither of them knew:

> There we were at the graveside, not quite knowing what to do, when I noticed some well-known faces, among them one or two people with good voices. Dai Baswr was there, for instance. So I ventured giving out a hymn forgetting that mourners aren't supposed to sing at funerals. For Dai and the others were among the mourners this time, and stood there speechless, leaving only Alban and me to do the singing. Alban here with his deep bass, and me a squeaky tenor. And when he went up, I went down, with neither of us meeting in the middle, and neither of us singing the tune. It was awful! But just then things got worse, for I got the giggles. We couldn't look at each other any more, but sang away, with our backs turned on each other across the open grave.

These teas and suppers yielded more than stories, for matters of controversy and debate, or the world's events and crises, were mulled over. The windows of the manse looked outwards. Likewise the newspapers were to be read and digested every morning, with my father at the head of the table in his enveloping armchair. Then there were the weeklies, the *Christian World* and the *New Statesman*, the denominational *Y Tyst* (The Witness), and of course the national weekly, *Y Faner*, which during the war-years published Saunders Lewis's varied diatribes in *Cwrs y Byd*, so often at variance with official government policy that attempts were made to censor them, and the paper itself.

My personal interest in politics and world affairs began there, and the habit of keeping in touch through the newspapers became deeply ingrained. But another channel of communication existed with the world outside. Tours by missionaries on leave were fairly frequent, and when they came they usually stayed with us. I knew the argument that missionaries could be part of the softening-up process that was a preliminary to economic exploitation, with trade following the Cross. Yet that objection was often overcome in me by the charm of those visitors, and the way they opened up to me a world so different from ours, and with its own horrible problems. Madagascar and China were the two areas favoured by the London Missionary Society. I recall the stiff gentility of Miss Myfanwy Wood, who tutored Chiang Kai-Shek's children, at a time when he was a rebel against the old order, rather than a has-been in his Taiwan enclave. There was the more homely touch of Gwenfron Moss, who had served in China as a nurse, or Gwyneth Evans who as a teacher swapped the children of Cardiff for those of Madagascar.

One aspect of Rhondda life that saddened me was the unwillingness of some to recognize the need for charity towards those who lived in what is now termed the Third World. Their cry was: 'We've got enough problems ourselves.' It is surprising that people who could unselfishly support the cause of the miners in Asturias, or the Republican Government in Spain, drew the line somewhere between themselves and the rest of the world. That was much less easy in the chapel community, where collecting for the missions was a regular feature. Certainly the misery and deprivation that gripped most of humanity was something you could not easily ignore in the Manse.

Were there any particular disadvantages? The main one was the misunderstanding of which you were the object, if not exactly the target. Being a minister was bad enough, for nobody could really understand what he did, or what he was for. As a minister's son, or daughter, you had no *raison d'être* at all, you were just an eccentric, a left-over. This led inevitably to a sense of isolation on my part, especially as you were the victim of other people's clichés. It was taken for granted that you would be a fuddy-duddy, narrow in outlook, intolerant and censorious of other people's behaviour. In fact, like others in my position I had been brought up to tolerance in politics, religion, and morality. Nevertheless, in the local coalmine another 'chapel-boy' and myself were regarded as very odd, since, we were informed, we 'didn't drink, or smoke, or run after women'!

On the other hand, I felt no isolation in Porth County School, partly because coming from such a wide variety of backgrounds, both social and geographical, we all took each other for what we were, and did not bother about the social niceties. But with the Rhondda's highly selective system of entry we were as a group an élite within an élite, with the majority of boys and girls going to the higher grade, or later the secondary modern schools. My pals had the advantage of being able to return to the life of the majority after school and at the weekends, so that their comparative isolation was reduced. In my own case I took my isolation back with me to play with in the seclusion of the manse itself.

What that unique environment had meant to me was most deeply felt when Bethesda manse was sold-up in the late seventies after the death of both my parents. The loss was personal, but significance lay in its being part of the final disappearance of an enriching way of life that the Rhondda had nurtured through the large number of chapels. Now the total number of ministers left in the two valleys was no more than three or four. I remember pacing my favourite rooms that day — the kitchen around whose deal table so many had gathered to entertain and be entertained, the walls and ceiling darkened by decades of pipe-smoking; the study in which the hush remained unchanged, although the smell of damp and decay was now rank; my own small bedroom upstairs, with its bed-side table and lamp, and its own supply of books — an even more formidable redoubt within the larger bastion. And how I missed the voices raised in welcome and farewell, the reverberating *'Shwd ych chi, 'te?'*, the interminable laughter, the boom of discussion and debate! I recalled my mother whose job it was always to keep the show on the road; and myself at that table, a visitor from a younger generation, looking in on a marvellous spectacle that would soon cease to exist.

Excelsior (1982)

T.J. MORGAN

Sheep in the Rhondda

Last year and the year before that, all through the Winter that lasts from September to April, I used to go once a week up to the top end of the Rhondda. For the whole of that journey, and especially after passing through Treforest, there is hardly a section of road without rows of houses, so that the old saying about a squirrel's being able to run the length of the valley on the roofs of the houses is no exaggeration. True, on some sections — between Porth and Trehafod, for example — a pretty long leap would be needed. It's not easy to understand how one village is distinguished from another. There was once a gap between them, that's to say, a part of the road without houses stretching from one cluster of buildings to the next, but the empty bits have now been filled in for almost every step of the way, so that there's only an illusory division between places that have different addresses. For example, after climbing from the centre of Porth, and without feeling you have left that place, you see a sign that says you are within a few steps of crossing into the territory of Trealaw. On the way back, you are surprised after travelling for miles along the main road from Trealaw that you are entering, or have already entered Porth. It was a long time before I realized that it's the same sign and that the two directions are on each side of it. This is not the only example of a sign dividing two places; there are two-faced signs between Trealaw and Llwynypia, between Llwynypia and Ystrad, and so on.

For those who are not familiar with the mining valleys of East Glamorgan, this will give some idea of how populous and unrural these valleys really are. There is hardly any need to mention the works and the coal-tips, the coming and going of pedestrians and vehicles, and the crowds of children playing. Despite all this, there wasn't an evening on the occasions I travelled up and down that I didn't see sheep on the main roads, standing or lying on the pavements, or rummaging with their noses in the ash-bins, and very often walking in the middle of the road without taking fright until the sound of a bus or car's horn turned their contented ambling into terrified escape.

They are to be seen not only in the evening, just before it grows dark. I have more than once been unable to understand what the two light-green eyes were that I saw shining at the side of the road, where the gleam of the car's lights met the blackness of the night at the edge of the beam. I thought for a moment they were cat's eyes, and yet I couldn't work out how cat's eyes could be seen so far down the street; after rejecting this theory, I realized that it was from the head of an unseen sheep that the two elements of leaf-coloured light were shining.

Well, there's a subject to write about, says the literary part of my mind; but the subject for what? says the critical conscience. What about some verses, says the upper layer of my brain, playing around with the idea that the sound of *Worthy* has bathed the valleys in the dew of the name of the Lamb over the years? But that would be a caricature, especially if I went on to talk about the lack-lustre lamb wandering the streets like someone out of work, past Nazareth and Calfaria and the Gospel Hall. It would be best to leave that idea alone.

Yet still I had a hankering to make some literary sense of these sheep; an impression of their oddness had somehow been engraved on my mind.

I have had a special feeling for the Rhondda ever since I was a child. Although I was born and brought up at the other end of the county, I can half-claim these valleys as my own. As a young lad my father had worked in the Hills; his brother had stayed and raised a family there, and the trips to see our relations had been the farthest journeys of my childhood. A man is able to claim many a place on account of connections similar to this, and of all the various places with which I can claim to have some connection, and feel warmly close to, I'd put the Rhondda second to my own native place. As a small child I knew the names of places like Llwynypia and Pandy and 'Trealo', and the nicknames of places such as the Cwtsh and the Cape; I heard stories of the explosions and the upheaval of the great strike, and about some tremendous floods that had surged down the mountain near Clydach Vale. Sometimes, although he wasn't good at imitating, my father would speak the Rhondda dialect, using its vocabulary and phonology. And one Christmas he insisted on taking me to compete in the eisteddfod at Bodringallt, in order to show me off to his relations and former work-mates.

I should have sufficient reason to write about the valleys, with warmth and admiration, and there's plenty of similarity between the coal-valleys of the Rhondda and the Swansea Valley (in one respect), so that I could venture to interpret, or at least to portray the life and times of my second habitat, getting its special flavour into a bottle. If I could, I should be glad to convey in words the bustle and the indiscipline; the wit and the coarseness; the heroism and the incompetence; the good times and the big money; the dust and the sweat; the pubs and the chapels; the greyhounds and the rough neckerchief and the revivals; *Worthy* and the great strike; the poverty and the works idle and the frequent emigration — all those essential things that go into the word 'Shoni-hoi-ism'. But even if I could, I wouldn't, because Shoni by now has become a 'character', an illusion in literature and on stage, and so much of a favourite that he has been pampered and spoiled. The 'character' has been made to sing the *Messiah* on stage and in books in spite of the fact that he no longer goes to chapel and doesn't know the Welsh words of the hymns that are sung on the rugby-field, nor even the English words of 'Guide me, O thou great Jehovah'; and it's difficult to go into raptures — except in reminiscence — about a way of life that has to a large extent come to an end, surviving mainly as a literary ritual. In the middle of writing that last sentence, and as I hesitated after finishing it, a story came to mind that I once heard from a friend many years ago, about a small girl at a school in the North of England, where my friend was a teacher, who showed him a photograph of her little sister; arms were to be seen in this picture, as if holding or supporting the child. When asked why the child needed to be held up like this, the little girl explained that her sister was dead. The parents had no picture of the child when alive but had arranged for one to be taken after she died, so that they would have an image of her after she had been buried and was lost for ever from their sight.

So here I am back again, empty-handed, with the commonplace, unclever idea that sheep wander from the mountain-tops, down into the streets, making their way, tame and stupid, along the tarmac roads despite the noise and traffic. I once noticed a crowd of people standing in a long queue, waiting for a bus, and close by in the gutter a tiny lamb sucking for its life, unaware of the lookers-on and the passers-by as if it had been in the lonely, undisturbed places of Epynt or Snowdonia. And here we have the oddness and the inconsistency, namely, that it is not the sheep which are astray among people in the noisy urban bustle; it is the bustle that's odd in places where sheep belong.

And one evening when I was coming home in my car, not driving too fast or carelessly, I saw a greyish-white piece of matter leap out of the darkness on the pavement, across the car's lights and into one of the wheels. When I went back to it, it lay quietly in the middle of the road, not dead and yet without bleating, and I should like to think it was not in pain. I dragged it as best I could to the side of the road, lest some passing vehicle went over it, and then hurried to look for a police-station to report the accident. Although the policeman was not hard-hearted — to be completely fair to him — as he helped me to move the sheep to a less public place, I was surprised at his calmness and to see him so unfussed as he took down the details. It was routine for him to record an incident in which a sheep had been killed on the valley's roads; what was surprising, he said, was that there were any left at all, considering how often these accidents occurred. Although the excitement I felt at the time had worn off as I started out again and resumed my journey, I could still feel in my right hand some of the shock of the collision, and in my mind's eye I could still see the helpless inertia of that sheep. And although I was not guilty in the eyes of the law, I couldn't rid myself of the uneasy thought that I had been responsible, albeit it unintentionally, for causing pain to a dumb creature; and what's more, that I had somehow contributed to the destruction of an innocent species on land that belonged to them.

translated by Meic Stephens
from 'Defaid yn y Rhondda' in *Cynefin* (1948)

R. BRINLEY JONES
Rhondda Serenade

To those, like me, who were born in Penygraig in the Rhondda, birth and upbringing were a privilege. I have always felt that breathing the air of Penpisgah and Carncelyn, watching the sheep, tired of the verdant pastures of Cow's Hole, devouring the lush left-overs from our tables in Mikado Street, playing rounders and marbles by the light of the gas-lamp outside Mr Rex Jones's house, being paid a penny for shopping in the Star for Miss Jenkins who was perfumed with camphor and snuff — all these in themselves were a marvellous start for a boy who might have been born, but for the pull of the coal, in the grey slate streets of Blaenau Ffestiniog. Both my parents were born there, in the North, but all I knew of it was that one of my forebears had been hailed as a poet in his day and another had shed the slate dust and had worked his way up to become editor of the *Manchester Guardian*. Penygraig was a place of beauty for me; the view that I remember from our mountainside, of Trealaw resting in the sun with the Tonypandy Methodist Hall like some giant phallic obelisk lined by the River Rhondda, would have made Canaletto wild with paint.

Apart from the privilege of living beside a brook and within earshot of the tennis balls and bowls that moved with grace on the greens of the Penygraig Welfare, there was Mrs Owen as a neighbour on one side — Mrs Owen who grew roses and white daisies — whose husband died a long death, pinched by asthma and smothered by enormous flower-pots of geraniums, and on the other side Mrs Bateman whose highly polished piano was my first acquaintance with music and whose husband slept in the afternoon and imposed on me quiet and self-discipline. And it was Penygraig that taught me reality and put the brake on in later life when one might have been carried away by colours and charms; in Penygraig the butchers were called butchers, not meat-purveyors, as they were higher up the valley.

There was the joy of the Penygraig Infants' School with its morning-milk served from jugs, Mrs Harris and her winning ways, and rests in the afternoon and the jump from units to tens under the guidance of Miss Jones the bell-room. It was there that I painted my first seascape, there that I learned 'Nicknack paddy whack', there that I dressed up as a gipsy and sang 'Hob y deri dando' and there that I knew the fun of playing bell-horses and discovered what friendship was all about.

After that it was Dinas Boys' School — or Tai School as it was called, with Mr Sam Howells, who hailed from Treorci, as Head and Mr Jenkins and Mr Ledbury as my teachers. How splendid a school it was, dampened only when my friend Leonard Salvanell died; the school 'dinner' in the canteen was a privilege I enjoyed only when the weather was too bad to climb to Mikado. It was there that I heard a tuning-fork for the first time and Mel Griffiths singing 'Danny Boy'; I can see him now, called upon to perform every time a visitor came, singing until the neck veins showed taut. I was a monitor and that involved keeping the books tidy, distributing them and putting small-coal on the fire in the winter, at the start of playtime. There I was drilled in the three R's and solved how and when one train driving at a speed of 50 mph in one direction, passed another travelling at 60 mph in the other direction. I have forgotten, now, what the answers were ... but I remember the decency, the caring, the thoroughness of the teachers. And the gorgeous smell of the pencils.

From there it was Tonypandy Secondary School which stood up-right like a prince behind Theophilus Fashion Shop and the Mirror of Gems. And the teachers arrived by car and wore gowns. I can hear to this day the remarkable and resonant voice of John Thomas sharp-ened by Players Navy Cut, who taught Latin; 'oppidum bar-bar-orum' conjures it all up for me. It was there that I discovered that I was Welsh. At home, though both my parents were able to speak Welsh, the language of the hearth was English. It was Mair Kitchener Davies, David Davies and Elizabeth M. Jones who converted me to the land of my fathers. It was there, too, that I composed my first poem — on Spring, 'Y Gwanwyn', thought out in the back kitchen of my auntie's house in Kerslake Terrace; I have never written as good since. And there in Tonypandy Sec. mutations turned into magic and the impersonal form of the verb brought to my mind the strength and independence of my people. The headmaster, Mr Edward Hugh, M.A., Mus.Bac., was a large man, mad about music — morning as-sembly, on occasions, was the length and breadth of a Beethoven Sonata and a whole repertoire of Welsh folk-songs: 'Syr Harri Ddu' and 'Mentra Gwen' rang through the corridors while prefects fainted and masters excused themselves. But how much more all those melodies have remained in my mind than the theorems and details of the reproductive system of amoeba. My gratitude to the happiness of those days in that red-brick citadel raised above Dunraven Street is unchanged and immeasurable.

There were Saturdays and Sundays: the school rugby match on Sat-urday mornings and on Saturday evenings the play at Maes-yr-Haf where I sniffed the smell of grease paint and watched from the wings. I belonged to the Garrick Players, housed in an old engine-house on the campus of Llwynypia Colliery opposite the statue of Thomas Hood. Mrs Matt. Lewis mesmerised the players for years and she was followed by Jack James who was kind enough to ask me to take part in a broadcast from Cardiff. It started with a play, produced by T. Rowland Hughes, in which Rachel Thomas, Prysor Williams and Moses Jones starred ... continuing with my playing a junior to Richard Burton ... and the contact with the BBC remains to this day. I owe a great deal to Jack James who had acted with Robert Donat and Sybil Thorndike. Wasn't I lucky? On other Saturday evenings there was a dance in the church hall in Tonypandy, where the sixth formers met; it has given me a fox-trot complex which I know will remain with me always — but the girls were good and some of the friendships everlasting.

On Sundays it was Soar Ffrwdamos, Penygraig. There, under the divine direction of the Reverend W. Dyfan Thomas and in the smell of gas, I heard the words of Pauline epistles first; it was there in the cold water under the big seat that I dived and was saved. It was there that I saw Lloyd George collars and was given sweets by Mrs George John for reciting the Twenty-third Psalm. And it was Mrs Powell of George Street who taught us to enunciate and Mr Roger Jenkins of Hendrecafn who taught us the scales in time for the Gymanfa Ganu at Soar, Moriah, Tonypandy or Jerusalem, Llwynypia. I can remember the different woods and polishes of those chapel seats now — a dry, a medium and a cream sherry of wood. I have never gone to a singing festival since without wanting to put Brylcreem on my hair ... and I still feel a deep resentment when there is no repeat of the chorus. But in Soar there was more to music than the mere matter of a Gymanfa Ganu. When I was a boy, Soar performed oratorios under the able direction of Thomas John Hughes ... 'Samson', 'Judas Maccabaeus', 'Elijah', 'Messiah' ... they were the high musical festivals of my calendar. The big-seat was platformed and there was an elaborate decoration of the pulpit with coloured crepe-paper; the choir was resplendent in blouses and black bow-ties and sat like the heavenly host in the upper-chamber, though I remember now how their heads wagged when they sang 'All we like sheep'. It seemed as if they knew what they were singing about. On that occasion, professionalism really came to our part of the valley — and the names Ceinwen Rowlands, Gwyneth Morgan, James Johnston, Redvers Llewelyn are imprinted on my memory as they were, with photographs and qualifications, listed on the programmes printed by Evans & Short or Robert Davies. I wish I had kept those programmes as a record of my musical nutrition in those years. They were splendid, memorable performances, when Soar came out of its shell and showed, for a mere three and sixpence, what culture was all about. The valley was exalted.

Sunday evenings had second sessions, too: in my early days, as a bonus after the solid sermons of Soar I was taken by hand by my cousin and brother to see a magic-lantern show in Trinity, Tonypandy, introduced by Mr Cook. The scenes of poverty and depression, of alcoholism and penance are with me still and my infant imagination was exercised for days and nights in an attempt to locate the setting. And then, when I was older, I was taken to the second service at the Methodist Central Hall in Tonypandy; its individual seats, wide platform and English hymn-singing were a new experience. It was there that I learned the word 'epilogue' and I liked it. It saddens me deeply to know that these places of worship, dedication and service are now ruins of their former glory.

Most of us were destined to leave Penygraig and it seemed that the G.W.R. were determined that we did so. It was not enough to have a convenient railway-line that took us from Tonypandy to Cardiff and the big, wide world; there was another, private way — direct from Penygraig Station (mastered in my day by Mr Edwards who had a passionate belief that the Welsh language was closely related to Hebrew) through the gentle fields through Tonyrefail, Llantrisant, Peterston-super-Ely, to Cardiff. It gave me a feeling of the superiority of Penygraig people, from an early age. But my departures had significance, too. My first trip to University College, Cardiff, puffed from Tonypandy Station with my father and his colleagues waving me off from the jetty of the Tonypandy Labour Exchange, alongside C.&G. Thomas, Painters and Decorators. My second departure was from Penygraig, heading for Oxford; my family lined up like a guard of honour high on the bank and saw me off with Penygraig Infants, Tai, Tonypandy Sec., and Soar Ffrwdamos safe in my heart, ready for the rigours and romance ahead.

When I return now, there are changes of course and so many have moved for quiet and eternity to Llethrddu, bordering the Brithweunydd Road. But when I was made an honorary druid by the Gorsedd of Bards of the Island of Britain a few years ago 'Ffrwdamos' was my obvious choice as a bardic name. After all, when you owe as much as I do to those brooks and streets and pits, to those friendships and experiences, you cannot afford to forget without losing something of yourself. What a privilege it was for those of us born in those days in that place!

from Excelsior (1982), the record of The Treorchy Male Choir

GARETH ALBAN DAVIES
The Fur Coat

'There were six or seven fur coats in Bethesda,' my father once re-marked, while referring to more prosperous years in the Chapel's history, back in the 'thirties. But perhaps I'm mistaken as I try to recall the voice of whoever it was made that statement. It would have been more in keeping with my mother's viewpoint, for she was more sensitive than he to the gradations in society and the lines drawn between one class and another. But there was no doubt about the facts: they were confirmed by my own childhood memory. Those coats were part of life's wonder.

Seated in our pew, with the waves of organ-music swelling the eddies of heat that swirled down the aisle, I was well placed to see the coats as they came into Chapel. On winter nights they would be pulled tight around the body, but of a Spring evening they billowed free, a fit adornment for their owners rather than a necessary garment. I wasn't well enough acquainted with the world of Nature to be able to say where these various pelts had come from, but it would be an irreverence to suggest that they had once belonged to cat or rabbit, since it was so obvious to the eye that they had adorned the backs of exotic creatures in the far corners of the earth — the rare Siberian fox, or Persian lamb, or the musquash about which I knew nothing save the fragrance of its name.

But who were the owners of these luxurious furs? A Marxist ana-lysis would lead inexorably to the conclusion that they were the wives and daughters of the exploiting classes, and in the Valleys during the 'thirties there was no doubt as to who *they* were, — the owners and managers of the coal-mines. It must be admitted that several of these were to be found among Bethesda's members, and that one or two had been elected to office in the Chapel. Let it not be forgotten, either, that a fur coat adorned the back and shoulders of the wife of the Ocean Coal Company's general manager ('Ocean, thou mighty monster' was the mischievous suggestion for the solo in one of the musical competitions at the Treorci Eisteddfod of 1928!). And to that fine, dark coat there was, moreover, a sheen very different from those others seen here and there in the congregation: sable has a sedate, unshowy quality which suits a woman who is well aware that she's wealthy, and that everyone else knows it too. There remains in my memory a picture of a beautiful woman, of well-bred comport-ment and manners, with the night's blackness closing like death around the whiteness of her flesh.

At the other extreme from this capitalist coat there was quite a different one, which at first beggars Marxist definition. It belonged to the wife of a collier and was made from sealskin. The family must have sacrificed quite a bit to have been able to afford such an expensive garment. The coat might even have been described as defiant, since it demonstrated that an ordinary collier could, with effort, rise to the same level as his masters. The plain truth is that this particular collier didn't rise at all, and perhaps the coat merely made up for his failure to realize a dream that had become reality only in the case of some of his fellows: after all, the manager of the Ocean had risen from the same community as he himself had.

One of my contemporaries at Bethesda remembers the sealskin coat well, for it had belonged to his grandmother. She used to keep it strictly for Sunday services. During the week it would be hung in state in the darkness of the wardrobe, with camphor-balls placed in the pockets to keep out the moths. When Sunday came round once more it would be taken out, and in its pockets would be a plentiful supply of mints, so that its owner could keep her grandchildren quiet during the sermon. Not surprisingly, some of the camphor's scent would stick to the mints, leaving in the boy's memory a Proustian stimulus that has remained frustrated ever since, for it's almost impossible in these prosaic days to hit upon the precise aromatic combination that would awaken the memory from its deep slumber.

Those two examples were to be found at either extreme of the phenomenon — in between there were coat-owners who were much more typical, mostly schoolteachers in their thirties and early forties, indeed, so many, now that I come to count them carefully, that I doubt the statistical accuracy of my parents in noting only six or seven. Among those wearers of fur there was a pit-manager's daughter, and a local schoolmaster's wife who was so small that she looked just like a feathery wren. But speaking generally, the rest were the womenfolk of ordinary colliers.

The fur coat itself set those teachers apart, but there was something else, too: they were unmarried. The most obvious explanation of this fact was that the Glamorgan Education Authority, during the years of the Depression, used to refuse permission for a woman to remain in her post as a teacher once she had married. In the cruel economic circumstances prevailing in those days it was very difficult to leave your job, because a whole family might be dependent on your salary. In some instances there was another explanation for this maiden state, of which I as a child was completely unaware. Among those teachers there were some who were old enough to have experienced what it was like to be a young woman during the years of the Great War. It had been part of the sadness of their lives to see their sweethearts going off patriotically to Death's great harvest in the trenches in France, from where many never returned. This experience had left a scar on the soul of some of these women, a scar left unhealed by the passing of the years, and people would sometimes be heard to comment that a 'tragedy' had occurred in the life of this one or that.

But how to explain that the majority were the daughters of colliers? First of all, a passion for education was widespread, often arising from aspirations that were quite materialistic. It offered boys a chance to escape from poverty and the dangers of the pit, and for girls there lay hope of another wage with which to supplement the family's slender purse. Such was the craving for giving an education to the children that it produced many more schoolteachers than local society could find employment for. As a consequence, it was coal and teachers that were for many years the main exports of the Valleys. And through the efforts of these young people, in London, and Birmingham, and elsewhere, some other member of the family would have a chance of higher education, and a teacher's certificate, later on.

Despite these losses to the local community, a small proportion remained to leaven it. It was easy enough to recognize them, and not only by the fur coat. That was a sign of their independence, and of the fact that they enjoyed a comparatively prosperous way of life. It must be remembered that the coat was a reward for years of thrift in a period when the ownership of a motor-car was not at all common: that was why the coat was worn by teachers of more mature years, rather than by those on the ladder's lower rungs. The wearers of the coat were an élite within a group that was already an élite in society.

I referred to their independence. That was to be observed in the very way they moved, in their self-confidence, in the *joie de vivre* that seemed to possess them whenever they found themselves in one another's company. Two other things should be noted about them: they had money and the spending power at a time when other people had but small means; also, in a society where the male was dominant, and traditionally the family's breadwinner, a woman with money in her pocket, and the right to spend it as she wished, stood apart from the rest. Another characteristic: some of these women used to smoke, doing so openly. But the most striking thing about them was their choice of holidays. In those days, long before people had acquired the habit of going to the Costa Brava — it wasn't until the 'fifties that they began doing that in the Rhondda — few families could afford to go on holiday, even for a few days. In contrast, some of these teachers used to take their holidays on the continent, or even further afield. I well remember one calling to see us after coming back from North Africa: for my part, I felt as if I'd met someone who had just returned from Annwn itself! I know of another who went on walking tours in the Alps, and of yet others who'd been to Belgium and Germany. Before the decade was out several had joined their Welsh-speaking compatriots on the cruises organized by Urdd Gobaith Cymru on board the *Orduña*, to Norway, Spain and Portugal, and Morocco.

I've already mentioned the prohibition on marriage. This rule was relaxed at the beginning of the Second World War, but it was too late for many of these women to think of marrying then: some had grown too fond of their independence, while others found themselves responsible for their parents, who by this time were elderly or infirm. In some instances the courting had gone on for many a long year, without hope of union in 'holy matrimony'. As a result some courtships came to an abrupt end, because one or other had tired of waiting and had met someone else who was readier to go to the altar. It was a sad sight, too, to see 'old' sweethearts wandering the paths of the Bwlch, or setting out on holiday in the company of other unmarried women. It should be added that some women had affairs with married men — which caused delicious scandal locally — and that between some couples there was a lesbian relationship, which was accepted without anyone's attaching much significance to it.

Some teachers flouted the ban by keeping their marriages a secret, in the hope no one would notice. In other cases a man and his prospective wife would move away from the area completely, and find work in one of England's cities. But it was more usual to conform, by marrying and giving up one's job. This created a different category, a rarer one, but one that was quite plain to see. 'Once a teacher, always a teacher' — so the saying goes. Although these ex-teachers had married and raised a family, they still had the stamp of authority that sticks to anyone who has ever stood before a class of children. And it could be said that a few had managed to retain something of the independent spirit that had been characteristic of them in their years of freedom. They knew, too, from personal experience — and this was in a society that was quite macho in its attitudes — that a wife has the same capabilities as her husband, and the right, to say the least, to some of his privileges. For some of the more old-fashioned colliers the thought of taking a wife who had once been a teacher was something hard to entertain. Many were ready to rag mercilessly any man who did such a thing. One such worked in the Maendy pit, and I remember the regular line of defence the poor chap used to come up with for those who teased him: 'My wife is an educated woman'. Fair play to him.

That story illustrates the gap between the uneducated majority and the privileged few. In a poor society where education offered a means of escape and the guarantee of a job, it possessed a special mystique. This was clearly to be seen in the home, for the educational process had created an inevitable gap between the privileged and the others. The goddess Education called for visible testimony of the cult by which she was worshipped, and these virgins became willing, well-mannered priestesses at her shrine. It may be that some women had encouraged the process, but it's easier to believe that it usually had its origins in their adoring and credulous parents. The fact is there was created sometimes, within the home, a special sanctuary for them. This minority tended to live separately from their family in a room that was set aside for them, a circumstance that was a sign of their higher status and the sacrifice that had been made for their sakes. Even in less extreme cases, a special respect was shown towards a woman who had 'got on in the world'.

There were dangers, to be sure, in such separateness. Snobbery was the most evident thing about it, but sometimes, I imagine, a tension would arise between the teacher and the rest of her family. There was also a quite natural temptation to exploit her advantageous position in the home. The fur coat itself was the expression of this snobbery, this feeling of social superiority. But it was manifested by other means too. For example, one or two used to speak in an unusual way. As a social group, they consciously identified with the Welsh language and its culture and took pride in them, but in some cases the pride gave rise to a strange phenomenon, namely a tendency to speak Welsh that was too correct, affected, and almost anglicized! It was as if they needed a bit of Englishness to maintain the authority of their Welshness. Given the nature of my relationship with this group of teachers, it was only their Welsh I ever heard, but I understand from other witnesses that one or two spoke an over-rich English, an effective weapon in a society where an English accent was a badge of power.

One aspect of this snobbery was the tendency to make a show of themselves. That probably accounted, at least in part, for one particular incident at a chapel in the Pen-y-graig area. Three fur coats were to be seen there, and their owners — because they wished to make a splash — always tended to arrive late for the service. The minister had become fed up with this performance, for it interfered with the course of things. One evening the three teachers arrived at more or less the same moment, whereupon the voice from the pulpit said sardonically: 'As the three bears have arrived, we can now proceed with the service'.

An unexpected manifestation of this snobbery — and yes, I'm referring here to a wider bourgeois class — was the success enjoyed by a dentist, a German Jew, who had fled his own country at the outbreak of the Second World War, and settled as a *rara avis* at the lower end of the Valley. Somehow or other he had become fashionable as a dentist. It was considered to be something of a privilege to go to him, as if this were a sign of your status in society. Indeed, some ladies used to travel the slow miles from the upper reaches of the Rhondda Fawr just to pay him wide-mouthed homage. Naturally, in such circumstances, it was often felt that the appropriate thing was to wear one's best clothes, including of course, the fur coat. But what these wretched women did not realise was that the dentist was an old Socialist, and that he had a unique tariff for his services. He charged according to the clothes you were wearing — a pound, say, for working-trousers, but five pounds for a fur coat! In this just man's surgery the most unwealthy of the exploiting classes paid dearly for their privilege.

I don't want to give the impression that these fur-clad teachers and their less fortunate sisters were all Welsh-speakers. And yet a very high proportion of them were, and it was quite definitely they who were the mainstay of Welsh cultural life in the two Valleys. Without them Urdd Gobaith Cymru wouldn't have taken such firm root, establishing its groups and branches here and there, and creating activity in the schools that was later to express itself in local and regional eisteddfodau, or in folk-singing concerts. Without them the local drama companies would have been short of leading players, and the same could be said of the chapels' drama companies in the 'thirties. It's only fair to note that some of them contributed with the same enthusiasm to those companies performing plays in English. Bearing in mind how barren the cultural life of the Rhondda is nowadays, one can only wonder at the bustle of those far-distant times.

Evening classes also flourished, where these women were just as ready to show their commitment. This continued right up to the beginning of the Second World War, and I remember several of them attending the weekly classes of T.J. Morgan on Welsh Literature at the Boys' Club in Treorci. In the life of church and chapel their contribution was equally indispensable.In their daily work, too, they kept the spirit of the Welsh language alive within an educational system that scorned it and tried to crush it to death. Later on it would be they, or rather a minority among them, who would fight to establish Welsh Schools in the two Valleys, and make efforts at producing text-books for the teaching of the Welsh language in the other schools.

The word today is 'feminism': *'ffeministiaeth'* didn't even get into the supplement of the first volume (1967) of *Geiriadur Prifysgol Cymru*. Is it right to mention the word in the context of this particular élite? Were they a protest movement against the condition of women in less fortunate circumstances? Were they in some way a sisterhood similar to an order of nuns? In fact, I doubt whether they had any group consciousness. If they did, then they saw themselves as dedicated teachers, or as keen Welsh people, and not as a group of women. As far as I know, they didn't consider their maiden state (assumed or real) as having any value in itself. Rather, as in the case of nuns, it offered them a wider freedom, and the spur to direct their sexual energy towards worthy ends of a different kind.

On the other hand, it was clear that they took particular pleasure in one another's company — the daily train journeys to and from school, the committee meetings and eisteddfodau in one place or another, and the tendency to go on holiday together. And this last gave them an opportunity of displaying their independence and status, since they usually put up at guest-houses or hotels that were of an approved standard. Indeed, the enjoyment of the status which they had earned was obviously important to them. And if we look closely at their contribution as a group, we can see that they placed before the imagination of other women a kind of life-style and behavioural possibilities that the rest wouldn't even have dreamed about had it not been for their example. Without any doubt, it was the need for female labour in the arms-factories after 1939 which was to create the greatest revolution in the development of Rhondda women. Nevertheless, there was something quite pioneering in the lifestyle of those teachers in the 'thirties, and in many ways the 'broadening of horizons' which came in their wake was a creative, nourishing process, rather than a vulgar one lacking in good taste.

The fur coats continued to keep their owners warm throughout the war years, through the greying of middle-age, and the wintry winds of old age. I don't recall ever seeing either blemish or spot on those everlastingly young pelts. They must have taken special care of them, placing them between warm, camphor-smelling sheets at each season's end. By the 'fifties the coat had ceased to be a symbol of defiance: it became, rather, a visible part of nostalgia for better days, for the verve and adventure of youth, for a way of life which had challenged the system.

Some time in the 'sixties it became the custom for students at English universities to wear their mothers' fur coats. Usually they were in tatters, even dirty and foul-smelling — an attempt on their owners' parts, perhaps, to demonstrate that they were in revolt against the bourgeois values of their parents. I myself felt a certain abhorrence for those furs, because they somehow brought into disrepute the forests of Siberia, Africa, the Himalayas, or the Andes. I realize by now that my aversion had a deeper and more irrational basis. After all, I had been used to seeing the fur coat as a sign of noble effort. It had somehow been a challenge to the grey poverty of the Depression, a coat-of-arms in revolt against a system that gave victory to others, a bright spark that would turn, in the fullness of time, into the bonfire of the feminist movement. And here was a barbaric pelt on the backs of women who had come to college as a matter of course, rather than by personal effort and family sacrifice. I could feel no respect for such a thing. Twenty years later those furs too have completely disappeared and a generation has grown up which sees the fur coat as nothing more than proof of man's cruelty to animals. I have to confess that there remains in me a sneaking admiration for a garment that was such a part of my boyhood. And I keep in my memory the fragrance of those golden creatures who walked with their heads held high down the aisles of Bethesda. Alas, like the russet-red fox of Williams Parry, their fate was to be, and then cease to be, 'like a shooting star'.

translated by Meic Stephens
Taliesin (75, 1991)

ALUN LEWIS
The Rhondda

Hum of shaft-wheel, whirr and clamour
Of steel hammers overbeat, din down
Water-hag's slander. Greasy Rhondda
River throws about the boulders
Veils of scum to mark the ancient
Degraded union of stone and water.

Unwashed colliers by the river
Gamble for luck the pavements hide.
Kids float tins down dirty rapids.
Coal-dust rings the scruffy willows.
Circe is a drab.
She gives men what they know .
Daily to her pitch-black shaft
Her whirring wheels suck husbands out of sleep.
She for her profit takes their hands and eyes.

But the fat flabby-breasted wives
Have grown accustomed to her ways.
They scrub, make tea, peel the potatoes
Without counting the days.

from *Raiders' Dawn* (1942)

MARY DAVIES PARNELL
The Mountain above Trehafod

Trehafod, especially the Tump which is the upper part of the village overlooking the valley floor and basically composed of three terraces (Bryn Eirw, Woodfield and Rheolau, or Bottom, Second and Top Streets to the locals), may not be much to look at but was a paradise for children growing up. When in my teens and a Porth County 'snob' (as opposed to a Porth Secondary 'sardine'), I occasionally went to tea with school friends from various parts of the Rhondda Valleys, Fach and Fawr, but nowhere possessed a mountain half as exciting as Trehafod's.

Thanks to the Lewis Merthyr colliery, the bowels of the earth had been deposited at intervals from the valley bottom right to the very mountain top, some eight hundred feet higher, covering in neat mounds the sandstone, limestone and millstone grit of which the South Wales coalfield is composed. Those at the bottom had greened over and it was difficult to see where mountain ended and bowel began. As the eye rose upward, though, it was to another world of dark, hostile, dusty shale where even sheep could not get a sure footing. Not that they wanted to, as only sparse, tough clumps of grass grew on these tips, and that with difficulty. This was a sombre, silent world, the only sound being that of circling hawks and other birds of prey waiting to pounce on a stray sheep with a broken leg and about to release its hold on life. Even the few men who worked up there rarely spoke, it seemed, as they carried out their tip maintenance work. Now and then a voice echoed eerily around.

Occasionally bold valley boys set off, grim-faced, silent and never alone, to climb to the Black Lake, said to lie beyond the topmost tip and in which, so it was said, all life — frogs, newts, and fish — was as black as the inhabitants of the deepest oceans.

'Where you going then, Billy Luckwell?'

'Mind your own business, Mary Davies.'

'Aw, come on, mun, say!'

'Up the Black Lake, if you must know, but don't think you can come, 'cos you can't, see?'

'I don't want to in any case.'

'Aw, don't tell yer fibs, you do.'

'No, I don't, see, 'cos my mother wouldn't let me.'

The verbal exchanges would continue until Billy and his friend were out of earshot, trudging off as if this was a journey they had to accomplish.

Witnessed a day or two later, strutting around the streets, they were looked on as heroes, as though they had trekked to the South Pole like Captain Scott or had scaled Kilimanjaro. To get a girl's attention in Trehafod, all a lad had to do was set off for the Black Lake and be seen and heard doing it. I never knew of any girls who had ventured there or even cared to. For all we young ladies knew, it might have been a male myth.

The west-facing hillside opposite ours on the far side of the river was tamed. It had farms, the big house and a tarred road. Carts and an occasional car went along it. Old ladies went for walks there. It was a relatively uninteresting place, populated by adults. It was respectable, whereas our hillside was wild.

Above the Tump, three feeder ponds filtered water down to the colliery. The top one, Coedcae, was fed by a mountain stream running from somewhere in the direction of Cymmer. This was the largest of the rectangular ponds where scores of dogs had been forced to learn to swim or drown, having been hurled in by their tough-minded owners. Thousands of minnows had been hauled from the pond, caught in jam jars which had been hurriedly and usually unthoroughly divested of their contents — Coedcae pond wild life had developed a sweet tooth! Brave men sometimes swam in its murky waters, and it was rumoured some had drowned, caught in the profuse, treacherous weeds in the middle, where there lurked, it was said, Coedcae's very own monster, a fish more than a foot in length, though no one had ever seen it for sure. Unwanted dogs in weighted sacks had met their Maker there too, and many games of ducks and drakes had visibly reduced the size of an adjoining mound of stones and pebbles. Early one Sunday morning Olly Pugh, pigeon-fancier extraordinaire of Lower Trehafod, but a Tump original, was walking with his offspring around Coedcae when he espied what he thought was a partly submerged sleeper near the bank. 'Funny, that's a wide log, aye,' he said to himself, then to his dismay realised it was a man's body.

'Didn't know who he was, mind, but oh, we ran as fast as we could, aye, down to Alice Lewis's, 'cos she got a phone, see. And we rang up the police, and they come and took the man's body down the Coll'ery in a tram. Jew jew, I'm stiff today after that run, aye.'

Doubtless they discovered who the man was — perhaps someone who had had too much to drink in the Vaughan's Arms, taking a short cut home over the mountain but cutting short his days in the process.

At the southern end of the pond, water spilled over into a conduit to feed the unoriginally named, smaller Middle Pond, which in turn fed the smallest, Bottom Pond. These latter two ponds were far more homely and manageable than Coedcae. There were no reeds, weeds or frogspawn; the water usually lapped right up to the level grassy surround and was clearer. In hot weather during the summer, Middle or Bottom, depending on the water level, became decidedly murkier as Tump children made it their own private swimming pool. Foreigners from downtown Trehafod were definitely not allowed in, nor dared they show their faces. Surrounding dense ferns provided natural changing rooms and discarded sleepers from the nearby tram railway were used as diving boards.

Accidents occurred with annual regularity. The bold ones would dive head first into the murk and occasionally a head would make forcible contact with a submerged bit of pennant and its owner be knocked out. Once a swaggerer dived in, caught the sharp edge of a rock in flight and opened himself up from the nave to the chaps, dyeing the water pink in the process. At such times, after the unfortunate person had been given juvenile first-aid, or in the case of the slit stomach an ambulance summoned, swimmers would vanish from the scene for a few days, warned off by anxious mothers, to return, at first surreptitiously then brazenly defiant, at the next hot spell.

My own mother, reluctant to see me join the rabble bathing in the pond, would at first try to dissuade me by reasonable argument: 'Nice girls don't go bathing in old mountain ponds.'

Then, aware of my downturned mouth and feeling my stubborn resolve: 'Don't go pulling those jibs at me. Boys pee in those ponds. *Ach y fi*! You can catch nasty diseases from that, you know.'

Then finally: 'Mary! You are not to go bathing in that pond!'

I was always 'Mary' when naughty or difficult, and 'Mari fach' when good.

So I would have to put my bathers on under my clothes and stuff a small towel up my cardigan, then slip out while my mother was busy with a customer in the shop.

So-called friends appeared to sense my mother's antagonism to my pond-bathing and would threaten to tell her if I didn't get them lollipops, gob-stoppers or licorice sticks from the shop. That was no problem, compared with the re-introducing of wet towel and bathers back into the house, not to mention their subsequent concealment, so I didn't worry too much about them.

During the rest of the year, the main attraction of the ponds was submarine races, the submarines being once again sodden sleepers which had formerly graced the incline. These were hurled in at one end, often taking their skinny launcher into the water with them, and the triumphant submarine was the one longest true to its name. Dripping wet small persons were often to be seen making their way shiveringly and apprehensively home, trailing spirogyra and other assorted weeds. Interested passers-by would say with relish to the unfortunate: 'Oh, fallen in Coedcae pond, have you? You'll cop it from your Mam!'

One of the hazards encountered before reaching the ponds was crossing the incline or tramway. The last words children heard as they left their houses and headed for the mountain were: 'You watch out for those trams. Don't you come back here injured, mind.' The trams — small pram-like contraptions, usually about ten or a dozen linked together — took waste from the colliery to be jettisoned high up towards the sky on the most recent tip. As one little train was laboriously hauled up by cable, another came hurtling down, the trucks bouncing, pitching and swaying independently of each other in a clatter of wheels and links and chains. Alas, they never collided, despite hopeful cries of, 'They're going to crash! Look, they're heading straight at each other!' There was a chicane where each unfailingly passed the other with a deafening roar, creating mini-earthquakes on the nearby land.

Tip maintenance men rode up perched on the shale in the trucks and waved to the watching children on the levées. They looked like inverted black and white minstrels with their white faces and coal-dust-ringed eyes. On the way down there was no time to wave as they clung on for dear life. Needless to say the bold boys would hitch lifts up to nowhere on unattended runs. Some must have been de-railed now and then, probably through the wiles of village boys, the 'rebels' as my mother called them, as the mountain around was dotted with old rusting trams, marvellous playthings, some up-turned, in which children made fern-clad dens, others upright and full of bright, orange water with oily iridescent streaks, wheels askew or missing altogether. The mountain was truly a haven of delight. There were former abandoned tramways, now steep-sided gullies with small streams, boggy floors and an amazing array of plants, wild flowers and crawling creatures. A rusty pipe spanned such a one and the daring would edge across from one side to the other in an awk-ward sitting position, giving many mothers extra patching work on trouser seats and occasionally causing a parent's puzzled look at a girl's underwear: 'Mary, what on earth have you been doing with your knickers? Look, the bum is all orange.'

from *Block Salt and Candles* (1991)

IDRIS DAVIES
Tonypandy

Dai bach, Dai bach, with your woollen muffler
Tight around your stout dark neck,
Why do you seem so sad and lonely
There at the corner of Pandy Square,
Now in this moist grey hour of twilight
And colourless streets and long black hills?
Are your eyes on those birds that have strayed from the sea,
Those few smooth gulls up from the Severn,
Floating and crying below the clouds,
Complaining and floating above the valley-sides?
Do the sea-birds awaken old sorrows at dusk
There at the corner of Pandy Square,
As they circle and sigh above the slag-heaps
And the narrow brown river trickling
Between the crooked streets and the colliery sidings?
Are they as poems from the Severn Sea,
Sad little lyrics borne on the dusk wind
Over the coastal plain and over the valleys
Up to the mountains and mists of Glamorgan,
Haunting the twilight, haunting the heart?
Or do they remind you, David, you son of Tonypandy,
Of summer afternoons on holiday beaches,
And cheap excursions to Weston-super-Mare,
With the steamer chuff-chuff-chuffing across the Channel
And the Flatholm in the distance, and the sunshine
Radiant over the Somerset cliffs and gardens,
And your Martha, with her mouth wide open,
Leaning against you on the crowded deck,
And the Sunday School parties all around you
Sweating with singing the sad, sad hymns?
And O it was sweet in the evening, Dai,
After the bathing and the dancing and the pastries
            and the ice- cream,
And the gardens of roses behind the coloured town,
And the nut-brown ale in the pub by the pier,
Ay, it was sweet upon the evening waters
To watch the sun go down in scarlet
Behind the far promontory, and gaze upon

The velvet undulations of the sea,
And sweet it was to dream, Dai bach,
With Martha warm and fragrant, close against you,
Martha from Treorchy nestled in your arms,
Sweet it was to coo of love and summer
To the rhythm and the moaning of the darkening sea,
And the pleasure-boat chuff-chuff-chuffing homewards
Toward the lights of Cardiff in the bluish distance,
And the waiting quays and the quayside station,
With your Day Excursion tickets sticky in your hands.
Or do I dream that you dream like this
There as you stand in the dreary dusk,
There at the corner of Pandy Square?

II

When you were young, Dai, when you were young!
The Saturday mornings of childhood
With childish dreams and adventures
Among the black tips by the river,
And the rough grass and the nettles
Behind the colliery yard, the stone-throwing
Battles between the ragged boys,
The fascination of the railway cutting
On dusty summer afternoons,
And the winter night and its street-lamps
And the first pranks of love,
And the deep warm sleep
In grandmother's chapel pew
On stodgy Sunday evenings,
And the buttercup-field you sometimes noticed
Behind the farthest street, the magical field
That only the heart could see,
The heart and rarely the boyish eye,
And the pride you had in your father's
Loins and shoulders when he bent
Between the tub and the fire,
And the days you counted, counted, counted,
Before you should work in the mine.
You never, never cursed your luck
Or desired to see another town or valley,

Or know any other men and women
Than those of the streets around
The street where you were born.
Your world was narrow and magical
And dear and dirty and brave
When you were young, Dai, when you were young!

III

The dusk deepens into the autumn night,
The cold drizzle spreads across the valleys.
The rubbish heaps are lost among the mists,
And where will you go for the evening, Dai,
For the evening in Tonypandy?
Will you count your coppers and join
The cinema queue where the tired women
Huddle like sheep, and comfort one another
With signs and sentimental phrases,
And where some folk blame the local councillors
For all the evils of the day and night?
O in the little queue, what tales are told
When we have shuffled off the burdens of the day —
What rancour, what compassion, what relief!
Or perhaps you will go to the prayer meeting down the chapel,
Where the newest member can pray for an hour without stopping,
The one converted at the last Big Meeting.
Or will you go to the pub at the corner
Where tongues come loose and hearts grow soft,
Where politics are so easy to understand,
Where the Irish labourer explains the constitution of de Valera,
And the Tory Working Man snarls behind his beer
At those who do not worship Winston Churchill,
And those who vaguely praise the Beveridge Report.
Or perhaps you will go back to your fireside this evening
And talk with your Martha of the children abroad,
The son out in Italy, the quick-tongued Ifor,
And the young quiet Emrys in the R.A.F.,
And Mair, with her roses and her laughing eyes,
So sprightly in her khaki uniform;
And you will be proud and you will be sad,
And you will be brave for Martha's sake,
And you will be Dai the great of heart.

IV

So much you have given, so little received,
O Dai, you miner of Tonypandy!
And 'blessed it is to give' the Bible says —
My God, then you ought to be an angel,
An angel in the Garden of Empire,
With wings of Red, White and Blue!
But to-night as you sit by your kitchen fire
You know in your heart how your life has been botched,
Been robbed of peace and grace and beauty,
Of leisure to dream and build and create,
Not the leisure of the shabby witless idler,
But the leisure that burgeons with proud achievement,
The leisure that marks an awakened nation
Exultantly singing the joy of the earth.
How silently and subtly and surely the chains
Have bound the mind and the body
To the status quo of the iron jungle!
Men have gone down unknown through the ages,
Down to the shame that is deeper than death,
Darkness behind them, darkness before them,
Ravaged by hunger to desperation
And goaded and whipped and tortured
For the sake of a pampered despotic few.
And here in your home in Tonypandy,
Tonight by this fire that flickers and dies,
You know that these words are not figures of fancy,
You know that they echo the thoughts in your heart.

V

Dai in his bed, and Tonypandy
Silent under the silent stars,
Silent and black and cold beneath the autumn night,
The night so full of mystery and memory,
The night of stars above the streets of Tonypandy;
And you shall listen to the footsteps crossing Pandy Square,
The echoes of the footsteps silenced long ago,
Dear, dogged footsteps marching to the sound of drum and fife,
Footsteps whose echoes were heard across the mountains,

TONYPANDY

Footsteps of toilers and rebels and dreamers,
And the echoes of bullets and galloping horses
And curses and desperate rallying calls.
And older far than all those echoes
You hear the battle cries of Celtic kings
And bearded chieftains in the virgin valleys
Riding in scarlet and yellow to the castles by the Severn Sea.
And the skies that look down to-night and to-morrow
On slag-heaps and hovels and little bowler-hatted deacons,
On square grey chapels and gasometers and pubs,
Once saw Cadwgan and his shining battle-axe
Rallying his warriors among the summer mountains,
And Owain Glyndwr sweeping southward to the feudal coast,
With colour and with music and with pride
And Dai's forefathers roused by song and banner,
Alive to the passionate lore of Gwalia,
Crowding and flocking and roaring to battle
Between the hills and the forests and the Severn Sea,
Martyrs to freedom and the Celtic dream.
And will that dream disturb one sleeping youth to-night
Beneath the roofs, among the streets of Tonypandy?
And shall the Future mock our simple, simple faith
In the Progress that has scorned the native culture,
The legend and the vision and the dream,
And a people that has nigh lost its history and language
To serve with blood and flesh the maw of Mammon?
O singers, singers in a thousand years to be,
Who shall sing of joys our richest hearts can never conceive,
Forget not the dreams of the few who dream to-night
Among the rubbish heaps of 1944!
And forgive and pity and remember those
Whose souls were narrowed by the joyless day,
The lack of bread, the sordid strife,
The penury inherited from father to son to son,
And men in chains who did not feel the chains.
And singers, singers in a distant golden time to be,
Remember a little of Dai and Tonypandy,
Dai and his Martha and his fireside,
Dai and his lamp in the depths of the earth,
Dai and his careless lilting tongue.
Dai and his heart of gold.

VI

And meanwhile, Dai, with your woollen muffler
Tight around your pit-scarred neck,
Remind us of the gratitude we owe you,
We who so easily pass you by.

Remind us of your long endurance,
Those bitter battles the sun has never seen,
And remind us of the struggles you have waged
Against the crude philosophy of greed.

And remind all who strut with noses high in the air,
How the proudest of nations would falter without you,
And remind us when we lie on fireside cushions
Of the blood that is burnt within the flame.

And remind us when we kneel to the unknown God
And turn and cry to the cold infinite heavens,
Remind us of the toil of the blistered hands
And the courage and the comradeship of men.

from *Tonypandy and Other Poems* (1945)

MARY DAVIES PARNELL
The Lewis Merthyr

Trehafod grew up dependent upon but not actually around the Lewis Merthyr colliery which is situated on the northern edge of the village. Most of Trehafod extends south of it, hugging the main road and broadening out a bit where the valley widens in the direction of Hopkinstown and Pontypridd. Although I had little to do with the colliery, I lived close to it for eighteen years, taking for granted its sights and sounds. Miners completely black but for the whites of their eyes and their pink lips, held no terrors for me as a child and I was never frightened by tales of bogeymen, although an evacuee friend from Finchley in London, Olive Hughes, ran and hid in the flood overflow pipe the first time she saw a blackened miner, and when the hooter blast was heard at the end of the afternoon shift, she would run home, saying it was time for tea although it was only three o'clock.

If men were practically unrecognisable in their Sunday outfits, they were completely unrecognisable in coal dust. I might be tamping a ball against the end wall of our house and a miner returning home would say, ''Ow be, Mary'.To my uncertain reply he would continue: 'Don't know me in my working clothes, do you?' and laughing at my shaking head say: 'It's Olly Pugh, gul. I dunno, I was only in your 'ouse on Sunday morning, aye. And you don't know me now. Well, well. And I brought you some lovely beans for your dinner an' all.' I was very sorry but, like sheep and Chinamen, unwashed miners all looked the same to me.

In later years pit-head baths were constructed, but by then the evacuees had returned to London with the notion that in Wales (pronounced 'Wells' or even 'Wews'), at a given signal, black sub-humans crawled from holes in the earth and that signal was also notification for sensible children to hide.

The only times I found the mining fraternity eerie was early in the morning. Men would get up in the grey dawn light for the early shift and some individuals would take on the responsibility for wakening their work-mates or neighbours. This they did by knocking loudly on doors, a noise which resounded and echoed hollowly in the still, silent, dark streets. I could hear the knocking from my bedroom a street away and quieter at first, then loud and insistent on the door of a house immediately behind ours in Second Street. There were never any voices, only the knocking, then the metallic, rhythmic tread of hob-nailed boots on the hill next to our end wall.

Apart from its topography, an extra hill above Trehafod, the Tump derived its name from the miners who spent hours squatting on their haunches, especially along what was called the New Road, a road directly connecting with Woodfield Terrace (Second Street) and after a gentle descent linking with the main road to Porth. They resembled monkeys sitting on their haunches on an elevated spot or monkey-tump — hence the name, or so it was said. Their shift finished, and after a bath, meal and a quick glance at the newspaper, the *Western Mail*, *News Chronicle* or the *Daily Herald*, *Mirror* or *Worker* and before going to attend to the care of their pigeons in the cote, miners would squat alongside each other and look out over their place of work, the football field and waterfall beyond, the Hafod Fawr hillside with the farms, green meadows and trees above, and the valley road stretching down over the river to lower Trehafod. They enjoyed the company of others but exchanged few comments or reflections, as they were a contemplative rather than a loquacious breed of men. Unsurprisingly, no sooner home and their needs attended to, they would be out of the house and squatting on their vantage point, enjoying the light and gratefully breathing the warm air after their incarceration.

Apart from this squatting position they adopted, you could always tell if a man's trade was that of a collier, as usually even when bathed they had black rings round their eyes and blue scars on their faces where a cut had healed without having been thoroughly cleaned.

Not counting the panorama from high on Gelliwion Mountain, along New Road was the best viewpoint on the Tump, and no doubt as a mother surveys her child's cradle the miners surveyed their colliery, where a special feeling of comradeship and belonging existed, like that among soldiers in times of war.

The Lewis Merthyr colliery was opened in the 1880s when the Hafod, Bertie and Trefor pits were sunk. It originated as the Coedcae colliery, but after being opened by Sir W.T. Lewis, chief administrator of the Bute estates and later Lord Merthyr, it was re-named. In August 1892 an explosion underground caused the deaths of fifty-eight men, but fortunately since then there have been no large-scale disasters.

Several of the Trehafod streets were named with the colliery association in mind. Two of them recall the philanthropic landowner, Lewis Morgan of Hafod Fawr. Wayne Street commemorates his nephew, Dr Wayne Morgan, who was also a churchwarden from 1893 to 1912 at St David's, Gyfeillion, built in 1853 on land donated by Lewis Morgan. On hearing the hooters blare for the shift changes, I was always amazed at the vast numbers of men who poured in and out of the main colliery gates on Coedcae Road because the view of the colliery yard from the railings at the top of Church Hill was always one of calm and peace with few workers to be seen about the place. Large wagons in the marshalling yards stood idle, full of coal, or moved slowly forward and gently shunted the one in front, which carried on the lazy movement down the line with a light high-pitched clang as they touched and sometimes a squeaking of axles like the braying of a metallic donkey.

This was the end of the coal production process, the wagons being filled with clean, shiny coal and emerging from beneath the big, black, wooden slatted building on stilts and lining up for the trans-portation of Trehafod steam coal all over the world. These wagons used to join others coming down from the hundred or so collieries scattered throughout the Valley, the Lady Lewis in Ynyshir and the Pendyrus in Ferndale, to name two in the Rhondda Fach and the Parc and Dare, the Fernhill and the Tynewydd, remembered for its big disaster in 1877, four among many in the Rhondda Fawr, but by the late 1940s of which I write only three or four pits were still working. Throughout the mining period, millions of tons of Rhondda substrata were borne to the port specially constructed to ship coal at Barry, and to Cardiff, for export all over the globe. In 1910, the heyday of the mining industry, nearly ten million tons of the Rhondda passed through Trehafod on its way to Cardiff and Barry, which in that year between them handled nearly twenty-three million tons of South Welsh coal.

It was a sight taken for granted in the village, but a magnificent one none the less that would stop strangers in their tracks when, shortly after the hooter, the huge wheels with wire ropes leading down into the winding-house began to revolve in their gantries, standing proudly, black, greased and stark against the sky — the ultimate symbol of industry and man's taming of his environment.

If one has relatives or friends to visit in Llwyncelyn, slightly north of Trehafod and on the opposite, south-facing slope of the valley, the official route is a good two-mile walk by the time you have crossed the river, passed the British Legion Club and doubled back under the railway after Temple Buildings. Then, striking off towards the water-fall under Cwm George, with the few cottages of Bridge Street on your right, you are on the Llwyncelyn road looking down on the swirling, fast-running river Rhondda and its rocky, convex bank and the football field next to it. The gaze rises to the colliery beyond, then up to the fine sight of the Tump. It is approximately another mile with a bit of an uphill pull at the end to Nythbran Terrace, the first of the three Llwyncelyn streets.

However, if you took the unauthorised route across the colliery, using its access footbridge over the river, you could reach Llwyncelyn in ten minutes, or five if a colliery official shouted at you in vain to come back, then chased you off the premises. The main colliery gates were huge and fairly intimidating to children, but when they were shut there was a little in-built wooden door, normally unlocked, around which you could peer guiltily to assess the lie of the land before stepping through into the yard. Bold boys spoilt the chances of other trespassing youngsters who simply wanted to get quickly across the river to Llwyncelyn, because they went on to the colliery for adventure, to play and aggravate the duty watchman, who naturally developed an antipathy to children.

During the day, when the machinery was at full throttle, the colliery was a truly dangerous place even for the people working there, let alone the uninitiated, and the din was ear-splitting.

Fans at ground level would be blowing out the warm, used air from the pits, coal being sorted rattled deafeningly in the screens, the stacks would hiss and steam, and the sudden blare of the hooter made you start as would the clatter and unexpected arrival on the surface of a cage from deep down, carrying weary men covered in coal dust, blinking at the light and wearing their helmets with lamps attached to batteries worn on belts. The winding mechanism, meanwhile, added its grinding, churning, cog-engaging rumpus to all this and you'd have to be on the alert for trucks of coal bumping along the tram-lines crossing the yard, and above all for the Red Devil, which might appear, swerving rapidly around a corner, causing you to jump quickly aside or get mown down.

The Red Devil was not I think a typical piece of South Wales colliery equipment like the winding gear, the tall stack or the water-dripping washery, but was peculiar to the Lewis Merthyr. It was a motorised vehicle that looked like a slightly shortened, speedy milk float, painted red. Perhaps it conveyed urgently required machinery or tools from one part of the yard to another. It always proceeded flat out, driven by a grinning fanatic bent over the steering wheel, who enjoyed seeing people taken by surprise and having to perfom a standing lateral leap. More than anything in the colliery, even the watchmen, I was wary of this Red Devil contraption and preferred to make my illicit crossing in the evening when the surface work was finished for the day. I would sometimes see the evil little machine parked near the clocking-on room, and even stationary it seemed to be watching you, ready to pounce if you didn't tiptoe past, avoiding accidentally disturbing the thing.

The clocking-on room was next to the lamp room, where hundreds of Davy lamps were lined up neatly on shelves and on the floor, counted out daily by the lamp man, and I always paused briefly to look in here and wave to Lew the Light, the night-duty lamp-man, a customer of the shop who bought ipecacuanha cough mixture for his bad chest.

Despite the noise during the day, there were never many workmen to be seen, and in the evening, apart from the man on night-watch duty, the only people you passed were those going the other way, from Llwyncelyn to Trehafod. Sometimes at the Llwyncelyn end of the covered footbridge miners would be going to or coming from the pit baths or canteens, but they never bothered anybody and wouldn't have cared if you held a Highland Fling in the place. It was strange to think that beneath you the earth was teeming with men manipulating coal-cutting machines, shot-firing, loading coal onto conveyor-belts and mine-cars, manning first-aid rooms and fire stations and shoring up tunnel roofs at the coal-face, because no matter what the time of day or night, a shift was working. In fact at night there was un-doubtedly more activity beneath the Trehafod ground than above it.

On Friday afternoons it was not uncommon to see women waiting outside the main colliery gates when the hooter went for the end of the day shift at three o'clock, because Friday was pay-day.

Before the pit-head baths were built the miners emerged through the gates with black faces and dusty clothes, helmet with lamp having been exchanged for a 'Dai cap', but some still wearing leather knee-protection pads and carrying their tin tommy-box for food under one arm and a log for the fire under the other. Occasionally the food-box and metal drink-flask would be suspended from their belt.

Hanging on a nail in the wall outside the kitchen door, every miner's house possessed a tin bath, either a long, thin bungalow-bath, rounded at one end and flat at the other, or a shorter, oval one with raised ridges in the bottom. Water was heated in buckets on the fire and as soon as one was emptied into the bath, another was put on to warm up. A great deal of the water ended up on the floor and the whole bathing business was quite a performance by the time the bath was fetched in, gallons of water heated in precariously balanced vessels, the miner washing with carbolic or coal-tar soap which now and then escaped and skidded over the floor, the final bucket being poured over the man's head by his wife to rinse him off, and finally the lugging out of the bathful of dirty water to the back yard to tip it down the drain. The pit-head baths, where men could shower in ten minutes, surely added months to a miner's life and a week to his leisure time in every year; it was one of the revolutionary inventions in coal-mining and must have been a marvellous inducement to recruitment.

When on Fridays the men hurried out, clutching square, beige packets, some were counting pound notes, others taking out the change, were making their way to Cobner's shop for a packet of Woodbines and yet others would be hurrying the eighty yards down the road to the Vaughan's Arms, open until half-past three, to slake their thirst with a few well-earned pints of beer. A few would head for a very anonymous-looking building with a brown painted window — the betting shop in the little clutch of buildings at the bottom of Bryn Eirw Hill between Eileen's fish-shop and the undertaker's. I thought the men met by women always looked a bit embarrassed and faintly irritated. Were these poor wives with lots of undernourished, skinny children, kept short of money by their husbands who would gamble away all their earnings? Were they men who drank so much beer that they would arrive home very late, unable to stand up, ready to beat their wives and offspring and with their pay packets empty, the result of temptation? They were probably neither — just wives on their way to town, Porth or Pontypridd, to do some shopping, and who had run out of house-keeping money, and the men hard-working, honest folk who enjoyed a fag and a pint.

from *Block Salt and Candles* (1991)

GWYN THOMAS
A Horse Called Meadow Prospect

It was Kitchener Bowen who made the suggestion. I was there in the Council Chamber when Bowen stood up and put the idea forward.

'I propose,' said Bowen, 'that Meadow Prospect show a smiling face to the world and buy a racehorse which will be given the name of our fine, old town, Meadow Prospect, carrying the colours of our national emblem, the leek, white and green, colours restful to the punter and stimulating to the horse. I know where I can get you a mount of mixed Arab and Welsh blood for little more than five hundred pounds, which will have the speed and strength to carry to triumph the hopes and investments of the voters.'

Bowen was our senior bookie and a sporadic politician. He had been on the Council for years but he had never learned to be truly coherent about anything but the turf and odds.

'The horse, Meadow Prospect, after five or six brilliant outings at meetings which I will choose with care, measuring carefully the state of the top soil and the hooves of the horse, will attract the eyes of industrialists to the town of Meadow Prospect. And, by God, fellow members, if there is anything this town needs at the moment it is the interested eye of industrialists.'

There were at least a dozen plain motives behind this statement by Bowen. A new mood of solemnity had just struck Meadow Prospect. The post-war hedonism, which had never been more than brittle, had begun to fall apart. A clutch of bettors in a gambling shop run by Bowen had been struck by a paralysing intellectual curiosity, had cancelled their bets, had stared at each other in a deepening disgust for half an hour, then sent off to the region's university for the services of an extra-mural tutor to guide them towards heavier themes.

Bowen accused the Free Church Council of having used some type of nerve gas to subvert these bettors, but the truth was that none of these people ever laid a bet on again, and they sat at least once at the feet of the tutor before they unlaced his shoes and went back to crib, a tepid compromise, by their standards, but, after a long look at Bowen, safer.

At the same time a deputation of local youths had set out to walk around the world on an anti-bomb errand. They planned to pause at every capital and look meaningfully at anyone rich enough to afford this type of weapon, and impulsive enough to use it. Bowen's answer to these pacifists was to demand that they be gaoled before they reached the town's limits. He also assured America that these marchers were loons and that the real heart of Britain was still sound.

Other strokes of gloom had fallen. A small colony of nudists, set up to ridicule the shyness and serge that had driven sex to cover, broke up and the members seemed to be walking about in thicker suits than usual. A mattress factory had run out of orders and was now prone on its last mattress.

So Bowen was out to inject a bubble of gaiety into the bloodstream.

'A horse, is it?' said Geary the Emporium. 'You'll buy it out of the rates, will you? And the dope with which you regulate the speed of these animals, I suppose you'll try to milk the ratepayers for that, too.'

Bowen, who had an appetite for libel like a cow's for grass, just smiled.

'We'd collect for it,' he said.

There were groans. Meadow Prospect was a poor place for collections. During the war when we had set out to buy our own municipal Spitfire the fund yielded resources for no more than a wing-tip, even with Bowen and the Treasurer going around the town explaining about the war and air power. For the horse called Meadow Prospect the pennies would have stopped rolling before we had paid for the first hoof.

But we were never to know. As Bowen sat there, complacent, waiting for the senate to give him an oxygen grant for the new project, Goronwy Franklyn stood up and pointed at Bowen. He did not say anything. He was a poor speaker, but at standing still and pointing you could have taken him hunting; he would have done as well as any dog; Franklyn was the best in the area. He had a shadowed, ravaged face that made him a first-class accuser.

I turned to my neighbour, Hadrian Mills, a newspaper reporter and a leading local archivist.

'What's Franklyn pointing about?'

'He hates horses. And he hates Bowen because Bowen loves horses. Every second he stands there the members will recall anything shady that was ever charged against Bowen and that adds up to a long night. Standing still and pointing also helps Franklyn with the trouble he gets with his back.'

The reference to Franklyn's back helped me to fill in his dossier.

In early middle age Franklyn had been a coal merchant, hauling coal about Meadow Prospect in a cart drawn by a huge stallion called Dewi. Franklyn, at that period, was a man of striking good looks and brisk sexual enthusiasm. He did not prosper. Money was scarce and many women, genuinely fond of Franklyn and coal, bartered their affections for a sackful. Exhaustion and guilt made a wreck out of Franklyn. For a short time he would drive about Meadow Prospect saying firmly, but in too weak a voice to be effective, 'Coal for money.'

His temper shortened by the day and he took to laying his whip on the massive back of Dewi. One day he was caught doing this by Bowen, and Bowen, always eager to win sympathy for horses, threatened to use the whip on Franklyn if he found him doing it again. There was a secondary motive for this. Bowen was a long-distance amorist and he had lost the love of many women to Franklyn.

This finished Franklyn off. He developed some psychosomatic ailment of the back and he took to a wheelchair which was pushed about by his son. The boy had pushed Franklyn up Meadow Prospect's longest and steepest hill. Franklyn was in a rancorous mood and between that and the heat the boy was edging towards delirium.

At the hill's top he paused. In an effort to drown his father's laments he began to shout over to a passing neighbour an account of a fight he had seen a few nights before between Tommy Farr and some Midlander. The neighbour wanted the boy to render in fuller detail the lightning left and right punches with which Farr had finally floored his opponent. To do this the boy had to take both hands off the chair and before he could drag it back again Franklyn was plummeting down the hill at the speed of sound.

The road was clear except for a cart, the grocery cart of the Cooperative store, drawn by Franklyn's old horse, Dewi, now called Divi. To avoid any possibility of collision, Franklyn, always clear-minded when travelling at top speed, leaned heavily to the right. But when he was about half-way down the hill Divi started to move and with its bulk and the cart's blocked the road.

Some people claimed that Kitchener Bowen had passed at that moment and had given Divi the whispered command that caused it to make a right wheel. Others believed that Divi had sensed Franklyn's plight and had arranged its position to give Franklyn a royal welcome.

Franklyn, who had now given up any attempt to guide the chair, was now heading straight for Divi. By an astonishing bit of crouching he passed under the horse with about an inch to spare. He shot over a bridge and up the slope on the other side of the valley. He leaped out of the chair as soon as it slowed down and he began running up the hill he had descended, waving a plaid shawl and shouting that he was going to stifle Divi and his son in that order.

Franklyn went on to do well in his second try at the coal trade. The experience of shooting through Divi's legs had made him Calvinistically uncordial in his dealings with women, and he told me a few days ago that in this career in public office he had known no moment richer then when he had pointed a finger of general denunciation at Kitchener Bowen and buried the prospect of our being saddled with a horse called Meadow Prospect.

from *The Lust Lobby* (1978)

BOBI JONES

The Rhondda

Don't keep saying the Rhondda's the pits of a place
  Because the works and the clubs are as nasty as furtive brothels:
Nowadays it's all polished up like the most modern
  Parisian locales.

Don't say it's a dangerous site for industry
  Because rebels are devouring Marx and defecating rights:
It's something that belongs to more extreme nations, and to the past,
  Such expending of thoughts.

Everybody's so nice in the Rhondda, just like everywhere else
          in England:
  You can purchase Max Factor there as in Piccadilly,
They've almost got rid of their Welsh accents; and as for sol-fa,
  Oh! don't be silly.

There's a cleanness in the Rhondda that's never been found before,
  The antiseptic cleanness of a surgeon who spread
A sheet across a patient's scrubbed body on the traditional table
  And cut off his head.

In the days gone by, strangers had a hard time knowing
  Where one village would end and the next would commence.
But today the inhabitants have a hard time knowing
  Themselves where the Rhondda is.

  translated by Joseph P. Clancy
  from *Tyred Allan (1965)*

RHYDWEN WILLIAMS
Mountain Streams

(For the children of Ynys-wen Welsh School and in memory of
three worthies of the valley:
John Robert Williams, miner and poet; Robert Griffiths, pastor
and preacher; James Kitchener Davies, teacher, poet, pioneer)

Listen.
Can you hear the mountain-streams —
Ynys-wen ... Ynys-feio ... Ynys-hir ...
all the way to Ilan,
and the holy well on Pen-rhys
as crystal as precious stone
still praising Our Lady —
the mountain-streams are virgin again!

  Stranger?
— Yes.

He was seated at the foot of Moel Cadwgan ...
cap ... stick ... cigarette.
I seemed to remember his face — what was left.

  — Lleteca? Oh, they've pulled the old place down!
  — He was a poet.
  — Ay, and a better collier you wouldn't find from
  Bwllfa to Maerdy.
  — An old hand in a hard heading.
Writing poems and cutting coal — chalked them on the coal face!
This mountain's first bard.
Onward. To the servile chapel.
  — Only a few women left — like the handful on
  the Third Day!
Enter ... halt ... observe.
  — This plaque is in memory of the old minister.
  — 'Prophet, shepherd, friend of all'.
  — A few left who remember him.
  —Spent a life-time here.
His grave is on a high hill in the cemetery — as though he couldn't
  let his Moriah out of his sight.

Onward. Gelliwastad ... Tyntyla ... Brithweunydd!
          — Oh, they were all poets around here once!
          — He died young.
          — For Wales, they said.
          — Black hair, large eyes, and a smile.
          — Handled a spade like he handled a pen.
          — Nationalist, poet, Calvinist, and contented rebel.
          — Fine voice for the open-air.
          — Soap-box or pulpit.
          — Theomemphus and a pint of beer!
When they laid him to rest in Rhondda earth one afternoon,
this valley had a vein richer than the coal.

Listen.
I was born here. The mark of the Cwm
as indelible as a sheep's identity ...
accent ... memories ... creed.
The Great War hampered my birth ... like breaking teeth
          ... like the whoop.
The Big Strike hampered my boyhood ... like sums ... like girls.
I was brought-up tenderly around the big-seat and the big-tip;
school-cap and hobnails weekdays, velvet and pearl-buttons
          Sunday:
known around foundry, cinema, football-pitch, bandroom
          and Gymanfa,
a chubby Welsh cherub fluent in the Bible and the obscene.

I remember ...
          lunatic hooters terrifying the defenceless birds;
          wheels, turbines, drams causing delirium at night
          and the repulsive pit — stretching alongside the river
          as vulgar as a sow with her teats in the water —
          and the burdened mothers helping their menfolk
          starkers in the tub in front of the fire
          — Shut the bloody door!
          — Wash my back, my luvly!
          And the children imitating Daddy and Mammy in the street...

Can you see now with me —
          here, the day of the red squirrel,
          wild pigeon, pheasant, and the swift partridge,

the mountain-streams a ready help in need
when there was only water and the good earth
to ease the hunger in their peasant eyes?
Can you see in that rural dawn,
a man as unhurried as his beast
toiling his life away between his fields,
a mind as narrow as his hedges
and his language music on the tip of the tongue?
Can you hear in this seamless silence
the chatter of stars as loud as the birds
and the hands that steered the plough
strumming a harp like Orpheus once in surges of song?
Innocence was as ordinary as dew
on these mountains then
and the goodness of man in the compound kitchen —
hens, cats, dogs, and the meddlesome sheep —
as warm as the egg in its nest.

A world of trees,
multitudes of trees to the horizon;
one lazy path zig-zag to everywhere
scraped by boot and hoof and paw,
leaves falling daily
like green rain,
and only the sun and moon and stars
and the occasional drover
calling — the sun come to stay awhile,
the moon on its way to Hirwaun Fair,
and the drover heading for Bristol
and his beast sighing
under cargoes of skins.

Leaves, the scents of wild flowers, and an eyeful of sky—
the limits of their world!
Earth, beast, bird, man, and God —
the only verities;
all else was supposition ... and the dark
at the end of the day
to grant the mercy of sleep!

Spring! Can you see the stars

tarrying to gaze at their image,
framed by fragile boughs
in the running mirrors of the streams?
Summer! can you see the heather and gorse
nymph-like aside the water
screening its virginity?
Autumn! Can you see
thieving fingers ransacking the forests
and pouring the loot
into deep turbulent pools?
Winter! Can you see
the assets and masterpieces
of Nature locked
in a river's vaults?

Our fathers fought
seasons and firmament and the sly soil
with raw hands;
their daily bread fleece on a barbed fence
and their prayer a bunch of fingers under the cow's udder.
From peak to peak,
slope to slope,
stream to stream — cartwheels turning,
horses steaming,
a lamp in the dark — long before dawn —
like a star gone astray,
a scathing scythe whispering to the corn,
and the croft and the barn and the tumble-down stable
huddled together on the hill.
Sometimes, a trace of blood in the stream,
a dead sheep nearby,
and ravens high in the trees
wiping their claws in their feathers
after the savage feast.

At close of day,
having clouted the hard clay
and sought the favour of the lively streams,
listening to a child's prayers before
sitting-down to supper,
and bundling-in for the night

in love's double-bed
as silent as two under the sod.

Pen-yr-englyn ... Glyncoli ... Parc ... Tyn-y-bedw ... Ton ...
Bronllwyn ... Bodringallt ... Ffrwdamos ... Dinas ... Porth!
Here, on native soil, their garments threadbare,
and the flesh taut around the hard-working bone,
only the lowing of cattle and the song of the birds to be heard,
a patient people waited
to greet the calf come tipsy out of the womb
and wash the wound on the side of the mare or the purse
            of the cow;
here, where the streams were as pure as the people
and their flow as merry as the children
who sang their innocence over these hills.

Listen.
Can you see how the forests ruined and the tall trees slain,
the squirrels lost on the bereaved mountain
and the dove bewildered in the sky
and all the birds berserk for their nests?

Can you hear now the hooters claiming the air —
air that once trembled with the song of linnet and lark?
And the trucks and carts and steam and tumult
mocking the tranquility that was once seamless and green?

Can you see the earth displaying its wounds to the sun
and the river dying on its bed and the trout on the surface
            of the water?
And the man who strummed his harp once on a homely hearth
descending like Orpheus into the industrious dark?

Listen.
This song is neither sentiment nor tears, but steel —
the farmstead was bought for a price —
animal manure thrown-in for luck!
Oh, the stable sewage was a lovely gesture ...
and from that moment onward,
the epileptic deep spewed into the streams,
stained the estuary,

as the river lost its virtue
and the water was disgraced under the stars.

> — I remember Dr Morris coming to Noddfa.
> — I was there when Ben Bowen won his first chair.
> — D'you remember Joby Culverhouse fighting in
> Scarrot's booth?
> — Mabon was a guest in my mother's wedding.
> — Siloh Chapel was packed with J.J.
> — Mr Davies Nazareth preached in America.
> — Did you hear Todd Jones? Now *there's* a tenor!
> — Noah Ablett wore himself out for the people.
> — I'm told there's a Northman opened a chip-shop
> in Ferndale.
> — Who sent the police to Tonypandy?
> — Damn, between the Irish and the Northmen, this
> valley's gone—
> — An' before London will give in —
> — Will John and Will Mainwaring will be in jail.
> — Mrs What's-her-name read all this in her tea-cup!
> — Mind, we got a lot to be proud of here!

Can you feel the atmosphere different?
Can you see the wheel of fortune turning?
Can you see the pattern changing?

Who is this coming down from Ynys-hir
red with rage, blue with pneumoconiosis,
his banner in the air and his Bible under his arm?
> — Oh Lord, send the Holy Spirit to Ainon!
English, mind! Fundamentalist, Military, Myth!

Who is this as delicate as the dawn
and as lovely as the moon,
standing in a doorway in Cardiff,
tainted, one of the girls of the street?
> — They say it's all his fault!
> — Well, you can't dress like that on the dole!
What's the trumpet I hear sounding
from Blaen-cwm to Blaenllechau?
And who's the drummer in Blaenclydach's jazz-band?

And who's the Carmen dancing with a red rose between her lips?
        — Her mother sang in Evan Roberts' Revival.
        — Her father died under a fall in the Cwtch.

Our nationhood is not an adornment but a struggle;
not entertainment, but a yoke we carry —
the yoke is heavy and there is no relief!
We saw the soup-kitchen aggravate our poverty,
our dignity bought with the pittance of the dole;
uprooted by the hundreds, we were transplanted all over the world
 —feeble old roots that would grow on any dump under the sun!

        — Our Morgan 'ave 'ad 'is B.A.
        — Oh, there's nice to see them gettin' on in the world!
        — Our Megan 'ave 'ad a headship in Stoke!
        — Well, she was always good with the children in Saron!
        — Our Percy is now a curate in Stepney!
        — Oh, he'll suit the élite to the T!
        — Our Dyfrig is a male-nurse in Uttoxeter!
        — I think Tommy Farr will be as good as Tom Thomas.
        —And if Jimmy Murphy gets a chance with West Brom —

Who will be left on these hills
to rust with the gear and the rails and the wheels
and grow old with the Chapel and the Cymmrodorion
          and the mother-tongue,
scratching a living like old hens in the rubble of past years?

        — I've got a new poem.
        — Now you take it easy.
        — Just let me have a sit-down —
        — Lean on my arm!
        — Steady now!
        — If I could only ...

Death's sculpture is meticulous — to the bone.
Passion! Muse! Soul! Where are they all gone
behind those big eyes in that wren's body?
He died — his poem his only concern,
the old Welsh on his lips
and the invincible dust conquering his cultured frailty.

— I must go to the service —
— But the doctor has forbidden —
— Sarah James and Annie Davies will be there —
— But you'd better rest —
—And Miss Thomas will be at the organ —
— Better you stay at home —

The faithful were there. He delivered his sermon. The last.
He fell in the big pew — his work done.
The funeral went up the valley. Streets hushed. Children weeping.
The people knew that this was a death the valley could ill afford.

— An open-air meeting in Trebanog!
— Pain, boy?
— Wait till we have home-rule —
— What about a drink now?
— There's more Welsh spoken in Trebanog now —
— Trebanog!
— There are *budgies* in Trebanog can speak Welsh!

One day more. Nobody could deceive him. Neither friend
            nor Death.
Teasing ... laughing ... debating ... dreaming ... till the
            Darkness embraced him.
Dear God! The brain behind the dream and the inspiration
            of the poetry gone!

Can you see now where pit and lamproom were
and the prayers and the hymns and the blasphemies at the coal-face
and the Hippodrome and Gaiety and Empire and Tivoli
and the strong-man from Glynneath pumping his muscles
            for a pound?

Can you see where the black man from Merthyr
swallowed knives and fire
and Nazareth Band-of-Hope acted the *Pirates of Penzance*?
and the siren from the East was sawn in pieces
and Pendyrus Choir won all the awards?

Can you see the sarsaparilla fountain on Dai Cenimo's counter

and Das Kapital the topic in Hebron and the Griffin Inn?
and the people flocking to the Grand Concert and Funfair
and the morning service and the singing-school at night?

Here, where the wild pigeon and pheasant nest again
and the resurrected trout make merry in the stream,
new lovers romp in the ferns on Moel Cadwgan
and the apples are ripe in the orchard on Pen-twyn.

Listen.
I hear the music of mountain-streams ...
Ynys-wen ... Ynys-feio ... Ynys-hir ...
all the way to Ilan,
and the holy well on Pen-rhys,
as crystal as precious stone
praising our Lady —
the mountain-streams are virgin again!

     — Stranger?
     — Yes.

He was seated at the foot of Moel Cadwgan ...
cap ... stick ... cigarette ...
I seemed to remember his face — what was left.
     My daughter's girl goes to the Welsh School now.
     — A young man come to our chapel straight from the college.
He made to go — as though defying a valley's fears,
his stick as firm as his faith.

translated by the author
from 'Y Ffynhonnau' in *Y Ffynhonnau a Cherddi Eraill* (1970)
and in *Rhondda Poems* (1987)

RON BERRY
The Fall

We stripped off in the gate road before going up into the face. It was quiet, the Meco cutter loader in the stable at the end of the run, two men changing the picks. The ventilation blew steady as Atlantic wind, wisping curls of dust right up the length of the face. The night-shift fireman came down under the white prop line chalked on the roof. 'Boys, be careful about fifty yards up the face,' he said cordially. 'There's a break running on to the coal from where we crashed the gob last night. Shove a couple of flats across it. Righto, lads, straight face, ah! Don't hold up the Meco when she's ready to come down. What's the weather like up top this morning?'

I said, 'Friday weather over in Daren. Christ knows what it's like this side of the mountain. Some of your Brynywawr blokes don't know the days of the week; they'd live underground if the NCB brought down a few old bags and a fish and chips shop at pit-bottom.'

'Rees,' he said, 'you're making good money on this Meco team. *Iesu*, when I was a kid we'd be holing over the stank all day to fill two trams.'

'Aye, we've heard all about hand-cut coal,' I said. 'Do you see any old colliers working on the coal these days? The poor buggers can't take it. Another few years and you'll be down-graded; they'll put you in charge of whitewashing manholes or some bloody thing.'

'Mechanization,' he said. 'You can't expect old men to operate these modern machines.'

'Is there a war on?' I said. 'Shove us youngsters up in the front line, is that the idea? You and the bastards who invented Meco loaders, you'll kill us off yet.'

He couldn't understand, and I don't blame him.

'Rees, what the fuckin' hell's the matter with you? Anyhow, I got no time to fuckin' argue. My shift's finished. Do your best.'

We were driving the gate-road stable on, cutting in, shovelling the coal back, posting and flatting the roof ready for the Meco after she made her first cut down the 180-yard face. When she started roaring Dicko Harding and Reg Page (one of Charlie Page's four Brynywawr brothers) went up to the break. Dicko soon came back to the gate-road stable.

'Give us a hand, Rees,' he said. 'Dowty post out of line, tight against the bloody coal. We'll have to double up on the back row, shove a few more bars on before we can extract. Won't be safe otherwise.'

'He kept his mouth shut about that Dowty,' I said.

The oldest man in our team raised his goggles to his forehead and landed another of his morning phlegms on the conveyor chains. 'Officials, I've shit better.' he said.

Star-bright far away up the face, cap lamps were shining and we could hear the Meco above the racket of the chains.

'First things first,' I suggested. 'We'll have to make it safe. They'll be down here ready to turn the machine by half-past nine, fresh picks and all.'

We went up to the break in the roof, our forty-nine-year-old stableman collier steadily effing the night-shift fireman. The Dowty post was inside the conveyor, eighteen inches from the coal. Rushing the job we doubled up on the last line of posts, sending steel flats across the roof break and free-end bars forward to the coal.

'Ent safe yet,' said the old bloke, 'not if you was to ask me.'

We were squatting like aborigines stuck in ritual, the Meco growling fifty yards away up the face.

'What else can we do?' asked Dicko.

I said, 'We'll tell the fireman. The Meco boys can stand clear and let the machine plough through. Any muck that comes down she'll load it on the chains. Shouldn't be too much.'

'Me, I'll be down in the gate-road stable,' said the old bloke.

So the Meco came through the bad spot, all clean coal swimming along the conveyor and while they were turning the machine in the lower stable we fixed a new line of Dowtys and bars up the face.

'That ent bloody safe at all,' warned the old bloke.

It wasn't either. The fall came before the second cut reached the break in the roof, soft coal mostly, trapping the electrician for a couple of minutes, but we dragged him clear. He had bruises on his left thigh, that's all. Shock, too. His jaw shivered and he couldn't talk much.

It wasn't a big fall, but the Meco cable and water pipe were under it. Careful work, mole scrabbling. We threw the muck back over the chains. The overman came, for morale no doubt, him and our old bloke chatting mining principles polite as two Q.C.s in chambers. Once we had the conveyor running again the electrician rode out to the gate road and went home. Cup of tea and a fag, that's what he wanted, just like any temporarily beaten infantryman. We were down ninety minutes on cutting, so the overman stayed in the face, him and the fireman helping out with the Meco loader. No doubt for morale as much as anything. They weren't like us, on tonnage.

We were posting the top-end stable when the big fall came, *behind* the Meco. Nobody there to cop it, thank God. The chains stopped running.

'There now, like I said,' pointed out the old bloke, old merely because at forty-nine he was the eldest.

'Right, men, let's have you,' the overman said. 'I want this face ready for cutting by the time the afternoon shift comes in.'

At two o'clock I changed places with Reg Page, working the coal inside the fall, soft coal, mashed soft, like a bag. We spragged as we cut in, but not enough. Not enough sprags. Neither was it the coal that did the damage. I rolled, elbowing inside the fallen coal — soft coal — rolled over on to my back for another squirm to get away, safe, clear, with nothing worse than shaken breath. Like the electrician. So when the stone came down off the inner lip of broken ground, I was flat on my back.

Thank the Jesus Christ for morphia.

from *Flame and Slag* (1968)

ALUN RICHARDS

The Scandalous Thoughts of Elmyra Mouth

Elmyra Mouth did not like BBC Wales. Either on the box or off it. Although she dutifully watched the programmes which involved her husband as assistant camera-man, she was always conscious of a great disparity between them and her. She did not like the announcers for a start. The women looked like something out of a Sunday School vestry and the men sounded phoney, half-London, half-Welsh, neither one thing nor the other, with the most unacceptable of getting-ahead acquisitions, posh accents.

Then again, on the few occasions when she went down from the valleys to Cardiff and waited for Davie in the staff canteen, Elmyra had increased her dislike for what went on behind the scenes. Take the bosses. They treated the more lowly technicians' wives like dirt, either looking through you, or rambling on amongst themselves in deep, book Welsh. Always jabberjabber, it was, never mind whether you understood or not. They had no manners, Elmyra concluded, but that was not the worst. From what she had heard from Davie who was inclined to exaggerate to please her, the place was a hotbed of sex. You never knew who was sleeping with who, and for all the air of sanctity which somehow got on the air, behind the scenes, Elmyra was sure, the place was like a rabbit warren.

Wasn't it full of strangers? Glamorgan people lost out all the way along the line. You seldom came across anybody from up the valleys, or Cardiff even, just the in Welshy-Welsh, catarrhal BA'd North Walians down for what they could get, Ministers' sons from everywhere, and girls from farms by the look of them, legs like bottles, all sitting around endlessly in the canteen, heads bent together and the hum of gossip rising like steam above a football crowd. Some of them *lived* in that canteen. It was an unhealthy atmosphere, Elmyra felt, and definitely not her style

But there was another side to it. Her Davie had a good job by valley standards. On top of what he was getting in take-home pay, he always managed a few bob on top, what with car allowance, expenses and subsistence — it was as good as the Police from that point of view. But she had put her foot right down when there was any talk of moving down to Cardiff. Her grandmother had left her a furnished house, the corner one in the terrace, and where they lived, they had a view over the town that was worth waking up for.

From the bedroom window, she could see right down Dan y Graig Street, over the rows of terraced houses below them, right down to the memorial park where the trees formed an avenue beside the confluence of the Rivers Rhondda and Taff. Further away, familiar grey mountains and brown tumps stood sentinel over other valleys, and everywhere she looked, Elmyra felt at home. Here she had a position and status, and although they used to call her Elmyra Mouth because of her not being backward in coming forwards in that direction, she was well content to be at home. She was a valley girl, was she not? She knew every brick of Dan y Graig Street, every shadow of the courting gullies behind the terrace, every blade of grass and *cwtch* on the bare mountain and tip behind, and although now you didn't hear the tramp of miners' boots in the mornings and the little front parlour shop around the corner no longer sold lumps of chalk for the colliers to mark their drams as they did in her mother's day, it was still home and here she felt comfy. So when Davie'd proposed moving to Cardiff as it would cut down his travelling time, she had a cryptic and typical answer.

'Travel, you bugger,' she said flatly. 'You'll not move me an inch!'

For his part, Davie did not much mind. He was from further up the valleys, easy going, placid, glad enough to be in any kind of job when it came to it, and the extras that came his way from the travelling allowance allowed them an income that made life more comfortable. He had met Elmyra in a dance when home on leave from Malaya. One of Templar's boys, he'd caught a packet up the sharp end, a burst from a terrorist's gun that left him with a slightly stiff knee, and when Elmyra looked at him, handsome and sunburned with the fusilier's dark patch hanging from his battledress, he didn't have a chance. She liked a man who was a man, and the wound, the campaign medals, the air of experience about him, and his close-cropped hair and engaging *shoni's* wink were enough. She also felt she could manage him, as her mother had managed her father, also an old sweat. Give the valley boys a good look at the world and it did them no end of good, and like many before him, Davie had returned home from the wars with that certain air which Elmyra found irresistible. The best Welshmen belonged to the world. They didn't stay at home picking their noses in beautiful Welsh.

Of course, Elmyra was a catch herself. Now at thirty-two, she could still go down the shop without a bra under her jumper and nobody'd know for sure. When she got her war paint on, with her slim hips, long, sexy legs and wide, insolent mouth, she had her mother's Saturday night at the Vic look, cocktail lounge, not the Two Foot Six, a touch of the Lauren Bacall's, in short. And despite her nickname, she never went too far with Davie. Marriage and two children had calmed her in that respect. Now she thought more and said less. She was perfectly happy, thank you very much, no need to give her a thought. But she did sometimes worry when Davie was out late. It was not that she feared competition — she'd go through the BBC canteen like a knife through butter if she'd occasion to — but there was an end to her patience in waiting. She didn't mind when he was away on location, but lately, waiting up for him had got on her nerves. It was the age-old wives' complaint. It was when he was not in when he said he was going to be in, that was the rub. So when Davie informed her he was going to be late one Friday night, she had a caustic reply.

They were sitting at breakfast, lolling about on one of his rest days. Karen and Sabrina, their two young daughters, were in school.

'Oh,' Davie said, 'I forgot to tell you. Friday, I'll be late.'

'I thought it was your rest week?'

He took care to keep his eyes casually on the centre pages of the *Mirror*. 'It is, but you know Fred Eckersley? He's off to London, a promotion, and we're going to give him a bit of a send-off.'

'Fred — who?'

'Eckersley. You know. He's going to Panorama.'

'You don't have to kid me with none of that stuff,' Elmyra said sharply. 'Panorama? You can keep it. You know you usually take me out Fridays?'

'Well, he's going on Saturday. It's just a send-off with the boys from the Unit.'

'That Film Unit!' Elmyra said in much the same way as her mother would have said, 'That pit!' or 'That club!'

'Well, I could hardly refuse, could I?' Davie said mildly. 'Fred's one of the best. It's just a get-together, that's all.'

Elmyra scowled. She knew the charm of that phrase. It could mean anything from a few pints and a game of darts to the back door stove in and him banished downstairs in a Worthington fug, a bucket and sheet of newspaper ready beside the settee. Lifeboat stations, as they said. About once a year, she knew, Davie let himself go as her father had done and still did. They were both capable of drinking without reason, stomach to stomach in the four ale, and then returning home with flushed red faces, hoarse from singing and as full as eggs. BBC

Wales would be sorry to know that the songs they sang were *Mexicali Rose* or, *I have been a Rover*, but that was beside the point. Where they got the capacity from, she did not know. She was a Snowball and Babycham girl herself. But she was careful to control her objections. If her mother had taught her anything, it was not to be a nag.

'Oh, well, I suppose you'd better go then,' she said resignedly. 'Just men together, is it?'

'Just the boys in the Unit.'

'Mind to be home at twelve then. Twelve sharp.'

'Oh, good Gawd.' Davie returned to the Mirror. 'I'll be home long before that.'

'You have to be up early Saturday, mind? I want to go shopping and Sabrina's got to have new pumps for her dancing lessons.'

'Rightho,' Davie said. And that was all.

But when the time came for him to leave and drive the twelve miles down to Cardiff, she noted he had his drinking suit on. It was an ancient Burton's Donegal tweed which he fondly believed did not show stains, but despite this optimism, she felt she knew the signs when it was produced. He wore it on the *beyond* nights and it looked like it, had stayed crumpled where he fell, spillages on lapels to boot.

'Twelve sharp then,' she repeated. 'And remember the breathalyser.'

'Oh, if I have a meal, it'll kill it. A good hot curry'll do the trick.'

He went to give her a goodbye kiss. She'd done herself up. All the more desirable to come home to!

'So long then, kid,' he let his lips linger on hers.

She studied him gravely.

'You watch your bloody self. I know the signs.' He repeated a family joke. 'It's not the drink, Auntie, it's the company.'

'I can see that by the veins on your nose.'

'Go on ...' he gave her a playful squeeze.

'Stay if you want,' she kept her hands behind his neck.

'No, I can't. It's Fred's last night.'

She bared her teeth and released him. Men, she thought; animals. If he didn't come up the stairs cat-footed, she'd turn the tap off that night. Shut shop it would be, him and his drink and his Fred! As her mother'd advised, there was such a thing as frostbite after closing. But like her mother, she didn't want to be thought a bad old sort. So she merely grunted; 'Get on with you. And come home with more than your bracers!'

When he had gone, she heard the familiar clunk of the car's gears outside and lit a cigarette before getting the children to bed. There was nothing for her on the telly as usual. With all the money they spent on it, you'd think there might be a show she'd actually enjoy now and again. Sometimes there was a serial or a play with which she could identify, but it was never from Wales and usually had to do with the Midlands or the North. Locally, she did not count, she supposed. Not that she gave a monkey's. Davie said you had to go to Bristol to get the Welsh edition of the *Radio Times* because nobody took it locally. But why should they? It had precious little to do with them, any more than it did the other commercial lot, who weren't even worth mentioning except for a passing sigh for the Dorchester film stars worrying about South Wales on their yachts. Who was kidding who? They were no bottle from the start. Mouths shut, remember the divi, and don't offend Bristol again. Where were the valleys in that?

She finished her cigarette and went up to inspect the bathroom which Davie had recently tiled. It contained a coloured bath, pink, with matching accessories, and luxury of luxuries, a separate shower attachment. Elmyra could remember what it was like not to have a proper bathroom and she thought her coloured suite a whizz and no mistake. Now she looked proudly at the hand towels, the matching floor mat and lavatory cover, and thanked God for Embassy coupons. It was the most hallowed room in the house.

Presently, she called the children in, and having bathed them and settled them down in their nightdresses, decided to bathe herself. If Davie but knew it, she spent hours in the bathroom, wallowing in the suds, endlessly combing her hair, and surveying herself in the long mirror she'd insisted upon. She often took her measurements. Two kids and hardly an inch on or off at either end. Boy, she was too good to waste, she thought. It was a good job she was faithful. There were always plenty of chances. She couldn't go down the market Saturdays without what seemed like a visiting team trying to look down her dress, but she'd developed a look that killed, she fondly imagined. And anyway, she wasn't interested. They said a slice off a cut loaf was never missed, but not her loaf, thank you very much. She was took, a one-man woman.

She did not dress after her bath, slipped a robe on and went downstairs where she attempted to read her horoscope from a woman's journal, but somehow she couldn't concentrate. She didn't know quite what it was, but her mind was on the itch. Was their marriage getting boring? Did they take each other too much for granted? She'd caught Davie looking at pin-ups a lot lately, his eye flashing to the ripe page of the *Mirror* before he so much as crackled a cornflake. What if his eye was beginning to wander elsewhere?

At first, she put the thought out of her mind and turned to the broken hearts column which she also read avidly. People's troubles were incredible. The best required a stamped addressed envelope for a confidential reply, but she was adept at reading between the lines. Some men were so crooked, they'd fox their own shadows. And slimy with it, pure slime. But not her Davie. She couldn't understand how she even gave it a thought. He was as good as gold always. As open as the day is long.

And yet it nagged, this thought. For some reason, her natural confidence began to ebb away. It was the BBC that did it. Of course, it was ridiculous and the Cardiff lot were nothing like the London lot in that respect, but it was the showbiz world even if most of it was in Welsh. Oh, why couldn't he get a job in the chain works or on the trading estate? They said travel broadened the mind, even twelve miles a day, but there was all the difference in the world in those twelve miles leading down to Cardiff. She saw them stretching out in her mind's eye, Treforest, the Estate, Taff's Well, Whitchurch, and then the environs of the capital city opening up like a red light district in some lurid American film. Downtown What-You-Call, she thought. She'd give him Downtown! Bloody Cardiff.... It was so cold compared to the valleys. Oh, why couldn't he get a job at home?

Then suddenly, her mind began to panic. It was as if a spring had begun to unwind, a coil slipping slowly from its point of tension, then exploding, thoughts expanding like rings of steel and spilling into every corner of her mind.

What if he was on the knock? All those stories about Malay girls. What did they call them? Taxi Dancers. And what about the divorces in showbiz? The Boss of the whole BBC had had one and now he was working for the commercials! There was no such thing as loyalty any more. You only had to sit in the canteen to listen to them tearing each other's programmes apart to know that. Everybody got stick, and the South Wales boys who were coining it on *Z Cars* in London got the most. That was one thing, another was that she'd refused to go to the Christmas party on principle. The poor bloody technicians always got the raw end of it with the bilingual production staff and the bigwigs ruling the roost. She didn't fancy being squeezed, pawed or patronised in that crush. It was like Machynlleth zoo. If they had a zoo in Machynlleth. And if they did, Glamorgan and Monmouthshire people had to pay for it. Like the bloody language. And as for what went on down in Make-Up after some of those *Ychafi* programmes, disgusting wasn't the word. Sometimes, they had actors there, and actresses, and the Make-Up girls said anything went. It was no good putting in to see Controller (Wales) either because he said London was worse and Glasgow the best, according to what somebody had told somebody who told Davie. At any rate, it was no place for a self-respecting valley girl. Even if they didn't have queers which Davie said were everywhere else. Like some places he knew where you had to stand with your back to the wall as soon as you got into the lift, by all accounts.

But what about Davie? If Fred What's-His-Name was on transfer to Panorama, he'd be ready to let himself go, wouldn't he? They'd probably have the riggers out drinking with them, and the scene shifters, and there was a commissionaire who could tell a story or two, she knew about them. Once they got the beer into them, there'd be no telling what they'd do. If they weren't at it with the Welshy lot, they might be down the docks and that was almost as bad, if not quite. The trouble was, once you got near Cardiff, the values changed. You could get drunk up the valleys like a man, but after stop-tap, home you had to come, boyo, one foot behind the other, or no place for you but the gutter. And there was something very comforting about the gutter. There was seldom room for two in it.

But Cardiff, the docks.... She thought about them obsessionally now. What she hated most was her sense of the city's anonymity, those cold wide streets, actual architecture, people pushing, sometimes stuck-ups with yet another accent and the girls in the better shops trying to sound like a lot of lezzes and looking down their noses at you if you ever had to leave your address.

'Dan y Graig Street and up yours too!'

What was good about the valleys from her present point of view was that there was many a fly that was never unbuttoned because it would be all over town the next day. You couldn't bend down to straighten your tights without half the street pricing your under-clothes. Walls had ears and bricks had eyes, and it was a good job too, made you feel part of the family, and keeping the old Adam down in all but the wilder spirits and they were usually Poles or County School boys. There was no creeping off and having it on the sly if you were married unless you were the Invisible Man or something. What worried her now was the thought of them all together, egging each other on. They said there were some rugby clubs who actually had a competition when they went on the Cornish tour. Who'd be the first of the married men to click! Thank Gawd for that Malayan terrorist anyhow! He'd put the shot in just the right place.

By eleven thirty, Elmyra was convinced that her marriage was threatened. If it could happen to Diana Dors, it could happen to her, couldn't it? They must be on the razzle. Must be.

As a matter of principle, she never kept drink in the house, except at Christmas. It was not that nobody called, but rather, that she knew very well who might call, and the men there were around here, you couldn't give them one drink. Oh, no. With them, it was one drink, finish the bottle. They were as Welsh as Welsh in that, out-and-outers, the bloody lot of them. It so happened that there was a half bottle of rum which her father had given Davie for his chest in the winter. She brought it out and poured herself a liberal tot and drank it with a swallow. She'd give him a going-over when he came in. If there was a hint of another woman, she'd give him a beating, the like of which the street had never known. There'd been some famous cases, one erring husband sewn in the bed sheets and laced with a broom handle in his cups, another wrapped up in wet wallpaper and pasted all over like a snowman before he got his. They didn't believe in sulking, the Dan y Graig women. Defiantly, she poured another tot, swallowed it, and then another. She'd give him sox!

But by one o'clock when there was still no sign of him, her rage turned like the weather cock to self-pity. She was drunk now, wallowing in remorse. All these accusations. It was her fault, she'd refused to move to Cardiff in the first place. What was the good of blaming him if he didn't have a home handy? All the temptations were put in his way. He was a boy-and-a-half as far as his attractions went. A wife's place was to follow her husband. She'd jibbed at the first thing he'd ever really asked her. And now what was she doing? Never a quitter be, her father always said, true to the pit always; neither a quitter nor a squealer. Now she was both.

By two o'clock, she'd finished the bottle. She got to her feet and staggered to bed. Now she was maudlin, disaster's victim. Dead, she thought, he was dead, neatly incised on the motor-way, or crushed under some truck. He'd told her once he'd seen a man cut in half by a lengthy burst from a sten gun, actually in half. Now she transferred the image into her own mind, but it was too horrible. He was normally the most careful of drivers, but then, they were the sort who always copped it. She could not remember going upstairs, or what she did when she got there, but she already saw herself as a widow, pale and grief-stricken in black with the entire street turned out for the funeral and perhaps a sight of one or two of the BBC celebrities who might be there. It was all over in her mind. Perhaps they'd fiddle it to say that he was working so she'd get a pension, no doubt Controller (Wales) would find a few words of English to cheer her up, but she was a widow all right. She *felt* like a widow. Thank Gawd her grandmother'd left her the house. She sobbed herself to sleep finally, lying naked on the coverlet, her long, black hair hanging down by the side of the bed.

It was in this position that Davie found her at three o'clock in the morning. He smelt the rum on her breath with some annoyance. There was no call for that, nothing wrong with her chest, but he said nothing, stripped and eased himself in beside her, taking care to throw the coverlet over her in case she would catch a chill.

In the morning, it was he who attacked first.

'You were lying there looking like a bloody book jacket. What if the children had come in?'

She felt dreadful, a mouth like a birdcage. Her temples throbbed as she looked at him blearily. She'd decided on something before she fell asleep, but now she could not remember what it was.

'You said twelve ...'

'I was late because I had to drive everybody else home.'

'Twelve, you said.'

'Well, I wasn't much after, but before you go on at me, have you seen the bathroom?'

'The bathroom?' she caught at her throat. She had a vague memory of disturbance, a sense of sin.

'Were you swinging on the light cord, or what?'

'Swinging?'

'The plaster's flaked on the ceiling by the switch, and the matching accessories are stuffed down the pan.'

'The pan?'

'The lav,' he said accusingly. 'What did you have, an orgy all on your own?'

In her frenzy, she must have tried to wreck her own creation! *Ychafi!* And even as he accused, the fact that he did not couple her with anyone else shamed her all the more. Thoughts was awful things when you came to think of them: nasty.

'Oh, lor'... Sorry kid,' she said guiltily.

'I should think so too.'

She thought for a moment, then looked at him. 'It's the bloody BBC.

I get worried. I don't know why you don't try and get a job at home.'

He looked at her startled.

'Hey?'

Then she said what everybody knew and Honours Graduates denied: 'You know you won't get on there. It's all clicks, and with your *shoni's* Welsh, what chance?'

He said nothing. They had discussed the matter before and what she said was right. It was just that he was easy going.

But now she pursued it.

'A little photographer's or something?' she said suggestively, as only she could. She slanted her eyes in a look she privately called, The Japanese Goodnight. 'If you had a shop, you could come home dinner times. When the kids are in School. You know....'

He sighed. He knew the signs. From now on, she'd get her beak on it like a jackdaw at a nut. Might as well say yes to a shopkeeper before she dressed.

'We'll see,' he said comfortably. 'Leave it at that for the moment.'

'Great,' she said happily, and later a sweet, intimate poem in monosyllables: 'Oh ... Oh ... Oh, *Duw-Duw*! Oh, help! Oh, Malaya! Oh, smashing!'

Further up the street where the houses had bay windows and the occasional colour television they said Elmyra Mouth was as common as dirt, but the most endearing thing about her was that she thought him, her husband, the most desirable man in all the world. He was hers, and apart from him and the children, she had but a single thought. 'If you was from the valleys, stay in the valleys.' Nothing else made sense.

from *Dai Country* (1973)

RON BERRY
Another Pit Closes

Back in 1960 we had no qualms about Caib colliery. The coal was there in the Four Feet, millions of tons of high-grade steam coal. Only two explosions in thirty-four years, the killed men forgotten, just about forgotten. Ours was a good pit. In 1960 we had a sharp lodge committee. Compo cases were looked after, we ran a tote for pensioners, gave them £5 hampers and a cheque every Christmas. Daren Dramatic Society was established in Caib Institute. We had ten chapels and a Welsh Church of England, two cinemas, a film society, three pigeon clubs, a dog fanciers' club, four soccer teams, cricket and rugby teams, the Women's Guild was a power combine, Daren and District Angling Association, a bowls team, motor-cycle club, Barclay's and Midland Banks were thriving on H.P. deals, and the railway tunnel under Waunwen was still open in 1960. We had a swimming pool. The Houghton Four X brewery flourished, serving nine pubs and two affiliated clubs, plus the Earl Haig and Daren Social and Welfare Club (bingo three nights, dances two nights, concerts two nights), and the borough council were planning their two-phase housing project costing three million pounds. Two thousand Daren folk, mostly girls, worked in a radio and television factory....

Then suddenly it all came to a stop, ended, men off every shift shouldering loaded tool-bars down to Harding's Square on the final day. The last NCB workmen's buses. No more hobnail boots clacking the pavements — some of our modest miner democrats washed at home, they refused to use the pit-head showers. No hooters any more from Caib winding-house. Sunday peace over Daren. A dozen or so familiar faces arrived daily, men whose names were picked out of the hat for dismantling down below and around top pit. Men on bare day-wages, so absenteeism slowly increased, hung high and steady — they were better off financially as sick or injured citizens, despite accusations and economic jug-tooting from Coal Board leaders puffing safe behind the lines. Economics, aye. Power economics, as if miners were fated serviles immured to endless servility, not simply individuals of all sorts, loving, loathing or negligent towards everything under the sun, from women to television comedians, everything from onion-growing to *Das Kapital*. But the NCB élite merely issue data and directives. They are the Napoleons of coal-killing, their family lives chimerical. Do they have black-sheep sons, queer Bronte daughters, Electra-bleeding mistresses, nostalgias, cultural afflictions, spites, paradisial moments, depressions? What's their antidote to the disinfected breath of the Holy Ghost? Any oglers among them ? Do they have sweaty feet, Pentagon morale, morality, or the yen to grow sideburns, or itches, earache, or lint in their navel-holes ? Does Saturn emulsify their zodiacs? Of course, they'll fall to oblivious dust, humanly anarchic like us all. Surely so. Left-behind day-wage blokes, though, powerless, dismantling pits where they've spent working years, are on to nothing from the NCB, nothing promising, no reversal of ends and means. At best they could hope for a win on Littlewoods, while their OMS records gathered dust in Brynywawr offices and in Hobart House, SWI.

Daren allegiances were stretching before breaking, pride found its price in clubs, pubs, chapels, football teams, among dog fanciers, cricketers, pigeon fanciers, gardeners, motorists, social pride, competitive pride, pride of place. The Women's Guild shrank, dwindled to pensioners and the size of its committee. Old age throve, flourishing isolated from Daren's diminishing youth population. Both cinemas closed in March, resorting to bingo one night a week. Our MP opened a plastic bag in the House of Commons to show the members a lump of steam coal. He evoked bumblings worse than cat-calls. Daren's advance factories remained a mirage bubbling comically off the lips of councillors. Two young doctors emigrated; they were replaced by poker-faced Indian doctors. Daren Miners' Cottage Hospital became an old folks' convalescent home. In April old Watt Howard had the sack from the housing site. Afraid of losing their jobs, craftsmen and labourers accepted tighter bonus targets.

Stormy April, Rollo & Sons' filter beds overspilling, the river flooding black for days on end while rumour hardened to reality and one morning the firm's lorries ceased running through Daren. Mr Rollo's crew moved away to more profitable tips.

Meanwhile the Minister of Labour lowered his eyes, entwined his fingers and preached mobility of labour for the sake of Britain, our production, our balance of payments — that modern myth strewn with the fangs and gore of Democracy, Communism, Capitalism, Socialism, Science, Theology, Utopia. But Ministers do not collect their cap lamps at six-thirty a.m. five days a week, fill shuttering with concrete, or bolt up steel girders on power stations, and neither do their wives de-gut cod in Grimsby nor disembowel capons in a chicken-packing station....

Five men left on Caib pit-head in June. Regular surface workers: banksman, three traffic men and the overman. The cages were tipped over sideways on massive baulks of timber laid across the shaft. Sheep slept in the workshops, eight smithy fires dead since March, buckets of rust-filmed water, tongs, formers, rusted mauls, wedges, chains, jig-plates, bits and pieces scattered in hundreds. Old Derby winners were chalked on the walls. Horses' names, obsolete reminders, alien jargon (BELT CLIPS FOR WEST I2. SEE MWCIN HOWARD RE CUTTER PICKS. BARHOOK PIN FOR RIMMER'S HEADING), film actresses, breasts and thighs, Ike Pomeroy caricatured with his dago moustache among confident illustrations of angle irons, brackets, drilling formulas, pulley ratios. Behind the smithy door, the World's Cup winners named in their respective positions.

Trampled sheep droppings everywhere and thieving beyond precedent in Daren. Street-corner gangs moved in as the five dismantlers came down the tump. Every Monday a storeman from Brynywawr accepted orders for corrugated sheets off the screens, washery and pit-head buildings. Archie Booth's sons brought a lorry fifty miles for two hundred sheets: they ordered two dozen. Schoolboys smashed what their fathers and elder brothers failed to carry away. Every window in the colliery, washery, baths, canteen and flocculation plant was broken; the main winding-house fortressed with breeze-blocks inside the panes, but these, too, were hammered down, further sledge and chisel work removing the engine's brass bearings. A smaller engine house on the surface disappeared entirely, asbestos sheets, windows and doors assiduously stripped to the concrete base which held the engine.

Mrs Cynon privately protested to Seymour Lloyd, the retired Police Superintendent advising her against sending a letter to *Daren & District Clarion*. He assumed the Coal Board wasn't interested in petty prosecutions — everybody knew about the electric motors and haulage equipment abandoned underground. Afterwards Mrs Cynon demanded a vote of bad conscience in the Women's Guild, but too many members were the wives or relatives of looters.

Red painted to last a decade, the steel door of the never-used powder magazine still lay flat on the grass behind the carpenter's shop. Sodden log-books were scattered on the site of the original old stone-and-mortar-built magazine, soiled records of every shot fired in Caib since 1958. Log-books, powder tins and ripped-open leather satchels for carrying detonators. Trodden sheep droppings from the threshold to the four demolished walls.

A weight-training enthusiast named Claude Prosser rolled a pair of tram-wheels through the length of Upper Daren. Next day he fell forty feet off the flocculation-plant tower — Claude the only scavenger who attempted stripping the steeply pitched tower roof. He and his widower father were unemployed, earning a few extra quid doing a song and patter act around the clubs.

Finally on Ist July (black Friday tailing Caib's history) the five surface workers came down the tump for the last time. Bunched in a chatty group, they reached our house without a backward glance, Mrs Cynon standing out on the unmowed lawn, calling each man by name, wishing him good luck.

I thought, the old lady's sad. Her Hayden died in Caib. It's part of her life, Selina's scar, big Percy hobbling on his stick, always there to remind her.

She returned to the kitchen. 'That's that, boy, *mae wedi cwpla*. I am now going off down to the infants' school to fetch Lizzie-fach.'

'I'll start the dinner,' I said.

'*Does dim yn aros, mae wedi cwpla.*'

Nothing to belong to any more, I thought. Change or die. The wheel has turned full circle. Our black and white days are over. Twelve thousand buried in Daren cemetery. Whole families of children from times of diphtheria, tuberculosis, typhoid and small-pox. Daren men killed in the pit, in the soft-coal levels. Men and women who gave up the ghost. Preachers, teachers, miners, aldermen, shopkeepers. Daren's map of the dead. Life is cheap. Change or die. Change direction.

Pilferers softly banged and rapped on Caib colliery while I scraped new potatoes in the kitchen. I remembered ambulance sirens, ambulances since childhood, whining up to the pit-head. Miners tramping the streets in the middle of the night, bringing bad news to wives and mothers. Now, from this Ist July, quietness. Clean, quiet, residential Daren, with twenty per cent of the men on hardship allowance and school-leavers taught to appreciate dereliction as a way of life by fathers and uncles with damaged limbs or lungs. Privilege of the underprivileged.

I thought, *we* can't change. If change doesn't come from outside, we'll gradually die off. Fade like a horse-and-cart ghost town. Our compo cases will meagrely survive on street corners or hide, mouldering in bedrooms, despair conquered because despair requires energy. We'll fade, responsibility diminishing to queueing once a week at the labour exchange, to grey mornings in doctors' waiting-rooms. Daren's councillors are feuding via letters to the *Clarion*, and Cledwyn Hughes is engaged in the finesse of double-think diplomacy, lucidly bland as a secular bishop on BBC Wales and TWW. Numbing phrases relating to footage, skills, manpower, a plethora of talk and paper campaigns for generations who have lived by weekly wage packets. In the national press, Coal Board and NUM last words, edited regrets about the closure of Brynywawr colliery: that's where they spent the big money. Unpublicized millions at the command of unknown men. Virtually unknown. Those mining experts with clean lungs, nostrils, toe-nails and finger-nails.

My face lifted unaware in the mirror above the kitchen sink: wooden mouth, inward eyes, greying hair. Mr Rees Stevens, house-man, scratched from the bread-and-butter stakes, scraping spuds for his wife and family.

What kind of a bastard life was I born for? I thought — the simplest curse, damnation against fate swaddling like a winding-sheet.

from *Flame and Slag* (1968)

MAX BOYCE
Rhondda Grey

One afternoon from a council school
A boy came home to play,
With paints and coloured pencils
And his homework for the day.
'We've got to paint the valley, Mam,
For Mrs Davies, Art.
What colour is the valley, Mam?
And will you help me start?'

'Shall I paint the Con. Club yellow,
And paint the Welfare blue?
Paint old Mr Davies red
And all his pigeons too?
Paint the man who kept our ball —
Paint him looking sad?
What colour is the valley, Mam?
What colour is it, Dad?'

'Dad, if Mam goes down the shop
To fetch the milk and bread,
Ask her fetch me back some paint —
Some gold and white and red.
Ask her fetch me back some green,
(The bit I've got's gone hard).
Ask her fetch me back some green;
Ask her, will you, Dad?'

His father took him by the hand
And they walked down Albion Street,
Down past the old Rock Incline
To where the council put a seat,
Where old men say at the close of day
'Dy'n ni wedi g'neud ein siar'
And the colour in their faces says,
'The tools are on the bar.
The tools are on the bar.'

RHONDDA GREY

'And that's the colour that we want
That no shop has ever sold.
You can't buy that in Woolies, lad,
With your reds and greens and gold.
It's a colour you can't buy, lad,
No matter what you pay.
But that's the colour that we want:
It's a sort of Rhondda Grey.'

'It's a colour you can't buy, lad,
No matter what you pay.
But that's the colour that we want:
They call it Rhondda Grey,
They call it Rhondda Grey.'

from *Max Boyce: his Songs and Poems* (1976)

TOM DAVIES
A Terrible Music

The winter of 1984 came screeching into the Valley, flinging out great armfuls of frost and snow, freezing up water pipes and cracking radiators. Even well into March the old harridan was still jabbing her ice pick into the Valley slopes, still turning cheeks blue and making noses drip like taps, still making the villagers creak with cold as they shuffled about the streets like dummies in an Oxfam shop beneath their veils of old scarves and layer upon layer of winter woollies.

But then, almost overnight, this vicious old harridan was vanquished by a brilliant cross of holy sunshine. It was still more cold than warm but no longer did every joint creak with the pain of movement. The coats of frost disappeared off the car windscreens and bandy-legged lambs made their first wobbly steps out of their warm wombs.

Yet, as the sun daily climbed over the volcano wall, making the opposite slope sing with warmth and surging weather, even a casual visitor would have been astonished by the stain of sadness all over the village. Each year now you could almost see the colour and vivacity continuing to drain out of the houses and buildings. You could almost smell the clogging aroma of decay curling above the terraces; almost feel the arrival of death among such life as was left.

There was terrible music in those padlocked streets. Two of the shops had been closed down and boarded up. The Co-op was festooned with iron bars and aluminium roll shutters. Whole sections of the roof of the deserted police station had been vandalised, and litter spilled out of the rubbish tip and over the outlying fields in ugly, haphazard avalanches. The Welfare Hall, once the proud heart of the community, was also visibly puttering towards death. Practically every window frame was rotten. The roof beams had been condemned as unsafe by the council. Even the one-armed bandits just inside the main door were locked inside cages to stop people robbing what robbed them. Such fresh faces as anyone saw these days belonged to marauding Jehovah's Witnesses or hopeful sellers of double glazing.

Soon after the disappearance of the incumbent, thieves and vandals had ripped the very heart out of the Libanus Chapel. The lead in the roof was the first to go followed by the pulpit and pews. Even the old organ had been unceremoniously chopped up for firewood. There were no sounds of old in the place any longer either; not a whisper of

Revival in any of its dusty corners — just the steady drive of cold draughts whistling past damp patches and jagged edges of broken windows. Of Rev. Mordecai himself there had been little to go on. Once he had been spotted walking, as neat as a wren, down a pavement in Chepstow. But, despite a prompt visit by Glynmor and the boys, old Mordecai continued to elude them and the police.

The days of the pit were clearly numbered too. The miners were still struggling to maintain their quotas; still battling against immoveable sandstone, flash floodings and sudden squeezes. It even looked, at one stage, as if they were winning. Then, right out of the blue, the pit manager, John Walsh, sent every Bont miner a letter.

> Dear colleague (the letter ran),
> The National Coal Board is running at an operating loss of £410m. a year. Our new chairman, Mr Ian MacGregor, is looking at ways of taking out 4m. tonnes of uneconomic capacity. This will entail a total loss to the coalfield of around 20,000 jobs.
> The plain fact is that Bont Colliery is currently losing £200,000 a week. It costs us £82 a tonne to bring to the surface coal which would never earn more than £47 a tonne in the market place. In fact Bont coal — once primarily used in steel production at the now-closed East Moors Steel Works in Cardiff — is probably unsaleable anywhere. Even if all the faces were now developed and worked they would be exhausted by 1991. In the circumstances it is my regrettable duty to inform you that the board intends to close Bont Colliery as soon as possible.
> Yours etc.,
> John Walsh, Pit Manager

The letter came as a considerable slap in the face to the boys in the pit, particularly as they disputed every fact and figure of it. 'Well, what do you expect if you put a bastard Englishman in charge of a Welsh pit?' Glynmor shouted at the next meeting of the lodge. 'Next thing he'll be joining those bastard Buffs.' That same day the lodge called on the said Englishman in his office demanding an explanation of his figures. But he had none. More maddeningly, he did not have a date for the proposed pit closure either.

Having failed to convince the board's doctors that he was a chronic invalid Glynmor had finally gone back down the pit and, within months, had become the disciple that Emlyn had long been looking for, quickly rising to lodge secretary where he surprised everyone by showing good organisational promise too. He was more than willing to pick up the telephone and send off letters. The pit manager was also scared of him which, Emlyn thought, was a very good omen indeed.

It was also especially important for Emlyn to have a good man at his side since, allied with their own local struggle to keep their pit open, a national struggle was beginning between the N.U.M., under the leadership of Arthur Scargill, and the N.C.B., under the chairmanship of Ian MacGregor. Each day now Emlyn was travelling to union meetings in various parts of the country and each day now a confrontation was becoming inevitable between a monetarist board who wanted to see profits and the miners themselves who were pledged to fight for their jobs, pits and communities.

Each week now Scargill, the fiery young gunslinger at the head of the most militant union in the land, was having some sort of skirmish with MacGregor, the ageing American sheriff, brought in by the Prime Minister to restore law 'n' profits to the coalfield. With every newspaper report it became clearer that a showdown was inevitable and it came sooner than anyone expected.

The catalyst of the conflict was the proposed closure of a pit in Cortonwood, Yorkshire, deemed by the board to be exhausted after losing £10m. between 1977 and 1983. There were many parallels between Cortonwood and Bont but it was the Yorkshire mine which became the centre of a national row after the local unions met the management only to storm out and prepare for battle. The unions called a meeting in the small parish hall of Brampton Bierlow where the branch secretary warned everyone present that the pit could have turned its last bucket of coal. Their pit of 111 years was now on the operating table and heading for the morgue. The meeting decided to fight the closure tooth and claw, asking the rest of Yorkshire for its support. Half the local pits fell in immediately and, within days, the whole of the Yorkshire coalfield was grinding to a halt.

Then, on Thursday 8 March, Scargill told his executive that, following the case of Cortonwood, the board clearly believed that 115 of the country's 179 pits were uneconomic. Now was the crunch. 'We are all agreed that we have to fight.'

A national strike was duly voted on and announced. And so began the longest industrial dispute in Britain's history.

The dance floor of the Welfare Hall was packed again that afternoon, not by the devotees of Smokey and his Sounds, but by the men from the Bont mine. Almost seven hundred of them crowded in for their first lodge meeting of the strike. Glynmor sat at a table on the side of the stage, preparing to take the minutes. Emlyn was shuffling with his papers, waiting for the men to settle down. A shaft of sunlight burst down through one of the dusty windows, dancing in the blue swell of the drifting cigarette smoke and the men's excited faces.

The news of the strike continued to make new blood surge through Emlyn's old Marxist veins. This was the right fight at the right time. Even as he stood there, checking the time on his fob watch and looking out over the smoky sea of all those familiar faces, he could feel his throat drying up and the flames of defiance flickering warm once more inside his belly. At last they had been given a chance to engage Milady Iron Drawers, Margaret Thatcher and her geriatric hatchet man, MacGregor. Emlyn had long thought that the old hated Tory coal barons had burned in Hades. But here was yet another, very much alive and kicking. Duw, the miners had brought down the last Tory government and they could do it again.

He tapped the microphone with his finger and stood waiting for quiet. His speech was extremely important, he knew. It was how the men would remember the start of the strike. It was his first opportunity to fire them up and he would clearly have to do that more than a few times before it was over. But he was up to it. He drew himself up to his full height. When I open my lips let no dog bark, his look said.

'Well the fight we've always wanted has come,' he said into the microphone, his voice thick with a musical power. 'And let it be known right at the start that when the history of this strike is written it will be recorded that the men of Bont — all the men of Bont — were there right at the very guts of it.'

His next words were drowned in ecstatic cheers. 'One thing is very certain,' he proclaimed. 'Bont will be rock solid. First in, last out — that's Bont. There will be no scabs here in Bont.'

Such words, the very manna of the socialist tribe, provoked a further outburst of cheering and clapping among men as diffuse as their multiple nicknames. Here they were, day shift and night shift together now: large, beefy types, force-fed by beer and black pudding, with bobble caps and round, generous faces; ratty faces with small mouths, devoid of mirth or charm; thoughtful types with soft voices and a copy of *Marxist Today* in their back pockets. Some had a surprising fairness, at odds with the more normal thick-set dark Celts.

'There are some fights which are over quickly,' Emlyn continued when the applause had abated. 'In 1912 the Bont miners gave the agents six hours' notice that, unless their demands were met, they would destroy the pit by pulling down the wheelhouse and filling in the shaft. And that, boys, is the real art of negotiation. Three hours after the delivery of that threat, the agents gave in and all the demands were met.'

The men all laughed and looked knowingly at one another.

'But this fight will not be like that,' continued Emlyn. 'Some of you must be wondering if this strike will be long. It will be long. Some of you may be asking if it is going to be a tough fight. It will be the toughest.'

He paused and raised a finger into the air, corkscrewing it around slow. 'This fight will be the longest and toughest ever. This Tory government has been preparing for it for six years. They planned this fight with the Ridley Report six years ago. We overthrew them once but then they began planning their revenge. They built up coal stocks. They planned coal imports. They adapted power stations to burn oil. All these years they've been planning the destruction of the National Union of the Mineworkers — the greatest and most powerful union in the land.'

He stopped speaking and raised both hands into the air like a champion boxer. 'This Tory government wants to whip us into the ground ... but we will never surrender ... they want to take our pride but the rank and file of this union will never bow the knee ... no matter what the cost — and the cost will be high — we will win in the end. Because the NUM will never give in ... the NUM will never hand over its pride ... never ...'

As each sentence rose in power the cheers of the men mounted until Emlyn's words were barely audible in the rolling crescendo. One man after another stood up to applaud the veteran warhorse. A few had tears rolling their cheeks — this was fighting talk such as the Valley had not heard for years. If there'd been more men like Emlyn perhaps it would not now be floundering so badly towards an early grave.

'But before we go out there let us be clear about one thing,' he went on. 'Let us be clear in our minds that this is not just a political fight — not just a scrap between Maggie Thatcher and Arthur Scargill. And neither, for once, is it a fight about wages. This strike is our very last chance to keep this pit open. This is our last chance to save our community. When our pit goes our community goes with it. This strike is about our right to life.'

More cheers and clapping interrupted his flow for a few moments.

'Half the South Wales coalfield is under threat at the moment by Thatcherism. The Tory proposal is to cut our coalfield in half, so we have to fight.' He paused and gave a hollow sardonic laugh before shouting, 'We have to fight because we have no other option open to us. We have to fight because we are redundant already. We have to fight because, when you've got nothing, you've got nothing to lose. We have to fight because otherwise we're as dead as dogs. And we're not dead yet are we? Well, are we?'

The men, all still standing, cupped their hands to their mouths shouting a great gale of defiant 'No's'. Emlyn stood back from the microphone and looked over at Glynmor, the lodge secretary who had found the polemic so pulverising he had not even taken any notes for the minutes. He had always known that Emlyn was good but never quite this good. He was proud to be at his side. The magician of oratory was still magical. Perhaps the old Marxist had finally met his moment.

Emlyn was not a man of God but had he been he would have given daily thanks for the life of Jack London since, no sooner had Glynmor stuck his nose into the old lefty spell-binder's novels, than he just seemed to wake up more and more by the hour. It was then a simple journey through George Bernard Shaw's Fabian days, then to Nye Bevan and the earlier works of Keir Hardie which had contributed so much to the birth of the Labour Party in the Valleys. After that Glynmor read more or less anything he could get his hands on and, oddly enough, Maggie seemed to join in with him too. Already Glynmor was puzzling out rosters for the flying pickets and talking of ways of fund-raising, while Maggie had already made the first few phone calls with a view to setting up a women's support group in Bont.

'And if anyone thinks he's going to sit out this strike in the bar he'd better think again. My branch secretary Glynmor Jones is going to be in charge of the pickets and, by the time he's finished, the pickets of Bont are going to be flying all over the country. And, boys, remember another thing — Bont pickets are like draughts. They can get in anywhere.'

The men were all laughing again now. Within the fishing net of his rolling rhetoric Emlyn could have got them to do anything.

'So let's remember the spirits of Ablett and Horner. Let's think on Senghenydd and those of our own families lost in underground explosions and floods. Let's think on history and remember history. The whole world came to this Valley to help keep themselves warm. The world came to plunder and exploit us. Now it's our turn to turn and say to the world and say, "You owe us now. But it's not much that you owe. You just owe the dignity of work, not the insult of your social security handouts. All we are asking for is the right to life, both for us and our families." So, boys, let's get out there and do it.'

As he sat down all the men raised their hands into the air in salute, shouting and cheering, stamping their feet so much it reverberated down into the rotting foundations of the Hall. It was a thundering roar of triumph: the roar of a defeated people who had begun a victory march at last.

'Well, boys, that was something, wasn't it?' It was Glynmor's turn on the microphone now. 'I'm going to be in touch with every one of you about picketing duties but, before we break up, the union has asked every lodge to take their own vote on the strike.'

'When did we ever need to vote?' shouted Danny Kettle. 'First out, last in, that's Bont. What do we want to vote for?'

'Well, if for nothing else, for the fucking minutes,' Glynmor replied, exasperated. 'I've got these minutes to write up. If you don't vote on it what am I going to do? Well, what am I going to do?'

'Sing us a song.'

'You can buy us a drink if you like.'

'As a striking miner with a missing thumb and a family to support' ... ironic jeers of commiseration here ... 'I can't afford to buy you all a drink but, if it's a song you bastards want, I've got a song for you. It's simple enough, even for you, and we'll sing it to the tune of *She'll be Coming round the Mountain*. You ready?' He unscrewed the microphone and lowered it a little before singing 'Oh I'd sooner be a picket than a scab: I'd sooner be a picket than a scab. Right, now you sing it.'

The men soon picked it up too. 'Oh I'd sooner be a picket than a scab,' they sang, 'I'd sooner be a picket than a scab.' They repeated it again and again, dancing about and clapping, hardly knowing that they had just given the first rehearsal to what was going to become the national anthem of the Welsh striking miners.

from *Black Sunlight* (1986)

DUNCAN BUSH
Summer 1984

Summer of strike and drought,
of miners' pickets standing on blond verges,
of food parcels and

hosepipe bans... And as (or so
the newspapers reported it) five rainless
months somewhere disclosed

an archaeology of long-evicted
dwellings on a valley-floor, the reservoir
which drowned them

having slowly shrunk towards
a pond between crazed banks, the silted
houses still erect,

even, apparently, a dusty
bridge of stone you might still walk
across revealed intact

in that dry air, a thing not seen
for years; just so (though this the papers
didn't say)

the weeks and months of strike saw
slowly and concurrently emerge in shabby
river-valleys in South Wales

— in Yorkshire too, and Durham,
Kent and Ayrshire — villages no longer
aggregates of dwellings

privatised by television, but
communities again, the rented videos and tapes
back in the shop,

fridge-freezers going back
— so little to put in them, anyway — and
meetings, meetings in their place,

in workmen's clubs and miners' welfare
halls, just as it had been once, communities
beleaguered but the closer,

the intenser for it, with resources
now distributed to need, and organised to last,
the dancefloors stacked

with foodstuffs like a dockside, as if
an atavistic common memory, an inheritance
perhaps long thought romantic,

like the old men's proud and bitter
tales of 1926, was now being learnt again,
in grandchildren and

great-grandchildren of their bloodline:
a defiance and a unity which even sixty years
of almost being discounted never broke.

from *Salt* (1985)

HARRI WEBB
Valley Winter

Under the gaslamps the wet brown fallen leaves
Glitter like glass of broken beer bottles;
The feast is finished, the hangover remains.
This is the time to walk the Welsh valleys
Under the rain that is falling forever
And the days that never dawn hiding the hills.
The mountains have vanished into another world,
The rivers boil black from hell under concrete bridges
And from the lost mountains ponies and sheep come down,
Ghostly refugees in the street that alone stand.
All the encompassing glory, the heroic crests
And soft voices of an older Wales are abolished
That we saw from every street corner of our brief summer,
And the black axemen have felled the dinging forests.
One day we will climb again the cliffs of clear air,
Walk by the carolling water, redeem our strength
On the high places of the old gods and battles.
But, for now, only the street are real
Where wet crowds shuffle shopping
And nobody sings or fights, not even the drunks,
Where we wait for buses that are never on time
And drag our feet through fallen, long-fallen leaves.

from *The Green Desert* (1969)

Gwyn Thomas
My Earth's Warm Centre

The mind, the body move in shrinking circles. My being has never edged more than a few inscrutable inches from the kitchen of the house where I lived as a boy, a teeming and tempestuous place, cocoon of myths and spinning absurdities. From its seemingly always open door we had a mountain in full view. It was called Arthur's Crown. Once, long ago, we had a sad and noble king called Arthur. This mountain had a sad and noble shape. So we called it Arthur's Crown. It was very beautiful. It was bare except for a fringe of stunted trees across its top, bent and crouched by the winds that blew in from the sea.

I felt sorry for those trees and I was relieved when I climbed the slope for the first time, touched them and found them stronger and happier-looking than they had ever looked from the valley-bed. That mountain became the centre of my heart and imagination. My father often pointed to it. He said that one day he would take us over it.

Beyond the mountain, with its magical velvet paths moving through the high summer ferns, in another valley, there was a town called Mountain Ash. There, said my father, we had a lot of aunts and cousins.

'They are beautiful,' he said, 'those aunts and cousins. As beautiful as that mountain. But shorter, you understand. And they are kind. They have a big house. Tall windows and flowers in them all. They will be waiting for us. They will see us coming down the hillside. They will come out to meet us. They have money. They will give you money.'

That last sentence clinched it. Things were tough. We were even borrowing from the mice. And they were appealing for protection to the International Bank.

A Sunday morning came when my father took us for the first time on the long hill-top walk to Mountan Ash. The path to the mountain-top was steep and treacherous underfoot. My father walked fast. To our small untrained legs the mountain seemed like a wall and we seemed like flies. Short of clutching my father's jacket and boarding him like a bus we could never have kept up. Fortunately my father knew everyone who passed and talked with them, discussing their problems without being able to do much to solve them.

As we approached the top we were full of a sense of an enchantment about to be revealed, touched, tasted. Enchanted it was. That sea of ferns, endless to the eye of a child. A world of kind and golden light. Larks singing with a force that made it seem they were trying to burst their way into one of the local choirs. And we would sing back at them. Larks and sheep looking so gentle and intelligent one spoke to them and got answers of a kind.

It was and is the land of my emotions. To the north stretch the ranges of mountains that make Wales a land of mysterious and exclusive valleys; to the south the channel that divides us from England, full, as dusk fell, of the winking, tempting lights of ships going to or coming from the great waters of the West.

A dozen times we started on that Sunday walk with my father. But we never got to Mountain Ash. We never got to see those aunts and cousins whose goodness and beauty would have brought new dimensions of joy into our lives.

Halfway across the plateau there is a village called Llanwonno. In the village is a pub called The Tavern of the Fountain. Near the pub was a spring and its water was sweet. This made no appeal to my father. He always considered water-drinking an inferior experience. By the time he got to the village he had developed a thirst it would have taken two fire-brigades to put out. He knew the landlord and landlady of the pub.

Although the pub was officially closed on Sunday my father was always welcomed in, and for three or four hours in the cool, stone-flagged bar he would sip beer and talk to his friends about the people they had known who now rested in the grave-yard just over the road from the pub.

'I can't think of a healthier place to be buried,' my father would say. 'No noise, no smoke, no traffic. A treat.'

As my father drank and chatted the afternoon away, the talk grew less solemn with the passing of every pint, and we heard the gales of laughter come rocking through the pub's closed door. We stayed outside, drinking lemonade and watching the wind make a kind of visual music among the ferns. If it were a day of great heat we would go to the shadowy banks of an ice-cold stream nearby. We would fish and catch nothing. Or we would bathe and catch colds. But even sneezing we never lost the sense of being in an unsmirched paradise.

We never managed to complete the journey to the neighbouring valley, to the big house where the group of fair and benevolent women and maidens would be watching for us in their flowered windows, to accord us a warm and silver welcome. After a session in the pub my father would be too weary even to start the second leg of his journey.

Using my brother and myself as two short crutches he would make his uneven way back to our house. There he would sit by the kitchen window, staring at the lovely mountain, a look of sad remorse on his face, vowing that one day, like a latter-day Moses, he would lead us all the way to that promised land in Mountain Ash where the cousins and aunts would be waiting to usher us into a heaven of affection, a blinding shower of tarts, toffees and threepenny bits. He never did.

I was at the Fountain Inn one evening last summer. Our intention was to cross the plateau all the way to Mountain Ash and fix once and for all the location of that shrine of loveliness that had slipped furtively in and out of my father's talk and dreams so many years ago.

The whole day had been a throne of sweet sensations. The walk over the mountain-top had been exquisite, the air and the grass a matching velvet. We had meat and wine in the dining-room. We were in a fine, rare mood of abdication. We talked of the futility of power and spoke with relish of Edward II who had been betrayed, captured in a dingle nearby and trundled to some English fortress, there to be abominably executed. So we were told by our teacher in the Primary School whose authority was total, and who had compiled a bulging dossier on local treacheries.

Then the inn filled up with a rush. It was a visit by the whole of the Pendyrus Male Voice Choir, singers of matchless passion from the Little Rhondda. There was pause for a drink of welcome and the pianist struck a rich chord for silence. A quartet of ancients were discussing parliamentary government with such gall the fabric of Westminster must have winced. Alongside them two men were trying to recall the year in which a brilliant black sheep called Caradoc had outsmarted a whole panel of sheep-dogs. It took three more rich chords to make these debators fall still.

The choir roared into a piece about the irrelevance of death and the certain prospect of renewal. They then eased the strain and brought all our doubts back with a very negative item called 'Ten Green Bottles'. Then, the midsummer dusk outstanding, they sang one of the loveliest of the quiet carols. The night put on a cap of gold. I was home, at my earth's warm centre. The scared monkey was back in the branches of his best-loved tree. I've never had any truly passionate wish to be elsewhere.

from *A Few Selected Exits* (1968)

Notes on Contributors

BENJAMIN HEATH MALKIN (1769-1842), antiquary and author, was born in London, where he was a headmaster and later Professor of History at London University. From about 1830 he lived at Cowbridge, Glamorgan, his wife's home, from where he pursued his interest in county history.

GWYN THOMAS (1913-81), novelist, short-story writer and playwright, was born at Porth in the Rhondda. He read Modern Languages at Oxford University, and became a teacher in Cardigan and Barry, giving up to become a full time writer in 1962. He was the author of nine novels and four collections of short-stories, as well as essays and plays and an autobiography, *A Few Selected Exits* (1968).

RHYS DAVIES (1901-78), short-story writer and novelist, was born in Clydach Vale in the Rhondda and educated at Porth. In his early twenties he left for London, becoming the author of forty books in all, mainly stories and novels, and a volume of autobiography, *Print of a Hare's Foot* (1969).

LEWIS JONES (1897-1939), novelist and political activist, was born in Clydach Vale, where at the age of twelve he went to work underground. He joined the Communist Party while at the Central Labour College in London, and as an organizer for the National Unemployed Workers' Movement he led contingents from south Wales in the hunger marches of the 1930s as well as demonstrations against the Means Test. A Communist member of Glamorgan County Council from 1936, he was prominent in the campaign in favour of the Spanish Republic.

ALEXANDER CORDELL (b. 1914), novelist, was born in Ceylon and raised in the Far East. He came to Wales in 1936 and lives now in Wrexham. He is the author of two trilogies about industrial south Wales.

J.O. FRANCIS (1882-1956), playwright and essayist, was born in Merthyr Tydfil and educated at UCW Aberystwyth. Though a civil servant in London for most of his life, he was in close contact with the amateur dramatic movement in Wales. His best-known plays are *Change* (1912), *The Poacher* (1914) and *Birds of a Feather* (1927).

J. KITCHENER DAVIES (1902-52), poet and dramatist, was brought up on a small-holding near Tregaron, Cardiganshire. Educated at UCW Aberystwyth, he settled in the Rhondda in 1926, teaching Welsh at various schools there. He was a tireless campaigner for Plaid Cymru.

IDRIS DAVIES (1905-53), poet, was born in Rhymney, Monmouthshire. He left school at fourteen to work underground, but later trained as a teacher. During the Second World War he taught at Treherbert in the Rhondda. His

Collected Poems (1972) include his famous sequence about the General Strike, *The Angry Summer*.

JACK JONES (1884-1970), novelist. Born in Merthyr Tydfil, he began work underground at the age of twelve, and later joined the army. He became active in left-wing politics in about 1920 and, as a member of the Communist Party, was elected miners' agent for the Garw Valley in 1923. Between 1928 and 1932 he was a member in turn of the Labour Party, the Liberal Party and Moseley's New Party. He wrote a dozen novels, the best-known of which are *Rhondda Roundabout* (1934), *Off to Philadelphia in the Morning* (1947) and *River Out of Eden* (1951), as well as volumes of autobiography, and plays.

HUW MENAI (1888-1961), poet, was born in Caernarfon, the son of a miner who worked in south Wales. In 1906 he began work at a pit near Merthyr Tydfil, where he became a political agitator and journalist. He published four volumes of verse, including *The Simple Vision* (1945).

T. ROWLAND HUGHES (1903-49), novelist and poet. Born in Llanberis, Caernarfonshire, a quarryman's son, and educated at UCNW Bangor, he taught English for two years at Aberdare but became a lecturer in English and Welsh at Coleg Harlech in 1930. Five years later he joined the BBC in Cardiff as a producer. He was the author of five novels in Welsh, all translated into English.

GARETH ALBAN DAVIES (b.1926), poet, was born at Ton Pentre in the Rhondda. A Bevin Boy from 1944 to 1947, he was educated at The Queen's College, Oxford, and was appointed to the Chair of Spanish at Leeds University in 1975. He is the author of two volumes of verse, an American diary and a collection of essays about the Welsh in Patagonia. He lives now near Aberystwyth.

T.J. MORGAN (1907-86), scholar and essayist, was born at Glais in the Swansea Valley. Between 1951 and 1961 he was Registrar of the University of Wales but then became Professor of Welsh at UC Swansea. He was the author of several major works of scholarship, including *Welsh Surnames* (1985), with his son Prys.

R. BRINLEY JONES (b. 1929) was born at Penygraig in the Rhondda and educated at Tonypandy Grammar School, UC Cardiff and Jesus College, Oxford. From 1969 to 1976 he was Director of the University of Wales Press, and thereafter until 1988, Warden of Llandovery College. He is at present Chairman of the British Council in Wales.

ALUN LEWIS (1915-44), poet and short-story writer, was born at Cwmaman, near Aberdare, and educated at UCW Aberystwyth and Manchester University. He taught for two years at Lewis Boys' School, Pengam, before volunteering for military service in 1940. He died in Burma. His *Collected Stories* and a volume of letters to his wife have been published as part of a uniform edition of his work. The *Collected Poems* will be published in 1993.

MARY DAVIES PARNELL (b. 1936) was born and brought up in Trehafod in the Rhondda. Educated at UCW Aberystwyth, she taught French in Cardiff until her retirement in 1991. She has published two volumes of autobiography, *Block Salt and Candles* (1991) and *Snobs and Sardines* (1993).

BOBI JONES (b. 1929), poet, short-story-writer, novelist, critic and scholar. Born in Cardiff into an English-speaking home, he learned Welsh as a schoolboy and graduated in Welsh at UC Cardiff. He became a lecturer in Welsh at UCW Aberystwyth in 1966 and was appointed Professor in 1980. He is a prolific writer; a selection of his poems has been translated by Joseph P. Clancy (1987).

RHYDWEN WILLIAMS (b. 1916), poet and novelist, was born at Pentre in the Rhondda, but moved to Chester as a teenager. After a variety of jobs he returned to the Rhondda as a Baptist minister at Ynys-hir. He won the Crown at the Eisteddfodau of 1946 and 1964. He lives now in Aberdare.

RON BERRY (b. 1920), novelist, was born AT Blaen-cwm in the Rhondda and lives now in Treherbert. After leaving school at fourteen he worked as a miner and later studied for a year at Coleg Harlech. He has published five novels and a number of short-stories.

ALUN RICHARDS (b. 1929), novelist, short-story writer and playwright. Born in Pontypridd, he was educated at Caerleon and UC Swansea. Formerly a teacher and probation officer, he has written for television and the stage. He is the author of six novels, two collections of short-stories, a memoir of his friend Carwyn James, and an autobiography. He lives in Swansea.

MAX BOYCE (b. 1943), folk-singer, was born in Glyn Neath, where he worked as a miner and where he still lives. Since the 1970s he has been a popular entertainer, his reputation based on material about the south Wales valleys.

TOM DAVIES (b. 1941), novelist and journalist, was born in Pontypridd, and now lives in Cardiff. The author of four novels, he has also worked on the *Western Mail*, *The Sunday Times*, *The Sunday Telegraph* and *The Observer*.

DUNCAN BUSH (b. 1946), poet and novelist, was born in Cardiff and educated at Wadham College, Oxford. He has published four volumes of poetry, and a novel, *Glass Shot* (1991).

HARRI WEBB (b. 1920), poet, was born in Swansea but has lived for many years in Merthyr and in Cwmbach in the Cynon Valley. By profession a librarian, he was educated at Magdalen College, Oxford. His main collections of poems — many of which are set in the industrial valleys of south-east Wales — are *The Green Desert* (1969) and *A Crown for Branwen* (1974).

Acknowledgements

For the story and excerpts from the work of Gwyn Thomas: the Estate of Gwyn Thomas.

For the stories and excerpts from the work of Rhys Davies, the Estate of Rhys Davies.

For the excerpts from 'We Live' by Lewis Jones, ...

For the excerpts from *This Sweet and Bitter Earth*, Alexander Cordell and David Higham Associates Ltd.

For the excerpt from 'Swn y Gwynt sy'n Chwythu', the Estate of J.Kitchener Davies.

For the poems of Idris Davies, Eben Morris.

For the passage by T. Rowland Hughes, Gomer Press Ltd.

For the essay by T.J. Morgan, Mrs Huana Morgan.

For 'The Rhondda' by Alun Lewis, Mrs Gweno Lewis.

For 'Rhondda Grey' by Max Boyce, by kind permission of Max Boyce. Copyright held by EMI Music Publishing, Charing Cross Road, London.